The Memsahib
& the Mutiny

The Memsahib
& the Mutiny

An English lady's ordeals in
Gwalior and Agra during
the Indian Mutiny 1857

R. M. Coopland

LEONAUR

The Memsahib
& the Mutiny
An English lady's ordeals in
Gwalior and Agra during
the Indian Mutiny 1857
by R. M. Coopland

First published under the titles
A Lady's escape from Gwalior and Life
in the Fort of Agra during the
Mutinies of 1857

Leonaur is an imprint
of Oakpast Ltd

ISBN: 978-1-84677-948-0 (hardcover)
ISBN: 978-1-84677-947-3 (softcover)

http://www.leonaur.com

Publisher's Notes

In the interests of authenticity, the spellings, grammar and place names
used have been retained from the original editions.

The opinions of the authors represent a view of events in which she
was a participant related from her own perspective,
as such the text is relevant as an historical document.

The views expressed in this book are not necessarily
those of the publisher.

Contents

I saw the youth become at once a man, the greybeard
Turn young again, the child grow to a lusty youth—
Yes, and that sex, the weak, as men most call it,
Show itself brave and strong, and of a ready mind.
Goethe

*Sah wie der Juengling auf einmal zum Mann ward; sah, wie der
Greis sich Wieder verjuengte, das kind sich selbst als Juengling
enthuellte. Ja, und das schwache Geschlecht, so wie es gewoehn-
lich genannt wird, Zeigte sich tapfer und mechtig, und gegen-
waertigen Geistes.*
From Goethe's *Hermann und Dorothea*

To the Reverend Henry Philpott, D.D..
Master of St. Catherins's College, Cambridge,
Canon of Norwich Cathedral,
And
Chaplain To His Royal Highness the Prince Consort,
Etc. Etc.

My dear Dr. Philpott,
Accept my sincere thanks for your kind permission to dedicate this volume to you. In doing this, I desire to express my grateful sense of your many acts of real friendship towards my husband, and also of the kind remembrance you have of him: the more valued as when alive he held no one in higher respect and regard than yourself.

The book pretends to no other merit than that of being a plain, unexaggerated account of the sad events which came immediately under my own eye, and are only a sample of what happened wherever the mutiny prevailed in India.

Your kind interest in my husband induces me to hope, that the history of his fate will not be a matter of indifference to you.

I beg to remain, dear Dr. Philpott,
Yours most faithfully and respectfully,
R. M. Coopland.

Thorp Arch Vicarage,
December 20, 1858.

Author's Preface 1858

Though the interest in India, which a short time since was so deep and absorbing, has lost its thrilling excitement for some, and its bitter suspense for others, and, though it may be thought presumptuous to add another book to the many already written, there may still be those who will be interested in learning further details of life in India during the Mutinies: first, how our peaceful calm was threatened; then how, in one short hour, many were bereft of all that made life dear, and the struggle that followed to hold and sustain that life when stript of all earthly joy and hope. India may yet hold a place in the thoughts of some, as the last home and resting-place of many near and dear to them.

In this simple narrative I have, of course, confined myself strictly to scenes and occurrences that have fallen under my own eye; many of which, as far as I am aware, have not hitherto found a narrator. It seems to amount almost to a duty, in the present unformed state of public opinion, that those who have been so unfortunate as to bear a part in the painful scenes in India should faithfully describe what they have themselves seen, leaving it to the public to draw their own conclusions.

By some my judgment of the natives of India may be deemed harsh; but I had little time to know them favourably, and have suffered too deeply from them, perhaps, to be a lenient and impartial judge. To me their character is a sealed book, beyond the sanguinary page which was the only one opened to me.

The Indian Mutiny we must all regard as one of God's heaviest and most awful judgments. Its cause, as yet, remains a mystery; but we will trust that out of such a fearful calamity, good will arise, but years must elapse ere we can look for it The next generation of India may be redeemed: the present is too far gone.

May the coming year of 1859 bring success to our arms in India; may peace be established there, and under the rule of our gracious Sovereign, may our Empire there be founded on a surer basis, and Christianity be spread throughout the land.

R. M. C.

Thorp Arch Vicarage,
December 20, 1858.

CHAPTER 1

Calcutta

We reached Calcutta on the afternoon of the 17th of November, 1856. The usual bustle and excitement, consequent on the arrival of an overland steamer, ensued. We all gathered on deck to view the rapidly approaching land. Some, who were returning to homes and relations, welcomed this country of their adoption as an old friend. Others, like myself, examined with a critical eye the new and strange land which they believed would be their home for many years. At last we anchored, and the friends who had been impatiently waiting on shore put off to the vessel. Some of the meetings must have been very trying; children in anxious suspense to see their parents after long years of separation, and parents in like anxiety to claim their children.

A friend of mine told me he once overheard two fine fashionable-looking girls, just come from some great school, say to one another, on seeing a boat approaching the ship, containing two yellow-looking, ordinary people, "Who are those old quizzes? what an antediluvian couple!" when, to their horror and dismay, the despised couple claimed the gay young ladies as their own children. I heard many such tales of former days, when India was not so easy of access: but now, in these times of weekly intercourse, when boys and girls go backwards and forwards for their holidays, and when it is merely a pleasant trip to see the "City of Palaces," the snow-capped Himalayas, or the romantic beauties of Cashmere, such things never happen.

My husband's brother-in-law now appeared, to our surprise, as we did not know he had arrived a fortnight before. At the same time, we were informed by a servant from the boarding-house, where we had engaged rooms, that a carriage was waiting for us; so without delay we bade *adieu* to our numerous friends, many of whom we were never again to meet, and getting into the boat, were soon on shore, and driving rapidly through the native part of Calcutta. I was much pleased with my first sight of the grand fort, the cathedral, the fine row of houses on Chow-ringhee-road, which is the "Belgravia" of Calcutta, the Maidân, or "Hyde-park," and the imposing-looking Government House, whose lofty dome was surmounted by some adjutants (birds) looking down on what was passing below, with grave, attentive dignity.

But it is not my intention to give more than a slight descrip-tion of Calcutta; I was there only five weeks, and abler writers than myself have so often described it, that Calcutta is better known to the generality of people in England than Paris or Rome. There is scarcely a family in the three kingdoms that has not some friend or relative in India, and who has not sent home an account of Calcutta, its splendid mansions, its balls, races, and the luxurious life of its inhabitants.

We arrived before long at our destination. Miss Wright's boarding-house, one of the quietest and best conducted estab-lishments of the kind. We much preferred it to the confusion of a great hotel: my husband too had been there before. Miss Wright we found a most pleasant and attentive hostess. Our large airy room reminded me of some in the German hotels. After the luxury of a bath, we waited for dinner in the drawing-room, which only differed from an English one in the quantity of its lights. By this time the room was filled with hungry peo-ple, ready for dinner, an agreeable mixture of civil and military, but no ladies.

A native appeared with meekly folded hands, and in a se-date voice said, "*Khana mez pur hi*" (Dinner is on the table). We then proceeded to the dining-room, which we had only been separated from by silken curtains. The table was surrounded by native servants, gaily attired in their winter clothing, of different coloured cloth. I only noticed a few odd things; one was the want of decanters: the black bottles were clothed in pretty netted covers, and the tumblers had small silver covers to keep out the insects. I remember sitting next to a poor young officer, who gave me an account of fever, ague, and other Indian drawbacks; he looked dreadfully ill, and was on the eve of embarking for England.

The next morning my husband went to call on the Bishop, and report his arrival; and also to hire a buggy for our morning and evening drives. I, in the mean time, was employed in selecting an *ayah*,[1] a difficult task, as I knew next to nothing of the language; but Miss Wright kindly helped me, and selected a clean-looking woman, who had the best chits (written character). I was very much astonished to see the number of servants we required, even in a lodging-house—a *kitmutghar*,[2] an *ayah*, a bearer, a *dhoby*,[3] and a *dirzie*.[4] After *tiffin* we dressed for our evening drive. The carriages and horses were equal to those seen daily in Hyde-park, and the ladies were most exquisitely dressed. Dresses from Paris arrive every fortnight, and the climate only requires a very airy style. We drove down Chowringhee-road, and on to the Maidân, or public esplanade, which extends several miles, round Fort William, and along the banks of the river.

Many dangerous accidents happen here during the year. One morning I saw a beautiful horse lying on the road, with its leg broken, and a lady whom I knew had two horses killed in one year. Sailors, when they get a holiday, invariably spend it in driving about recklessly in a wretched hired buggy with tumble-down horse in the midst of the splendid equipages, and as they are often intoxicated, accidents of course follow.

I was told that a sailor made the following excuse the day after one of these accidents:—"I saw two lights ahead, and steered

1. *Ayah*, lady's maid.
2. *Kitmutghar*, butler.
3. *Dhoby*, washerman.
4. *Dirzie*, tailor.

straight between them."

Calcutta was not then lighted up after dark with gas, so there was an order for all the carriages, at a certain hour, to carry lamps. The aspect of the river was very interesting: it was crowded with vessels of all nations, from the well-built English and American frigates and steamers, to the picturesque craft from the Persian Gulf, and the queer Arab boats, with their strange, wild-looking crews and gay flags. The scene was more striking here than in London, or any English port, on account of there being nothing to take off your attention.

A Calcutta "turn out" deserves a description. The carriage is like any London one, but the pair of glossy, graceful Arabs are worth looking at: they are stud horses, with the stud mark branded on their flanks, and though rather small, make up for it by their grace. The coachman is a stately individual, in a white dress, and gay *cummerbund*,[5] made of two different coloured bands, twisted together. The turban is not, as we fancy, simply a piece of muslin wound round the head, but is regularly made up, turban fashion; and obliquely across it is a corresponding band, with the master's crest in silver, like the thistle on a Scotch cap.

The European children were all assembled in the Auckland, or as they were often called, the "gardens of Eden," the Miss Edens having planned them: poor little things! they looked pale and sickly, and sadly overdone with grandeur. Fancy a tiny child, gaily dressed in the Highland costume, followed by an *ayah*, and preceded by a *syce*,[6] leading his diminutive steed, and a bearer [7] holding a large white umbrella, and two *chuprassees*.[8]

After driving for a couple of hours we returned to dinner.

I will describe how each day passes in Calcutta.

We rise at daybreak, half-past five; the morning is heralded by the cawing of myriads of crows, the sharp squealing of kites, and the twittering of sparrows: very different from the awaken-

---

5. *Cummerbund*, sash

6. *Syce*, groom.

7. Bearer, valet.

8. *Chuprassees*, Goverent servants.

ing in a quiet country-house in England; and instead of thinking and indulging for an extra half hour, we start up, hurry over our bath and dressing, and then go out for a drive of an hour: and woe betide your head if you remain out too long without the buggy hood up. We then loiter as long as we dare in the garden; return in and partake of *chota hazerie*, bread and butter and tea; bathe, and dress for breakfast at 9 o'clock: after that, most ladies occupy themselves with their households and children. My husband went out to the shops to buy things for our journey up the country.

At twelve, a dead calm falls on the whole city. The delicate European lady in her lofty chamber, the poor *coolie* with his head wrapped in his turban, and curled up in some corner, or basking in the sun, even the animals, are alike slumbering. At two there is *tiffin*; we read and amuse ourselves till five, when we again drive out, dine at seven, and retire to bed at ten. But the gay inhabitants of Calcutta don't keep such early hours: the cool time of the year is their "season," when they keep as late hours as "Londoners."

The houses in Calcutta are very fine ones, from fifty to sixty feet high; many of the rooms are forty feet long, and very lofty. The white *chunam*,[9] contrasted with the green verandas, has a dazzling effect The floors are made of white *chunam*, and carpeted with light, pretty matting. Many of the entrance halls and dining-rooms are paved with marble. I was much struck with the number of outside staircases, or ladders, for the natives to reach the upper stories without going through the house.

Our room opened into a pretty garden, where we often walked, and the old gardener used regularly to give me a nosegay every morning.

My husband went one morning to a large clerical breakfast at the palace, and returned with a kind invitation from the bishop for me to breakfast there. So, on the appointed day, we drove to the palace; a large well-built house. The bishop was very kind and friendly in his manner, and talked much about England,

---

9. *Chunam*, a fine stucco or cement.

and some friends of his whom I knew. We then went into the chapel, a small room, filled with benches, where the bishop read the psalms for the day, and a long extemporaneous prayer. At breakfast the bishop told my husband the station he was to be appointed to was Gwalior, which both he and Dr. Pratt seemed to consider a very good one.

The Bishop then turned to me, and said, "I have given your husband this station, which is a very desirable one, as he suffered so much in Burma." After breakfast he asked us to stay in the palace, but as we had engaged our rooms for some time at Miss Wright's, we refused his kind invitation.

We often went out to the shops to buy things we should require at Gwalior. Some of the bookshops were very tempting, with all the new publications lying on marble tables, and the rooms so cool and dark that it was quite a treat to rest in them after the dusty, glaring streets; but it was very dangerous to linger long, as the books were double the price they are in England. I was very much amused with the Exchange, a large place, where everything is sold; the shopmen here are natives, but they speak English very well. I know 5*l.* seemed to go no further than 1*l.* in England, everything was so dear. I now felt what a pleasure it was to receive letters from home, and often solaced my home-sickness, or, as the Germans more poetically call it, "*Heimweh*," by the "sweet singing nightingales of the pen of correspondence."

A steamer arriving, the fresh influx of people crowded every hotel and lodging-house to overflowing. My uncle. Colonel Stuart Menteath, his wife and daughters, arrived. They had to stay a day or two on board before they could get rooms, and then they could only get unfinished ones at Wilson's, up a steep flight of stairs. I went to see them, and the confusion was tremendous. Part of the house was a large shop, where everything could be got, from a wedding trousseau downwards.

One morning we went with Colonel Goodwin to see a school he had established to teach the natives modelling. Some of the models were wonderful. When they did them very well they were allowed to sell them. Colonel Goodwin gave me one or two: I remember one was a model of a little mouse.

My husband's bearer was a perfect specimen of a "mild Hindoo" (so much raved about at home). He was lithe and slender, with beautifully formed hands and feet, clear olive skin, well-cut features, and white, regular teeth. His movements were most graceful and refined, and he was most particular in the fashion of his dress.

We asked some friends what sort of a place Gwalior was, and found it was not under the Government, being in the Mahratta states of Gwalior and Indore; the *rajahs* of which are each bound by treaty to maintain a body of troops, officered from the Company's army, and under the sole orders of the British Residents at their respective courts. Scindiah's Contingent consists of five corps of artillery, with thirty guns, two regiments of cavalry, seven of infantry, in all about 7,300 men. This Contingent was called into the field during the disturbances in Bundlecund, and did very good service. A good description of Gwalior will be found in *Blackwood* for 1844; and for a panegyric on the *sepoys*, people must read Alison's *History of Europe*, vol. 10., page 370. We were told Gwalior was considered, though very hot, a healthy station, and the society there very pleasant; for, being a Contingency, the officers and their families did not change so often as at other stations.

We missed; in the flat country, the graceful undulations and hill and dale of our own home scenery. There is no hill which you may ascend and have a good prospect of the surrounding country: you cannot see beyond the flat, dirty-looking plain, and your eye soon wearies of the extensive cotton fields, only varied by miserable native villages, with stagnant pools and open drains. We had often to turn back when attempting to pass through some of these villages, the dense feeling of the air and smell of malaria making it unpleasant to proceed. I was sorry we could not see Barrackpore, my relatives who had formerly been there having left, for I heard the park and Governor-General's country residence were very fine. Lord and Lady Canning seemed to prefer this residence, as they only occasionally came into Calcutta for a state dinner, &c. Many of the Calcutta people spend their Sundays at Barrackpore.

The gentlemen at our boarding-house often spent their evenings at the opera or other public places of amusement The opera-house is an odd-looking building, built of bamboos, and thatched.

We often used to watch the cricket-matches on the Maidân. Cricket and races seemed the principal amusements of Calcutta. The natives, whose only amusements are sleeping, smoking, or watching the dance of the *Nâtch* girls [10], who soothe them to sleep by the tinkling of their ornaments and their languid movements, must have laughed at our toil after pleasure.

We went one day to see the Mint, and were fully initiated into the merits of gold *mohurs*, *rupees*, and *annas*, by Dr. Boycott, the *assay* master, to whom we had an introduction. I thought the device on the gold *mohurs* very pretty—a lion standing near a palm-tree; though the former seemed rather out of proportion. Many ladies make bracelets by stringing these coins together; and they often have ornaments made of *rupees* melted down: one *rupee* will make a thimble. The effect of the nearly nude black figures of the natives flitting about in the darkness, dimly lighted by the forge fires, was very unearthly.

We spent another day very pleasantly at the Bishop's College, founded by the Society for the Propagation of the Gospel, with Dr. Kay, whose society we much enjoyed; he was very clever and agreeable, and my husband had met him before. We walked in the evening of the same day to the Botanical Gardens, in which I was rather disappointed, having formed my ideas of tropical plants and gardens from the splendid conservatory at Chatsworth.

We now began to make preparations for our departure from Calcutta. We bought a grand piano, a buggy, and stores of glass, &c, and then "laid our *dâk*,"[11] which is necessary in order to

---

10. *Nâtch* girls, dancing girls.
11. Laid our *dâk*, i.e. arranged our relays of horses.

have relays of horses. The great number of people who were on their way up to the North-west Provinces made it necessary to bespeak a *dâk* carriage.

Some ten years ago, when people travelled up in *palanquins*, they used to have relays of bearers at every stage, and arrangements made. The money is always paid beforehand. I think our journey altogether up the country cost us between 50*l.* and 60*l.* We could only go as far as Agra by *dâk* carriage; from thence to Gwalior we were to proceed in the old way by bearers' *dâk*. We then hired a *kitmutghar*, but I could not hear of an *ayah* who would leave Calcutta. We bought a mattress, pillows, lamps, and blankets, to fit up our *gharry*,[12] as we were told not to depend on the supplies of the *dâk* bungalows. We then sent all our boxes, except two portmanteaus, by bullock train, as we are only allowed to take a certain weight of luggage on the *gharry*.

I was much amused at the way the Calcutta people spoke of our going up the country; they considered it banishment Many of them had never been beyond Barrackpore or Dum-Dum.

We had an invitation to a ball at Dum-Dum, to which my aunt and cousins went, and also one to Government House; but we could not stay, as all our arrangements were made, and our boxes sent off. I was very much disappointed at not seeing Government House, as I had heard so much of it, a relation of my father's having been Governor-General.

I went to say goodbye to my aunt and cousins—my uncle had just left for Mooltan; they were not going to Simla till after Christmas, which is always a gay time in Calcutta. The indigo merchants and other grand people flock in from the country to enjoy the gaieties, and every one buys presents. Wilson's shop, which is brilliantly lighted up and decorated, is a great resort for buying Christmas gifts. My aunt told me she had written to her sister, Mrs. Douglas Campbell, who was at Gwalior—as her husband, Captain Campbell of the Engineers, was superintending the completion of the road from Agra to Indore, through Gwalior—to ask her to receive us, till we could get a house of

---

12. *Gharry*, carriage.

our own. I was very glad to hear we should have such a friend at Gwalior, as I had often heard of Mrs. Campbell.

We left Calcutta on the 21st of December. Altogether I did not think Calcutta looked much like the capital of a country called "The Queen's penal settlement for paupers."

We were anxious to reach Benares by Christmas Day, which we wished to spend with my husband's sister and brother-in-law, who had left Calcutta soon after our arrival.

Chapter 2

The Mofussil

We started in a *palki gharry*[1] for the ferry, which we crossed in a small steamer, crowded with people going to the railway station—some, like ourselves, beginning their journey—and hosts of natives. We saw floating down the river many bodies of dead natives, all in that state described in the song of the "White Lady of Avenel," which so terrified the poor Sacristan; only a crow instead of a pike was diligently picking at the fishy, horrid-looking eyes of the dead bodies. The river was crowded with different vessels.

I was quite pleased on arriving at the railway station to see again the engine with its long row of carriages. My husband here met some friends of his, a young officer and his wife, who had been his fellow passengers to England the year before by the "overland route." They had just returned by the Cape, and were on their way to their station. I now saw, for the first time, some elephants; for they are not allowed to come into Calcutta, as they frighten the horses.

The railway carriages were very comfortable, and quite luxurious in their fittings up; you could draw out a board between the seats, and so recline: very different from the narrow, closely-packed carriages in England. We enjoyed ourselves very much talking to our friends. My husband talked to Captain F—— and I to his wife: she was very pretty and engaging, and I found her conversation most agreeable. She talked all about Indian society,

1. *Palki gharry*, palanquin carriage.

and seemed to prefer it to what she called the "cold, formal English manners!" She also gave me a great many friendly hints about travelling and station life. About six months afterwards I saw her name in the long list of Cawnpore victims.

We passed many small stations; at one we got out, and had some refreshments. If it had not been for the view from the windows, I could have fancied myself travelling from London to York.

About five in the evening we reached Raneegunge, 121 miles on our journey, and there bade *adieu* to all comfortable travelling; not without a strong wish that they would soon continue the railway on to Agra, and so facilitate travelling, and make India as much like home as possible. No one can imagine the benefit it will be when India is traversed by this gigantic system of communication. The hotel was a few yards from the railway station; before it stood several *dâk gharries*, and a travelling carriage belonging to some officer, who preferred travelling in it to a *dâk gharry*.

After a bath and dinner, we all commenced packing our *gharries*. I was much amused to see how our friends packed theirs; they were "up to" all manner of travelling "dodges," and very kindly helped us to arrange our small quarters, where we were to pass the night At last we all started: about six *gharries*, one full of young officers who seemed to enjoy the fun.

I never saw our kind friends again; they reached Agra before us. Captain F—— went on to the Punjaub, and his wife first went to stay with some friends at Delhi, and then at Cawnpore, so her poor husband was in uncertainty as to her fate for months. When he at last heard the dreadful news it nearly killed him.

The drivers began to blow their shrill horns, and make the night echo to their wild music. The horses went a tremendous pace at first, but soon relaxed their speed, and required incessant flogging. We changed horses every six miles, and it was rather annoying to be awakened out of a sound sleep by the process of changing. The horses are very troublesome: at time, they will rear, kick, plunge, back, and go through a series of gymnastics by no means agreeable to the occupants of the carriage, and disturbing all their little arrangements.

The next morning we stopped and breakfasted at a *dâk* bungalow. These bungalows have been so often described, that I will only say the first I saw struck me as being very dreary and desolate: near it were two tombstones erected to the memory of two unfortunate travellers, who had, I believe, died of cholera. Our route now lay through a rather more picturesque country. It was very dull work, however, as we could not read on account of the jolting; we did try to make up a few Hindoostanee sentences with the aid of a dictionary, but it was very puzzling: my husband knew very little of the language, as Hindoostanee is not spoken in Burma, and he had a Portuguese servant there. I always felt inclined to speak to the natives in German or French.

About midnight on the second night we met with an unpleasant accident. When we were both fast asleep we were suddenly awakened by the sensation of falling from a height, which was followed by a roll over and tremendous crash. Then came sundry ominous bangs, caused by the horse's kicking, and the wails of natives. We, after some difficulty, opened the door, and extricated ourselves, and I mounted the bank we had fallen down, with my husband's help, as it was very steep.

It was bitterly cold, and my husband threw up to me some wraps to cover myself with, whilst he picked up the *kitmutghar*, who lay groaning on the ground, declaring his leg was broken; he had really hurt himself, having fallen from the top, where he had sat amongst the boxes. We found out that the cause of the accident was the driver having fallen asleep over his *hookah*.[2]

We then both set to work to scold him in Hindoostanee, and not being sufficiently fluent in that, had recourse to English; which we had been told natives disliked more, as they did not know what it meant. What they consider the most opprobrious epithets in Hindoostanee are "*khala sour*," "*hurrumzadu*," and "*mourgeu*" (black pig, infidel, and fowl).

The *syce* and driver began to shout and yell, which in about

---

2. *Hookah*, a pipe; the smoke of which passes through water.

ten minutes brought a flock of *coolies* [3] from a neighbouring *chowki*; [4] and then began the process of dragging up the shattered carriage and horse (the latter being much hurt), and collecting our scattered goods, by the light of a single lantern which we had brought with us. The *coolies* afterwards dragged the carriage to the next *chowki*, where we got a fresh horse; further on, at Shergotty, we procured another *gharry*. Our adventure prevented us from breakfasting with Colonel Goodwin's son, near Shergotty; which was very provoking. We afterwards heard that the place of our accident was the haunt of tigers, being near a jungle. Some travellers had had their *syce* carried off by one the week before, and had been only disturbed by the poor creature's shrieks when it was too late to save him.

I saw some awful specimens of eastern diseases—leprosy and elephantiasis—at Shergotty, as this place is a great resort for beggars, who extort alms from travellers passing by. They thronged round our *gharry* as we were changing horses, and showed off their hideous deformities. I tried to get rid of them by throwing out handfuls of *pice*,[5] but they only surrounded us the more.

The country beyond was very wild and desolate. The only civilized thing we saw was the telegraph wires, sometimes supported on high stone pillars, by which a message can be transmitted from Bombay to Calcutta in less than three-quarters of an hour. The natives have a great idea of its magical powers. The first thing they destroyed in the mutiny was the telegraph.

We had been warned not to trust to the commissariat of the *dâk* bungalows, so had brought with us a good supply of eatables—hunter's beef, biscuits, preserves, and one of Wilson's Christmas cakes; Miss Wright also had given us some mincepies and other Christmas dainties. We eat our Christmas dinner at one of these bungalows, instead of at Benares, as we had intended. Our accident having made us nervous about travelling at night, we did not get on so fast, as we passed the nights at the

---

3. *Coolies*, common labourers.
4. *Chowki*, hostelry, stage.
5. *Pice*, copper coin.

bungalows. Such everyday matters as eating and drinking are of no consequence in England, where you can have as many meals as you like; but people travelling in a country not quite civilized, are obliged to attend to such matters.

No one ought to travel in India without tea, sugar, a flask of brandy, quinine, and opium. I think the way dinner is got at a *dâk* bungalow is most ridiculous. As soon as you arrive, you hear the most lamentable cackling and screaming amongst the feathered tribe, and speedily an unfortunate fowl is caught, killed, plucked, and grilled for your dinner, and generally turns out to be some tough old grandfather.

We arrived at Benares on the morning. of the 26th. It was a beautiful morning, and the view down the Ganges very picturesque, with hosts of natives bathing in its sacred waters; its banks lined with mosques, steps, and *ghâts*.[6] We found our friends well, and already comfortably established in their new home. Their house, though not so grand as the Calcutta houses, which are rented at the rate of from 300*l*. to 600*l*. a year, was a very comfortable and elegant one, far surpassing many officers' bungalows,[7] though it was a missionary's. It was large, well built, comfortably furnished, and the veranda, supported on pillars, was surrounded by a pretty garden, in a large compound,[8] where were two or three other missionaries' houses, equally comfortable and commodious.

Benares is called the Oxford of India, as it is a great place for learning. There are no less than eighty schools in which Sanscrit alone is taught. It is more eastern in its appearance than many of the Indian cities; most of the streets are so narrow, an elephant can hardly pass through them. It is held in great veneration by the Hindoos, who call it the "Holy City," and are constantly making pilgrimages to it, to bathe in the sacred waters of the Ganges. The Brahmins [9] (who occupy 8,000 houses) and the Brahmini bulls rule the rest of the inhabitants with an iron rod.

---

6. *Ghâts*, landing places.
7. Bungalow, thatched house.
8. Compound, enclosure, garden.
9. *Brahmin*, first of the four Hindoo castes.

One of these bulls may eat the *gram*,[10] exposed for sale in the streets, that belongs to some poor *bunyan*,[11] or enter a man's garden and devour his vegetables, and they dare not drive him away: they are even expected to feel highly honoured at the beasts condescending so far as to favour their property. These creatures are very pretty, with humps on their backs, and long dewlaps, and look sleek and fat; but many of them are very vicious, from being so petted and indulged: they keep the people in awe of the awkward poke of their horns.

The next morning my husband went with his brother-in-law into the city, to see all over the temples and other holy places; some he could not see, being too sacred. On his return, he gave me the usual account of the nonchalance of the overfed Brahmini bulls, who required a *chuprassee* to keep them from molesting people. In the evening my sister-in-law and I drove out, and our husbands rode. The road swarmed with sacred monkeys, who jumped about, and even leaped right over our carriage, till I expected every instant one would pop into it: their grave faces and odd antics were most absurd.

As we returned, we heard the most unmusical sounds, which proved to be the peculiar notes of the Brahmins' horn, issuing from all the temples where they were worshipping. Benares is a wide field for any number of active missionaries and zealous followers of Henry Martyn. I saw a native Christian, called Nehemiah, who was really a most gentlemanly and polished man; he had been all over England, Scotland, and some parts of the Continent, and spoke English perfectly. He had given up a huge property to become a Christian, and lived in a small hut in the Christian compound.

He was dressed in his native costume, and when he entered the room, took off his shoes. I thought that, now he was a Christian, he need not submit to such a degradation. He talked like a connoisseur of pictures and books, and, to my delight, said he preferred England to India. On Sunday we went to the station

---

10. *Gram*, grain.
11. *Bunyan*, shopkeeper.

church, as the service in the church at the missionary compound was in Hindoostanee. My husband knew the chaplain, so we spent a few hours with him and his wife after service, and had *tiffin*.

We left for Agra on the 29th. We passed numbers of natives going to their work in the fields, all "horrid with caste marks." The weather grew colder the further we advanced: they had fires at Benares, it was so cold.

We met a man carrying a large snake, apparently about two yards in length and ten inches in circumference, twined round his neck like a comforter. He wanted to sell us some stones for charms, but found a better customer in our *kitmutghar*. This man had complained dreadfully of the cold, and looked a most absurd figure, curled up, and rolled in his *rezai* [12] on the top of the *gharry*. He complained so much of his injured leg, that we got a doctor at Benares to look at it, who said it was only sprained; so we gave him some embrocation to rub it with. He made this leg a never-ending source of annoyance to us the whole way, making it a plea for excusing himself from his work.

We afterwards met a man leading two beautiful Persian cats, with splendid fan-like tails. He asked 2*l*. for each—rather too much for a cat; though at home he might have made a good market of them, where some old lady, with a cat-mania, might have found them a valuable addition to her collection.

I have never described a *dâk gharry*. It is something like a small caravan on four wheels, and is drawn by one horse. There is a well inside, in which all the provisions and packages are placed, and at night you cover this well with a leather cushion or mattress, which serves for a bed; but it requires a great deal of preparation, and you are obliged to stop to get out to arrange it. The vehicle is lined with a strong, thick lining, and has capacious pockets and a shelf for books, biscuits, oranges, &c.

We reached the *dâk* bungalow at Allahabad in the evening. This is a favourite station; and is said now to be chosen for the seat of government, instead of Agra. It is well adapted for this; as,

---

12. *Rezai*, wadded wrapper.

being situated on the Grand Trunk Road, at the junction of the Ganges and Jumna, 498 miles from Calcutta, 1,151 from Madras, and 831 from Bombay, its facilities for travelling and communication are many. Lying at the extremity of the *Doab*,[13] the country is fertile and well wooded; and, escaping the hot, scorching winds of the "up country," it partakes more of the humid Bengal climate. The gardens look fresh and luxuriant, as it rains here when other parts of the country are parched up.

Allahabad is the first station in the "Upper Provinces;" all to the eastward of it, being called "down country." Troops are continually passing through in the cold season, which adds to the enlivenment of society at the station. We drove a long way by the side of the cemetery, which, with its lofty tombs of Asiatic architecture, looked very different from an English one: these closely crowded reminiscences of our poor countrymen, made me think that India was truly called "Scotland's graveyard."

Our drive, however, gave me much pleasure: the military cantonments [14] surrounded by trees, the grassy, park-like plain, the English-looking houses, and tastefully laid-out gardens, formed a picturesque scene. How little did I then think, that that pretty, homelike station, in a few short months, would be a scene of devastation and ruin.

The road from Allahabad to Cawnpore seemed to me the extreme of barrenness. We halted part of the day at Cawnpore, and dined at the hotel. I was much struck with the dreary, depressing look of the place, which seemed fitted for the cruel tragedies so soon to be enacted there. The cantonments extended six miles, in the middle of a sandy plain; and when I saw the long rows of blank-looking barracks, the neglected houses, surrounded by bare mud walls, so different from those of Allahabad, I felt thankful that our lot was not cast in such a dreary waste. We met many travellers on our way, and constantly English ladies and children unaccompanied by male Europeans.

We reached Agra January 3rd, and visited the military chap-

---

13. *Doab*, a tract of land between two rivers.
14. Cantonments, place where the Europeans reside.

lain, to whom we had an introduction. He very kindly asked us to stay with him till we had made arrangements to proceed to Gwalior: for here the *dâk gharry* stopped, the road to Gwalior and Indore not being quite finished. I must here remark, that the Grand Trunk Road, when it is complete from Calcutta to the Affghan frontier, a distance of 1,500 miles, will be one of the best roads in the world.

Unfortunately it rained heavily all that day, so we could not do anything. Rain generally falls after Christmas in India, cheering and refreshing everything, and making a pleasant change in the air.

On Saturday we commenced the troublesome and worrying business of buying furniture.

In India when any English officer leaves a station either to return home or remove to another, it is customary for him to sell all, or part, of his furniture, horses, and carriages; he makes a list of the articles and their prices, leaving a margin for the purchasers to write their names in against the article they have chosen. In this way we procured a large portion of our furniture; for the remainder, we ransacked the European and native shops. The native shopmen tease and torment you dreadfully, trying to pass off painted deal for real mahogany, and cotton for silk-velvet One man, who was particularly imposing and cunning, afterwards made himself very active in the mutinies, firing on our troops, and inciting others on; but he met his richly deserved fate in a ditch near Delhi.

In the afternoon we drove to the celebrated Taj Mahal. The whole country we passed through looked so barren and wretched, that when we found ourselves in the midst of the lovely garden that surrounds the Taj, and saw before us, towering aloft into the clear blue sky, this wonderful pile of snow-white, glistening marble, contrasting with the solemn, dark green of the cypress and myrtle trees, our feelings of delight and surprise can hardly be described.

This stupendous edifice more than realized my expectations of eastern grandeur; and I thought no description in the

"Arabian Nights," of gorgeous palaces, exaggerated. One could scarcely fancy it built by mortal hands: it seemed as if it had been dropped from the skies, so exquisitely ethereal did it look—too sublime for this lower world.

Entering through a gateway into a large court, round which ran a range of arcades, occupied by horses and their attendants, we alighted at a flight of steps, which we mounted, and passing through the massive brazen doors of a splendid vestibule, where some natives were waiting to conduct us round the Taj, we entered the garden.

And now, picture to yourself—if you can realise such a scene—a long avenue bordered by sad-looking cypresses, fit emblems for the place where so much beauty and ambition repose; and at the end of this *vista* a vast platform of solid masonry, forty feet high, from which rises proudly to the heavens a structure of the clearest white marble, glittering and sparkling in the bright sun; four minarets, like sentries watching over this "crown of edifices," and tipped with shining gold, like the dome and four cupolas surmounting the edifice. We ascended the steps leading to the terrace—which, with the Taj and four minarets, is entirely built of white marble—and lifted the curtain, that guards the sacred interior from the common gaze.

At first, the soft light streaming in from the "clerestory" windows, casting a hazy indistinctness over everything, prevented us from clearly defining objects; but gradually the interior became more distinct, and we saw, round the octagonal-shaped centre hall, small cells, like side chapels in a cathedral. We descended into the vault, where are the tombs of the Emperor Shah Jehan and his queen, Mumlazi Mahal Begum, who lie side by side. Immediately above, under the dome, are the cenotaphs, enclosed by a marble screen, which is carved in the finest fretwork, like lace, and said to be unrivalled.

The cenotaphs are inlaid with costly mosaics, of wreaths of flowers formed by precious stones of cornelian, jasper, agate, and lapislazuli, the shading being so delicately and elaborately finished, that a single flower is often composed of several dozen stones; and also with sentences from the Koran in black letters.

The walls are panelled and inlaid with mosaics of the same description, only the patterns are larger, and the arabesque designs more profuse; but I should be wearisome were I to dwell long on each separate beauty. After spending some time in alternately examining these wonders, and reflecting on the time (200 years) this building had lasted, and which still showed so few signs of age, we went to the back of the Taj to see the remains of a bridge which Shah Jehan had commenced building, of white marble, to connect this Taj with another intended for himself, when his imprisonment and death cut short this grand design.

We saw the fort in the distance, at a bend in the river.

We strolled in the gardens till late in the evening. They are kept up by Government, and beautifully laid out in groves and alleys of peach and orange-trees, intersected by walks of white marble and free-stone, and borders formed in patterns of stone work, and adorned with fountains. Down the centre of the principal avenue runs a marble channel, with *jets d'eau*.

We sat on the marble steps watching the gathering darkness stealing on, and the fairylike Taj glimmering from amongst long shadows of the trees; and enjoying the soft, balmy air, like an autumnal evening at home, the scent of the orange and myrtle, and other tropical flowers, which, like all eastern fragrance, is so redolent of luxury and magnificence; brilliant green parrots were flitting about, or bathing in the channel, vying in brightness with the gold and silver fish; and we remained listening to the liquid, murmuring coo of the doves, and the twittering of the humming-birds.

On Sunday we went to the military cantonment church, where my husband preached both morning and afternoon. On Monday we looked over the fort: and little did I then think how I should again see it, alone, and under what circumstances. In the evening we dined with the brigade-major.

Mr. French was out on a missionary tour, so that I could not see him, much as I should have liked it.

We drove round the camp of the commander-in-chief, who

was on his way up the country. His wife and daughter had accompanied him so far, and stopped to see the Taj before proceeding to England. This, my first sight of the pomp and pageantry of war, was very novel and interesting. The tents were pitched on the parade ground, in rows like streets, the sentries at their fronts, and the horses picquetted about.

Aides-de-camps were riding about with orders, some men were cooking their supper over the fires, some unloading the growling camels, and others preparing the tents for the night and cleaning their accoutrements; the huge elephants were consuming their vast heaps of fodder before them, the goats being milked and fowls killed: altogether, it was a stirring scene. The "course" that night was crowded with carriages and equestrians; and when we went again to see the Taj, its silent, solemn repose was sadly marred by the loud laughter and comic songs of light-hearted people trying the echo.

Captain Garston, an officer on the commander-in-chief's staff, and his wife, spent the day with Mr. Hind. Mrs. Garston gave me a most amusing account of the march. She and her children had a large carriage, called a *palkee gharry* (something like the *dâk gharry* which I have described, only more comfortable), drawn by a splendid pair of bullocks. These animals are most useful for draught and agricultural purposes; they stand about fourteen or fifteen hands high, and are not to be surpassed in size and sleekness; many of them have queerly twisted and curved horns, which are sometimes painted red. This lady had many camels to carry her furniture, and enjoyed moving about very much; the only trouble, she said, was the early getting up, as they usually march from two in the morning till the sun rises: but sometimes they continue again in the evening. Forced marches are, however, very trying; many of the soldiers die of apoplexy and cholera.

Miss W—— arrived at the Hinds, on her way to join her brother, a judge, who was on his rounds in his district; and she went out to the shops to see the new Parisian fashions. On Tuesday we drove to the civil cantonments, which were some distance off. They also had a church and chaplain. Agra is the principal civil station in this part of India; it is, like Delhi, situated on the right bank of the Jumna, and is 800 miles from Calcutta and 150 from Delhi. The native city is very large, containing an enormous number of inhabitants; it has been in our possession since the year 1803, and was the head-quarters of Government in the North-west. The then Lieutenant-Governor, Mr. Colvin, resided in the Government House.

We saw the beautiful Roman Catholic Cathedral, which quite put to shame our station churches; and I was told the singing and service were most beautifully done, and much pains taken with them.

The Roman Catholics here have a bishop, a sisterhood, and a school, for both European and native children.

I thought the houses and gardens much better and prettier than those of the military cantonments, more like the Calcutta houses, with their flat roofs, and built of stone.

The civilians here have very high pay, from 2,000*l*. to 5,000*l*. a year; and many of them go to the Hills in the hot season: those who cannot afford to send their children to England, send them there also, where there are schools. I frequently met people who had never been out of India. It is much hotter at Gwalior and Agra in the hot season, .and colder in the cold season, than any other part of India, except the Punjaub. Peshawur is the hottest place in the north of India: I was told that residents there dug holes under their tables and sat in them, as the English did at Thyat Myo, in Burma, where my husband was for a short time; and where they used to dig deep pits, and retire to them in the heat of the day. There is a bad kind of fever at Peshawur, from which my cousin, in the 70th Queen's, suffered much when he was there. This fever, with apoplexy, causes so much mortality that the place is called the "Grave of the English."

We left for Gwalior on the 7th of January, and though I was wrapped in a cloth jacket and plaid, I was glad of a warm Siberian rug, the weather was so cold: perhaps I might have felt it more, after my illness in the Red Sea. We were accompanied by a tribe of thirty natives; *banghy wallahs*,[15] to carry our boxes, two torch-bearers, and additional ones for the *dhoolies*;[16] they were headed by our *kitmutghar* in a warm *lebada*,[17] or tight kind of cassock, brilliant green turned up with red, and a shawl turban ot red *lui*,[18] or native blanket; he rode a queer little pony, which looked as though it had not a leg to stand upon, and was attended by a village boy, screaming and yelling, and unmercifully thumping the poor animal with a thick stick, the boy shivering with cold, and complaining it made his *pêté*[19] ache.

At some distance from Agra the country was well cultivated and the crops looked fresh and green after the recent rain. The roadside was planted with *peepul*, mango, and *toon* trees; from the latter most of the furniture is made: it is something like the ash in foliage.

We passed several villages. My husband and I spent our time in reading *Macaulay's History of England* and *Westward Ho!* I felt grateful to the famous authors of these books for giving us so much interest and amusement when away from civilized life. You can read so much better in a *dhooly*; the motion caused by the jog-trot of the bearers is rather pleasant, and makes you sleep a good deal. In the evening we kept to our English custom of walking. We stayed the night at the bungalow at Dholpore, which is a large dismal looking place.

We had now passed from the Company's dominions into those of an independent (at least in name) native *rajah*.[20] A Mahratta soldier appeared, sent by the *Rajah* of Dholpore, to know if my husband was a "*lord padre sahib*,"[21] for if he were, he would send him a guard of honour; but on my husband saying he was only a "*chota*[22] *padre sahib*,"[23] he vanished, but soon returned

15. *Banghy wallahs*, porters for luggage.
16. *Dhoolie*, a litter.
17. *Lebada*, quilted cloak.
18. *Lui*, blanket.
19. *Pêté*, stomach.
20. *Rajah*, king, prince.
21. *Lord padre sahib*, bishop.
22. *Chota*, little
23. *Padre sahib* clergyman..

with one or two troopers, who were to guard us, as Dholpore is a celebrated place for thieves, and whom we rewarded with liberal "*bâksheesh*." [24] A friend told me that when she and her husband were in tents near Dholpore, halting on their journey, they had everything stolen; her jewels, the tent-furniture, and equipments; and in the morning she had nothing but her habit to travel in.

We passed through the town of Dholpore, and in the distance saw our attentive *rajah's* palace. The natives here were a robust, warlike set, well dressed in warm quilted *lebados* and trowsers, and gay turbans; they seemed to prefer the brightest reds and yellows in their attire, and were well armed with short daggers, matchlocks, and swords. I could not help thinking, when I saw these tall, stout, fierce-looking men, larger and more muscular than many in Europe, of the absurd notions many people at home have of the natives of Hindoostan; they think India is solely peopled with "mild Hindoos," dressed in white garments, gliding about with graceful movements, and cringingly submissive: I only found them obsequious when they wanted anything from me.

Many also think there is no greater difference between the inhabitants of Benares, Calcutta, and those of Rajpootana, Bundlecund, Rohilcund, and all the North-west Provinces, than there is between a native of Yorkshire and Wales. The inhabitants of Bengal are exclusively "mild Hindoos," if they can now be called so: but the Mahrattas, Bheels, and Pindarees, are a strong, savage, martial race, and eat as large a quantity of good substantial food as an Englishman: they differ widely in appearance, dress, and manners, from the Hindoos.

They are not bad-looking, with their black hair and moustaches, and rather harshly-marked features; but at heart most of them are cruel and bloodthirsty, and are only kept by our superior power from burning alive, swinging on hooks, crushing under the car of Juggernaut, and otherwise sacrificing victims to their vile religion: were it not for this, they would again return

24. *Baksheesh*, present.

35

to thuggism, sutteeism, and burying alive. I think we have had sufficient proof of their treachery; yet actually, since my return home, people have asked me if I did not think the "poor Hindoos much maligned and harshly treated!"

We were ferried across the Chumbul in a rough boat, and I much regretted my inability to sketch the scene: the clear Chumbul, the fort in the distance, the picturesque banks, and wild-looking natives with their camels and bullocks flocking down to the river. The following lines, copied from a missionary's book of travels in India, will give you a better idea of the beautiful Chumbul than any description of mine:—

FAQUEER'S SONG.

Since the days of my youth, oh, how far have I wandered!
How strange seems the way I—oh, how much like a dream!
But where are the scenes, like the scenes of my childhood,
When all heedless I roamed by the Chumbul's clear stream?

I have climbed the steep sides of the lofty Hamála,
And gazed on the their summits in morning's bright gleam;
I have strayed through the sweet-scented groves of Bengála,
But I sighed for the gay banks of Chumbul's clear stream.

Gently and softly flows the Nirbudda,
Pure are its waters, and holy they seem;
And lovely the banks of the far-wandering Kistna;
But to me, oh, how dearer the Chumbul's clear stream!

Broad is the Sutlege and rapid the Chenáb,
And whirling the Indus runs to the main;
But true as the chakwá [25] *turns to the moonbeams,*
My heart wanders back to the Chumbul again.

Rich are the fields by the slow-winding Ghumti,
And fair are the lands that are laved by the Sone;
But fairer and dearer the banks of the Chumbul,
Where my thoughts dwell with fondness on days that are gone.

Through gardens and palaces glides the fair Jumna,

---

25. The *chakwá* is a species of water-fowl, often to be seen on. the Ganges sitting with its head turned to the moon at night.

And royal the cities that rise o'er its tide;
But to me, oh I how purer the sweet rippling Chumbul,
Where gladsome I bounded in youth's early pride!

Divine are the Gunga's all-nourishing waters.
How glorious they shine in the sun's setting beam!
And lovely the scenes on the green banks of Dewá;
But lovelier by far is the Chumbul's clear stream.

These lines give by no means an exaggerated description of the rivers of Hindoostan, so much grander than those of Europe.

We travelled the whole day, winding through narrow ravines and fording rivers, or crossing on crazy native rafts. ,The air was very sharp and keen. Our bearers were oddly wrapped up; their legs were bare, and their heads muffled up. They each carried a blanket, in which they rolled themselves at night; but too much clothing would encumber them. I was amused to see them put on their shoes whenever their turn for a rest came, and trot by the side of the *dhoolies*, vigorously smoking a "hubble bubble" and munching *gram*. They must have carried us forty miles a day, as Gwalior is eighty miles from. Agra.

We halted at a village, and dined under some splendid trees, where I gave a small boy a packet of English and Egyptian coins; he ran off highly delighted and greatly astonished at the sight of a penny. We saw the fort of Gwalior looming in the distance; it is called the "Gibraltar of India."

CHAPTER 3

Gwalior

We arrived at Gwalior at twelve o'clock on the 8th of January. I was aroused from my slumbers by the *dhooly* being suddenly set down before a large white house, and was surprised to see a sepoy keeping guard, and several more lying on the ground asleep. The door was opened, and a servant appeared, saying our rooms were ready, and he would prepare us some tea; which was very welcome, as we had felt the cold greatly. I had not the comfort of smoking cigars like my husband. Captain and Mrs. Campbell had retired for the night, but sent their *salaam*, and hoped we would make ourselves comfortable.

Early next morning I was awakened by the cackling and screaming of poultry, and jumping up to see the cause of the excitement, beheld Mrs. Campbell, who had just returned from her drive, surrounded by about a hundred hens and cocks, fifty or sixty guinea-fowls, and ducks, geese, pigeons, and turkeys in like proportion, which she was feeding. She afterwards told me that if she did not daily see all the animals fed, the natives would steal them, or starve them by appropriating their food.

My husband went out to see what he could do about a house; but none were then vacant. There was only a chance of our getting a small house, when Major Macpherson, who then occupied it instead of the residency, left it; and a regiment was shortly expected to leave for one of the out-stations.

I was very anxious to hear what the station was like, and was relieved when my husband said he thought it a pretty one.

It surprised me to see what a nice large house the Campbells had, after the unprepossessing accounts I had heard of bunga-lows—that they were "low and dark, not to be compared to the *pucka* [1] houses." Bungalows are, however, cooler and better suit-ed to the climate; having thick walls, thatched roofs, and sloping eaves, surrounded by a wide veranda, and a portico for carriages to drive under. Though they have not so many rooms as a *pucka* house, they contain a dining and drawing room, one or two small sitting-rooms, two or three bed-rooms, bath and dressing-rooms, all on the ground floor; also *godowns* [2] and bearers' rooms. The rooms are only separated from the roof by a piece of white-washed calico stretched tightly across, which looks quite like a ceiling.

I was agreeably surprised when I entered the Campbells' large, beautifully furnished drawing-room. Most of the furniture was English; but there were some curiosities from Burma—solid sil-ver cups, alabaster ornaments, and a bell and *kezee*, [3] exactly like those my husband brought us to England from Burma. Some armchairs looked very odd, with their arms extending out for people to rest their legs on. The most curious things were some teak-wood sofas and chairs that Captain Campbell had brought from Burma, the elaborate carving of which would have been admired even in a medieval German town: two cabinets were carved all over with figures of Gaudama (the Burmese deity). The Burmese *poongie*-houses [4] are famous: I saw one being erected in the Auckland Gardens at Calcutta. A description of a Burmese pagoda, taken from a diary my husband kept in Burma, will give a good idea of the carving, &c.

We mounted our spirited Burmese ponies, and rode up to the Dagon Pagoda; on arriving at a flight of black gran-ite steps, we dismounted and began to ascend. The whole was covered with an arcade supported on solid teak-trees,

---

1. *Pucka*, stone.
2. *Godowns*, store-rooms.
3. *Kezee*, Burmese musical instrument.
4. *Poongie*-houses, priests' houses.

and in many parts covered with leaf-gold, or painted red. Emerging from this, we entered upon the large enclosure which occupies the summit of the hill and surrounds the great Dagon Pagoda. The scene here was extraordinary.

In the centre rose the vast spire of the pagoda, surmounted by the golden umbrella, to the height of 320 feet, resting on a base, whose deep shadows and projecting angles and mouldings of every variety gave one the idea of the greatest strength and massiveness; while the ample court was crowded with a confused assemblage of smaller pagodas, elaborately carved and gilded *poongie*-houses, gigantic images resembling lions in a sitting posture, and covered with scales of silvered glass, wooden representations of the human figure upon birds, elevated on long poles; temples erected over immense bells; sacred trees, hung with all manner of decorations, some of which were long tubes of fine muslin stretched on hoops or metal pipes, or figures of elephants made of tinsel and paper: and smaller buildings of various shapes and sizes.

Two bells there were larger than any I had before seen, and supposed to weigh between twenty and thirty tons; they were each surrounded by a carved and gilded canopy, supported on pillars made of gigantic teak-trees, and produced, when struck with a stone or brick, a very melodious sound. Mr. Bull pointed out to me a most remarkable and large sacred banyan-tree, probably a hundred feet high, from the highest branch of which a perfectly straight 'drop' had gradually grown downwards and taken root Around the base of it was built a sort of altar, shaped like a crown, the interior being filled up with earth; and it was hung with muslin tubes and paper ornaments.

The elevated platform of the enclosure commanded a most beautiful view of the surrounding jungle and winding river. Altogether the scene was the most striking that I had yet witnessed, and made me feel as if I were upon a different globe, and among a different race of beings from those to which I was accustomed. The interior of the Burmese pagodas are, like some of the Egyptian pyramids, solid, containing only a few small gold and silver images embedded in the brickwork, or, as they report, 'a tooth or lock of hair of Gaudama, the object of their worship.' Those of the Burmese who became possessed of wealth in times past, generally devoted it to the building and decoration of pagodas, and to the services of religion; and at the present time the great Dagon Pagoda is being re-covered with leaf gold by the contributions of the inhabitants of Rangoon, at a vast expense.

But to return to Gwalior. About two o'clock I was amused, at the ringing of a bell, to see about half a dozen horses appear with their *syces*, to be fed; then the goats and the fowls went through the same process: about three o'clock we dined. At five we drove out in a pretty carriage and pair to see the station. My first view was a pleasing one. The cantonments consisted of a row of large thatched houses in compounds, like pretty, gay gardens, on each side of a wide road bordered with trees, and about a mile long. The road had an English look: the people were driving and riding about, and the pretty, healthy-looking children (so different from those of Calcutta) also riding or driving in little pony-carriages. We passed the church, which looked exactly like an English one, and is very well built.

Early next morning I walked with my husband to have a good survey of the church; it was not surrounded with verandas, nor had it windows down to the ground, or Venetians, or a flat roof, like the other churches I had seen. These omissions added to the beauty, but not to the coolness, so important to an Indian church. It was small, with open benches, and the chancel paved with encaustic tiles from England.

The windows—though not Waile's or Hardman's—were very prettily painted. The pulpit was of Caen stone, and the reading desk oak, with velvet cushions. On the communion-table was a velvet cloth, and books bound in Russian leather. There was an organ brought from England five years ago, but quite out of order. The architect was Major Vincent Eyre, of the Engineers.

On Sunday the 11th, my husband had a very kind note from one of Sir Robert Hamilton's brothers, saying that he and his brother (also a chaplain) would be very glad to assist him in the service; so the three chaplains divided the morning and evening services between them. The church was very well filled.

On Monday, according to an Indian custom, my husband began his round of calls. The inhabitants of the station consisted of the resident, the brigadier, the brigade-major, about thirty officers and their families, some men belonging to the telegraph office, and a few sergeants and drummers, all Europeans: there were four native regiments of the Gwalior Contingent, the rest being stationed at Jhansi, Sepree, and one or two other small stations. These troops belonged to the Company, and were officered by them, but were paid by the Maharajah of Gwalior, to whom the whole of that part of the country belonged, though under the surveillance of political agents.

The ladies then all called on me, and I returned their calls.

Our first week at Gwalior was very gay, owing to the arrival of Sir Robert Hamilton, Agent to the Governor-General, on a tour; and with him General Havelock and his Staff, on their way to Persia.

We went to a large dinner given by the Gwalior officers to Sir R. Hamilton. Though I entered the room not knowing a single person in it (as Mrs. Campbell, being ill, could not go), my Scotch descent soon made me feel among friends; for every one nearly in India is Scotch or Irish: I met many of the former who knew my father's family in Dumfriesshire. I do think there were only half a dozen genuine English in the room, including my husband.

The mess-house was a large bungalow, containing a fine dining and drawing room, a billiard and several smaller rooms.

Of course the gentlemen outnumbered the ladies; and all the former being in uniform, there was nothing to contrast with the gay dresses of the ladies, except a few black velvet dresses which some of the ladies had wisely attired themselves in. I was struck with the youthful look of the whole party; very few had passed their *"première jeunesse,"* all were nice-looking, and not many unmarried; there was not one lady unmarried.

The rooms were brilliantly lighted and prettily furnished, and the dinner just like an English one, for what could not be procured in India had been brought from Europe; including hermetically-sealed fruits, fish, and meats, and preserves, with champagne, &c. The evening ended with music, singing, and games.

A few days after, my husband went to a dinner in Sir Robert Hamilton's tent, and was introduced to General Havelock. I remember (being uninitiated into such things) asking him, on his return, "if the tent was cold," and was told it was very luxurious, carpeted with thick Mirzapore carpets, and heated by stoves, and that the dinner reminded him somewhat of a Cambridge feast.

Then the Resident gave Sir R. Hamilton a dinner, to which we all went. My husband went to a *durbar*[5] held by Sir R. Hamilton and the Maha*rajah*, in the latter's palace. I need not give a description of the *levée*; such things are well known now: there was the usual amount of *nâtch* girls, fireworks, &c., and my husband returned with a wreath of yellow jessamine, with which the natives always adorn their guests, and some packets of sweetmeats, and *pawn*,[6] and pieces of fine muslin scented with *atta* of roses, all of which I delighted my *ayah* by giving to her. My husband said he had seen many of the neighbouring chiefs, who had come to make their "*salaam*," and thought them fine-looking men.

Unfortunately the *rajah* was a Hindoo; therefore, the cow being sacred in his eyes, we were not allowed any beef, except it was brought occasionally from Agra; but the distance and heat not being favourable, we seldom tasted any. We subscribed to "the mutton club," however.

I wish the *rajah* had known what a grudge I owed him for this troublesome prejudice. These Hindoos are the most inconsistent people: I have frequently seen them starve and ill-treat their sacred animals in the most heartless and cruel manner; and

---

5. *Durbar*, a court *levée*.
6. *Pawn*, a nut wrapped in a betel leaf, and chewed by the natives.

have seen a poor bullock in a dying state, and in such suffering, that it would have been a mercy to put it out of its misery; but if you dared to do such a thing they would never forgive it, or let you forget it.

I was astonished at the fine appearance of the *sepoys* whom I saw drilled and exercised every morning. They were tall, well-made, intelligent looking men; many of them more than six feet high. They looked a soldierly set in their gay regimentals.

Their lines [7] were rows of neat small houses on each side a road, planted with trees, and kept clean by *mehters* [8] Each regiment had its separate lines and parade ground. They are well paid and handsomely rewarded, have a chance of promotion and of retiring on a good pension; all their fancies are humoured, and their religion and caste are attended to: even their festival days were kept, and (so far as I saw) their officers always treated them kindly; yet these very men were in a short time butchering their officers in cold blood!

Many of the Gwalior *sepoys* were natives of Oude, and recruits were daily coming in.

Soon after our arrival at Gwalior, we went to a picnic at the fort; and started early in the mornings at gun-fire. I must here remark how startled I was when I first heard the gun-fire at Gwalior; it was such a loud report, and so near the Campbells' house, it literally shook the bed; and then commenced the most absurd "row," beating the tattoo, sounding the bugle, and practising the artillery. The gun is fired at sunrise, noon, and sunset. But to return to our picnic: it was bitterly cold. Captain and Mrs. Campbell rode, and we drove. We passed over the bridge; the *nullah* [9] was nearly dry then, but during the rains it swells to quite a river. We were amused to see the quantity of *dhobies* [10] beating the clothes in the water, or drying them on the banks. The country beyond was very ugly: nothing but low sand-hills; not a tree or blade of grass, and so dreary, it was difficult to

7. Lines, where the native soldiers live in huts.
8. *Mehters*, sweepers, low caste natives.
9. *Nullah*, brook, river.
10. *Dhobies*, washermen.

believe it we had left such blooming gardens and comfortable houses in the middle of it. Gwalior was certainly an oasis in the desert.

We saw the telegraph office and the place where the railway was to be continued to Indore from Agra.

We met parties of natives carrying *gram* and vegetables for sale to supply the small bazaar there. The road was very bad, not being made of *kunkur*. [11] When we reached the Lushkur,[12] six miles off, we found an elephant waiting, as the road was no longer fit for a carriage, and the ascent to the fort was steep. At the *mahout's* [13] order the creature knelt and we climbed its huge sides by the help of a ladder, on to a pad—a large cushion on which four people could sit *dos-à-dos*.

It was my first ride on an elephant, therefore the rough jolting pace was rather fatiguing, but not so bad as I expected. The animal was so intelligent, and picked its way so carefully, I felt quite at ease. The *mahout* talked to it just as though it understood every word (perhaps it did), calling it by endearing names, such as "my little son" and "my brother." The road here became so narrow there was only just room for the elephant, and the steps were very long and steep. The entrance to the fort was decorated with blue and variegated tiles, which still kept their colour. The fort is in ruins, situated on the summit of a rock four miles in length, rising with perpendicular sides in the midst of a flat plain, and about two or three hundred feet high. This fort was thought impregnable till it was taken by Major Popham, in 1778; but it was afterwards ceded to the Mahrattas, and had to be retaken.

The steps we ascended were formed of immense masses of stone, much out of repair, and ran sheer up the ride of the rock. They were formerly defended on the side next the city by a wall and bastions. We wandered amongst the ruins of vast masses of masonry scattered about; some part of the building was still standing, and I thought what it must have cost to take it. As the

11. *Kunkur*, dried earth or lime.
12. Lushkur, native city of Gwalior, where the Maharajah lives.
13. *Mahout*, elephant driver.
14. Mora, place where the Europeans lived at Gwalior.

sun was getting hot, we returned to some rooms in that part which had not been destroyed, and where the officers had lived when the fort was garrisoned. They were large and cool, and sometimes the families from the Mora [14] came up and occupied them for a short time for change of air. We found here the Alexanders and their merry children. Captain and Mrs. Gilbert, Lieutenant Cockbourn, Captain Cosserat, and several others.

After breakfast we continued exploring the ruins, under the shade of large white umbrellas. There were some queer little caves cut out of the solid rocks, where the *faqueers* [15] used to live. We had a good view of the sandy plain stretched out below, where was a Mahratta encampment, the tents looking like little white dots, so far were we above. The large white palace of the Maharajah appeared some distance off: the Lushkur looked picturesque and large. This fort is dreadfully hot in the hot season, there being nothing to break the force of the scorching winds which blow over the low sandy country. We went into some of the halls, lofty and carved in stone; and into a dungeon sort of place full of rubbish and bats, where we broke off some of the coloured glazed tiles with which the roofs and walls were covered: but "sight-seeing" in India, under the heat of the dazzling sun, is very fatiguing, and we were soon glad to retire again to our pleasant shelter, where *tiffin* [16] was preparing.

We sat on the bastions watching the children playing about as merrily as any at home, and heard the distant hum of the natives rising from the plain. I was amused to see the host of natives required to bring up the tables chairs, &c., from cantonments. Many of them were women, and they made a tremendous chattering, jabbering, and squabbling.

An Indian picnic is very different to an English one, where you can scramble about as long as you choose, and where you are not obliged to rest in the cool nearly the whole time. The breakfast and *tiffin* were very good; both given by some officers of the mess.

---

15. *Faqueers*, Mahommedan religious mendicants.
16. *Tiffin*, luncheon.

At last we commenced our return home, and again climbed our trusty elephant. The rest of the party followed, some on elephants, some in *tonjons*,[17] some of the gentlemen riding. I remember Captain Cosserat riding his sure-footed Arab (a great favourite of his) down the steep steps after us. Poor fellow! he afterwards died of wounds received before Lucknow. Our descent was rather disagreeable work: though the elephant stepped very cautiously, its immense strides were rather disturbing to one's equilibrium.

I enjoyed our picnic very much; though it was rather fatiguing to dress for a dinner party immediately after our return: but we spent a most pleasant evening at the Stuarts'. Mrs. Stuart was a most amiable person; young and very pretty, and so kind and friendly that I took quite a fancy to her. She played very well, and promised to teach me to tune my piano when it arrived, as it would not do to depend on a piano-tuner coming from Calcutta. Captain Stuart was very clever, and my husband enjoyed his conversation much. He played on "the musical glasses," and their ethereal tones were very soothing.

They had a little boy and girl, who came in after dinner, as is the custom in England. We met Captain and Mrs. Hawkins, both agreeable people. They had just come in with the artillery from one of the out-stations. Captain Hawkins gave my husband some good advice about visiting the out-stations, and said he "should be glad to see him at Seepree; and as travelling in the cold weather very delightful, he must bring me with him."

We also met Dr. Kirk, a thoroughly kind, hearted Scotchman, who was just going his visits into the district, being superintending surgeon. Mrs. Kirk had gone to Calcutta to see her children off on their way to Scotland.

It is really strange to see how people meet again in such different places. One day we went to call on an officer, and I was astonished to see my husband shaking hands in the most friendly way with a (to me) strange gentleman. I soon found out he was Dr. Christison, whom my husband had met before in

---

17. *Tonjons* chair with a hood, carried by four men.

Burma, and at Cambridge.

I was much annoyed at the time; for our boxes, which we had sent off from Calcutta before we set out ourselves, had not reached Gwalior, and I had no evening dresses; all our wearing apparel being contained in two portmanteaus and some travelling cases. At last we heard they had arrived, and much disappointed we were on seeing only eleven great packing cases of books, linen, and crockery sent over by the Cape. One disadvantage to Gwalior was, it not being situated on the Grand Trunk Road, so that all our boxes and furniture had to be brought from Agra by *coolies*; but there was a corresponding advantage: we got our letters *via* Bombay, only four weeks *via* Marseilles, and five *via* Southampton.

The immense improvements that have been made within the last few years in the postal system are really surprising. Formerly a letter—that can now be sent from Calcutta to Bombay from the extreme south to the extreme part of the Affghan frontier, for the low rate of three farthings—cost one shilling; and now a letter can be sent from the centre of India to any part of Great Britain for sixpence. In former days you would not receive an answer to a letter sent by the Cape within a year; so it was like banishment: letters from the exiled one were like "angels' visits, few and far between."

My husband found great amusement and occupation for a fortnight, in taking to pieces and replacing the church organ, which, as I have before mentioned, was quite out of order: a note could not be struck without the accompaniment of a ludicrous groaning kind of noise. He had studied a book on tuning, and being of a mechanical turn, and finding it hopeless to wait for the " timer from Calcutta," he set to work, and got on very satisfactorily; till one morning he came to me in a great state of perplexity, saying, if I did not come and help him, the organ would not be ready the next day (Sunday).

I accordingly accompanied him to the church, and was very much astonished to see the different parts of the organ lying all about; however, as he had marked all the pipes and their corresponding places, I had nothing to do but hand them to him, whilst he replaced them, and soon all was accomplished to our great satisfaction. The next day one of the ladies played, and we arranged a regular practising day. Some of the ladies had been members of the Simla choir, which is a very good one. We learnt some of the very best chants and hymns, which added much to the beauty of the service, and I flatter myself that our church and service might have been compared with those of any small church in England.

The officers also were very useful and kind in taking parts and blowing the bellows. At last my husband persuaded the church bearer, by the promise of extra *rupees*, to undertake it; who evidently thought it was himself who played: often, when I was practising, he would stop suddenly, and peep round the comer grinning, as if to show me how helpless I was without his assistance.

At last the small house was vacated for us by Major Macpherson, who went to Calcutta with the Maharajah. For six weeks we had been lookers-on, but now we gradually became initiated into the *minutiæ* of life at a small station. Most people kept from twenty to thirty servants; those who had children kept a bearer or *ayah* for each child. We kept about twenty; they cost from 100*l*. to 200*l*. a year, even in a station (and in the large towns like Calcutta they cost more), and we were told we should require more *coolies* in the hot season, to pull the *punkahs*.[18]

We were obliged to keep a great number, as they will do only their own particular work: it required three to cook the dinner, one to wash, one to sweep, one to attend to the rooms, one to sew, one for the bullocks, one for the fowls, one to carry water for the animals, one for the goats and cows, two for each horse. Besides those I mentioned we required in Calcutta, and a gardener, my husband had a bearer and I two *ayahs*: a high-caste woman for a lady's maid, and a low-caste one to do the under work.

---

18. *Punkah*, a large wooden board and curtain suspended from the ceiling, and pulled by ropes.

This is to gratify another absurd prejudice; for the natives think you are not "correct" if you employ a low-caste woman about your person: a high-caste native won't stay in the same room with a low-caste, or touch or take anything from him. A lady told me she once sent her *matrané*[19] with a note to a *sepoy*, when he commanded her to throw it down, as he would not "defile himself by taking it from her." Many people keep *chuprassees* and others, to perform what one man would do in England, but in Madras and Bombay so many are not required.

We bought a share in "the Mutton Club," which is managed by an officer and hosts of satellites. The arrangements are as follows:—

> A flock of sheep is kept, and separated into three divisions; No. 1 is a lot of fresh sheep to be added to the others, called *jungle-wallahs*; [20] No. 2 are *grass-wallahs*; No. 3 are *grass and gram wallahs*, or those given both grass and *gram* daily, ready for killing; as we had a plentiful supply of mutton—a shoulder one day, and leg the next: it was " mutton hot and mutton cold, mutton young and mutton old, mutton tough and mutton tender" every day, occasionally varied by fowls, fish, and game.

We also subscribed to the Book Club, which a very good one considering the distance it from the chief emporium of civilization. We had many of the new publications *Blackwood's* and *Fraser's* Magazines, and several Indian papers, *viz., The Delhi Gazette, The Friend of India, The Mofussilite,* and a stupid thing called *The Delhi Punch,* a bad imitation of its witty namesake in England: but it required a more perfect knowledge of Hindoostanee than I possessed to understand its would-be witty sayings and pictures, which all referred to "griffs" and their mistakes.

There always are plenty of funds to be subscribed to in India; one for watering the roads, another for the band, &c. My husband had the partial superintendence of a school for natives kept

---

19. *Matrané,* a woman of the sweeper caste,
20. *Wallahs,* follows.

up by the officers, who all paid a native Christian to teach them; my husband often used to go and hear the children read: some of the mistakes they made in translating were most amusing.

The officers were getting up a band, and even were sending to England for the musical instruments, which the *sepoys* were to be taught to play; but the mutiny put a stop to it, and all other improvements.

It was now the middle of February, and very cool in the morning and evening, and not oppressively hot in the middle of the day; indeed, we made all our calls from 12 o'clock to three.

Some of the ladies walked a great deal: I knew one or two who used constantly to walk quite round the "Course," four miles long, either morning or evening. We all wore warm shawls and cloth dresses, and kept good fires in our rooms.

The station looked its best, and a walk down the road was very pleasant, with the fresh, fragrant gardens on each side, filled with sweet-scented flowers; the magnolia, with their rich fragrance, and the bright scarlet blossoms of the pomegranate contrasting with its glossy green leaves, the soft puffy golden-coloured flowers of the *barbul* (the "wax flower," as it is called, from the waxy look of its dark green leaves and white flowers), the Indian scented jessamine, various sorts of roses, and a large flower with petals like scarlet leaves, besides mignionette, larkspur, and other English flowers.

The native flowers have either an overpowering scent, or none at all. The vegetables were all kinds of melons, potatoes, yams, cucumbers, and many others, the names of which I have forgotten. The trees were the neem, different species of acacia, mango, guava, orange, and lime, a few bamboos (but no palms, as they do not grow so far north), and a tree which blossoms like a laburnum. These gardens were divided by green hedges. The bungalows were either whitewashed outside, or coloured accordingly to the inmates' taste; they had no doors, as at Calcutta, but gates, and gravel walks: most of them were occupied by pet animals of some kind, deer, doves, &c.

The road was a good one, made of *kunkur* and planted with

trees; the "Course" was edged with grass, and the whole kept in order by a staff of *bheesties* [21] and *coolies*. There were no natives in Mora, as our cantonments were called, except the *sepoys* and bazaar people; but plenty at a few villages two or three miles off, and the Lushkur was densely populated, where the Maharajah lived, about five or six miles from the Mora.

When the novelty wore off, it was very wearisome to take the same drive every day, with no change, and to meet so frequently the same people.

Having described a few of the floral beauties of Hindoostan, I must say a little for its animals; but it must be a brief mention, as I was not long enough in India to make the acquaintance of all its birds, beasts, and reptiles.

I quite agree with the words of the song, "our birds have a plumage like coloured gems;" with the exception of the vulture. I often saw this monster waddling about, gorged with food, and felt a strong inclination to shoot it. What horrid feasts they have lately been making on the bodies of our unburied dead, left exposed to their mercy, in many a forsaken station! But they act the part of scavengers in a country where putrescence is poisonous.

There are many kinds of doves, some just like our tame Barbary doves at home, others bright brown, with gold burnished breasts. The parrots are pretty, lively, but sadly mischievous creatures; bright green, with red legs and beaks, and a short purple ring round the neck. The mango bird has a brilliant yellow breast; sparrows, crows, and kites abound. The natives are very fond of a small quail, which, being of a very pugnacious disposition, they amuse themselves by teaching to fight like cocks at home. I have often seen them carrying these birds about in cages for the air.

Many people keep a bird something like a magpie with white wings and tail feathers, and a bulbul, or Indian nightingale; also a bird that only sings in the dark. The brigadier kept several of these birds, and used to send them out every day to hear the

21. *Bheesties*, water-carriers.

other birds sing. The hoopoo is very pretty, with its yellow crest, which it can expand like a peacock's tail

Tigers are not so plentiful as they used to be; but as I knew some ladies who had shot them, I suppose they are still extant. Bears and monkeys retire further into the interior, and do not frequent the stations as they used. Deer are to be found, and grey foxes; though not such fine ones as ours, with their splendid tails: but I need not recount the advantages of India as a sporting country. The squirrels are very pretty, striped grey and black, though troublesome: they squeak like guinea-pigs, and get into the "choppers"[22] of the houses. I once tried to tame a young one; but its parents and brothers made such a squeaking for several days, I was obliged to restore it to them.

The howling of the jackals at night is most disagreeable: I often used to lie awake listening to their unearthly yells, while feasting on some dead animal, or the half-burnt body of a native floating down the *nullah*. I saw several snakes, and some were killed in the garden and near the bathrooms, which they frequent for coolness. I never saw a cobra *di capella*, but I heard of some people, mostly natives, who had been bitten by them, and died.

We once had a scorpion killed in our room, and immediately had the carpets taken up, and the house searched. I knew several ladies who had been severely stung by these reptiles; the best remedy is chloroform, or laudanum. Frogs croak in chorus during the rains. Small lizards, rats, large red spiders, cockroaches two or three inches long, swarm in the house, and crickets; not only "on the hearth," but chirping in the most excited manner all over the house.

We amused ourselves during the cold weather with riding and archery. The gentlemen often went out hunting foxes and deer, and for want of nobler game, jackals and porcupines. Some of the ladies shot very well, and as my husband was very fond of archery, we intended sending for our bows, &c., which we had left at home, thinking such athletic sports could not be practised in India.

Everyone now looked healthy, and the rosy, pretty children

22. Choppers, thatched roofs.

played and laughed as merrily as they do at home. Their attendants were most kind to them; no English nurse would have
borne with them, when they were fractious and irritable, as did
these natives. I have seen a tall bearer carry an infant about for
hours, and sing it to sleep, handling it as tenderly as possible: they
watch by the children's beds at night, and if they awake, hush
them to sleep, or fan them, and bathe their heads; tending them
most carefully. The children are very fond of their own servants,
and will cry to go to them; and the *sepoys* are very proud of their
officers' children: I have often seen a little boy riding through
the lines, and all the *sepoys* saluting him and talking to him most
pleasantly. It was a very interesting sight to see a deaf and dumb
native talking on his fingers to the children, with whom he was
such a favourite, it was considered quite a treat to ask him to
spend the day with them.

Some of the regiments were reviewed during the cold
weather, and I used much to enjoy watching them; particularly
the Irregular Cavalry, with their small red turbans, often worn
over a muslin or silk skull-cap, spangled with gold, their dark
blue tunics turned up with red, red *cummerbunds*, light yellow
trowsers, large top-boots, bright arms, and well groomed horses.
The native saddle is made of cloth, the bridle of twisted cloth, and
the saddle-cloth of two colours sewed in a pattern.

Captain Alexander and Lieutenant Cockbourn had much improved their regiment, and took a great deal of pains with it Captain Alexander rode a very pretty horse, and looked very well in his
gay regimentals. Some of the *soubadshs* [23] were fine-looking men,
quite old and gray; they wore thick gold chains round their necks,
had good-conduct stripes on their arms, and medals on their breasts.
It was very amusing to see the recruits being drilled: they were not
in regimentals, and "marked time" with their long bare legs and feet,
which stood out in strong relief. The *sowars* [24] were very fine-looking men, and seemed fond of their horses, and as if they liked their
profession. Strange to say, these men never attempted to shoot their

---

23. *Soubadahs*—native captains; native officers of the highest rank.
24. *Sowars*—troopers, horse soldier

officers in the mutiny, but let them ride off to Agra, and even sent their baggage under a guard: indeed, but for the force of example, they might have remained faithful.

The *sepoys* were exercised every morning on the parade ground close to the "course;" and it was rather nervous work to drive by, with a spirited horse, as they fired with blank cartridges right across the road, at a mark.

We really had enough of soldiering at Gwalior; bugles from morning to night, sentries posted all over, a guard to each house, and all the *sepoys* saluting whenever you passed them.

I have dilated sufficiently on the bright side of war; the dark side has yet to come.

All this time these honoured, trusted *sepoys* were hiding their dread secret under the mask of submissive friendship, and lulling their unconscious victims into a fatal security; but soon they will become demons, and show their real characters, when the word is given for the slaughter! Can the massacre of Cawnpore, the struggle at Lucknow, the deaths of brave men, and women and tender children, ever be forgotten? Though India may again be a safe home, can it ever be a happy one? when the thresholds of our houses have been bathed in the blood of our friends and brothers? But enough has been said on this subject

We had some trouble in procuring horses, and were obliged to return some sent from Agra, they were such miserable creatures; but we bought a little Arab from an officer who was leaving, and one for our buggy from another officer. The horses in India are a great trouble, being so vicious. Captain Campbell had one called "Blazes:" a very suitable name for it. Horses are sometimes brought from England, but they don't thrive: in the rains they suffer from a disease in the hoofs; they are also subject to fits, falling down suddenly. I have been told a bottle of hot beer is the best restorer in such cases. They suffer much from the heat, and are not nearly so active in the hot season. You can always tell when the rains are coming, they get so skittish and play such tricks.

We heard by letters, and through the papers, of the grand "doings" of the *Rajah* at Calcutta; how he was enjoying himself and lavishing money, and gaining golden opinions: they said he spent a *lâc* [25] of *rupees*.

I was much amused to see in *The Times* the following paragraph from "our own correspondent" relative to the *Rajah* and his proceedings:—

> The Maha*rajah* of Gwalior, the chief of the Mahratta princes, is on a visit to Calcutta. He is an irascible, self-willed lad, very difficult to manage. He went the other day down the river to visit the Fort Gloucester mills. On his way he was particularly boastful, until he passed the house occupied by the King of Oude. The sight sobered him in an instant, and his zeal for civilization instantly increased. He has been well educated, but seems falling back to the true native style of thought. In England there is great sympathy for these men. In India it seems horrible that a boy of this description, without principle or restraint, should exercise, by our favour, power of life, and death ever some millions of people.

How differently is he thought of now! He is called the "Saviour of India," "the firm friend of the English," and "the wonder of faithfulness;" but I have good cause to think otherwise of him: I feel certain he might have helped us more than he did in the mutiny at Gwalior, else why did he not come down and try to stop the massacre the next morning, when he knew of it the night before—not too late to save many? One reason given for his (lukewarm) adherence to us is, his previously seeing our power at Calcutta.

About this time some of our friends—the Meades and Murrays—went out to live in tents, some miles from cantonments. They seemed to enjoy it very much, as the ladies could relax from household cares, the gentlemen shoot and fish, and the children have more air and exercise. It seemed a pleasant sort of life, and though not quite under "the greenwood tree," it was not a bad attempt at gipsying. The weather became much warmer, and we gave up fires and warm dresses.

Mrs. Alexander and her children went up to the hills, and talked

---

25. *Lâc*, ten thousand pounds.

of going to England next year, as she had children six and eight years old. Major Hennessey's sons also returned to their school in the hills, and Mrs. Stuart talked of taking her children there.

We now removed to a nice large bungalow, surrounded by a broad gravel walk, as a precaution against snakes: it stood in the middle of a very pretty compound, and was approached by a small avenue. The sittingrooms were only divided by curtains hung across archways; the walls were light yellow, the mouldings picked out with white, which gave it quite a gay look. The garden was very well laid out, and filled with flowers and trees, and had a pretty walk, sheltered with an archway of vines.

We were soon settled in our new home, and had *dirzies* [27] to make up the carpets which had been brought from Agra, where they were made by the prisoners. Our buggy and my piano arrived, and, above all, a box of German and other new books, and the remainder of my husband's college books. Russian leather is the best binding for India, as the damp and insects spoil all other bindings.

We heard of the arrival of General Havelock and the officers of his division in Persia, and afterwards of their brilliant campaign, and General Sir James Outram's victories.

The shadows of the "coming events" now began to cast a gloom over us, and our calm was slightly ruffled by hearing of some disturbances at Dumdum and Barrackpore, about the cartridges for the Enfield rifle. Government had ordered mutton fat to be supplied by the contractors; but as they used pig's and bullock's fat, the *sepoys* soon found out the cheat, and made a "row" about "caste;" however, after a speech from the brigadier, they quieted down, and we soon ceased to be interested in the affair, thinking it only some trifling explosion about that bugbear, caste.

Then we heard of a mysterious affair about some *chupatties*. [28] It seemed that a *chowkedar* [29] of Cawnpore gave to a *chowkedar* of Futteghur two *chupatties*, with an order to make ten more, and give two to each of the nearest *chowkedars* to distribute in like manner. In

---

27. *Dirzies*, tailor.
28. *Chupattiee*, unleavened cakes.
29. *Chowkedar*, watchman.

57

this way they spread from village to village, and from province to province. Government was quite nonplussed. Some thought it was a ceremony to avert cholera, which had been frightfully prevalent in the North-West Provinces the year before; others said it was of superstitious origin; and some hinted at treason. But like everything connected with the natives, it was wrapped in mystery: certainly they were veiled under a marvellous cloak of caution, considering the deep and sanguinary plot they were hatching.

During April the weather became much warmer, and we were obliged to alter the hours for service on Sunday to half-past six, morning and evening; indeed we were soon obliged to vacate the church entirely in the evening, and have service in the mess-house. Many people began to complain of fever, and all to look less blooming and healthy. We rose earlier in the morning, gave up walking, and never remained out after 7 a. m., nor ventured out till after sunset We also had our *punkahs* and *tatties* [30] hung now.

The latter are made of a fragrant grass that grows in the jungles, and, as they retain water a long time, make it pleasant and cool. All began making or repairing their therm-antidotes, a thing very like a large winnowing machine; it is covered at the top and sides with a frame of wet woven grass, and the hot air passing through is coded by evaporation. The Campbells' were made of brick; and though they kept the thermometer in the house down to 60° when outside it was 120°, they quite spoiled the appearance of the house. These cost about 50*l.* each; but some are made of wood, and are cheaper.

These are of no use at Calcutta, as they have no hot winds there. The following passage, taken from MacFarlane's account of the Mahratta campaign, will give the best idea of the heat in the provinces:—

The country was everywhere swept by a burning wind, called by the natives 'the devil's breath.' It sweeps over the great sandy plains of this part of the country, and imparts to the atmosphere an intensity of heat which astonishes even those who had long been accustomed to the fury of a vertical sun. Westward

---

30. *Tatties*, a screen of thatch kept wetted for the hot winds to pass through.

of the Jumna this pestiferous current, this fiery blast, finds no rivers and lakes to temper its severity.

One of the officers, who was scorched and withered by it, compares it to the extreme glow of an iron foundry, in the height of summer. Major Thorn says, though, even that is but a feeble comparison, since no idea can be formed of the causticity of the sandy particles, borne along with the wind like hot embers, peeling off the skin and raising blisters wherever they fall. The heat was so great the soldiers died by tens and fifteens daily. Young men, who went out in the morning in the full vigour of health and spirits, fell down dead immediately on reaching the encamping ground, and many were smitten on the road by the noonday sun, whose rays darted downward like torrents of fire.

It was very dull to sit before the *tatties* all day reading; for we could do little else. Not a sound was heard after seven or nine in the morning. Even the birds seemed scared into silence; but the great heat did not commence till the end of April, and was at its worst during May and June, The first warning we had of the coming heat was a curious phenomenon in the shape of a dust-storm. Suddenly one afternoon a violent wind came on, filling the air to a great height with fine dust, rendering it almost dark, and casting a lurid light over everything. The servants said it was the "*tufân.*"[31] The trees bent and shook, and the storm came on in all its fury. It grew darker and darker, and felt quite suffocating; everything was covered with fine sand, and the doors and windows shook and rattled. After lasting half an hour it grew lighter, and the servants opened the doors and began dusting the sand off the furniture. These storms are very frequent in India, and are said to do good by clearing the air.

Some very agreeable people passed through Gwalior, on their way to Sepree; Dr. James and his wife. They had only just been married and arrived from England. Mrs. James was admired by everyone, and thought to be very pretty and engaging. They stayed a

---

31. *Tufân*, probably the original of Typhoon.

few days with the Kirkes. Poor things! they were shortly afterwards killed in the mutiny at Sepree, in a very shocking way. I could relate many horrible things that happened to people whom I knew, and describe how they were killed; but I wish to spare the feelings of their friends at home.

This I know, from authentic sources, that people were mutilated in the most frightful manner: a friend of mine saw two ladies in Calcutta who had had their noses and ears cut off. These facts are doubted by many people in England. A natural aversion from dwelling upon deeds of atrocity and human sufferings, renders sensitive persons reluctant to credit horrible facts, and disinclined to hear of the miseries of even their own countrymen. They exclaim, "Oh, how dreadful; but don't tell me! I can't bear it!" But the truth must come home to them at last.

Death will come, it matters not in what shape; whether as it comes to some, lying quietly on a bed of down, with kind friends around, or as it has come to others, equally tenderly brought up, who have been left by a cruel enemy slowly to gasp out life on some sandy plain, with not a drop of water to quench their agonising thirst, or a hand to close their eyes, and at the mercy of jackals and vultures; or mangled, torn, and tortured, after seeing those nearest and dearest to them put to a shameful death, from which there is no escape. We cannot always lie on a bed of roses, sipping the sweets of life, and taste not of its woes and pangs.

I have not mentioned a very kind friend of ours, Major Shirreff, who used often to come and see us, and lend us newspapers: he told us what he thought was the cause of the disturbances at Barrackpore and Dumdum, and explained the *chupatty* mystery; he also gave us valuable hints about our garden and servants, and would walk in our garden, telling me the names of birds and plants strange to me. He and my husband used to have long talks about the "Overland route," and we lent him *Murray's Guide*, describing the route *via* Trieste, as he wished to get home as soon as possible. He anticipated with great delight his approaching departure for England: yet he liked the natives very much, and always had a good word to say for them.

When my husband occasionally dined at the mess on their public nights, I joined the ladies, who always met together during the absence of their husbands, and talked about their children, books, and the news.

One evening we dined with the Meades, and met Major and Mrs. Blake, who had just returned to India. Major Blake had done much good service in Bundelcund, and received the well-merited thanks of Government; he had also raised his regiment (the 1st), which was considered the best in the Contingent He was a kind, good man, tall and soldierly looking, with a very benevolent face, and a brave, excellent officer: he was a great favourite with his men, who, during his absence, used constantly to come to his brother officers to hear news of him; and even prayed for his safe and speedy return.

Poor Major Blake! he met his death by the hands of these very men—or at least, men of the same Contingent; for, like a true officer, he fearlessly rode to the lines to see what could be done, when he was instantly shot. He was sincerely regretted by all who knew him, for his kindness of heart had attached many friends.

We went to a musical party given by Captain Pearson, one of the few unmarried officers. His house was one of the two *pucka* houses, built in the Elizabethan style, by the architect of the church. The evening passed very pleasantly in singing and playing the piano, concertina, violin, flute, &c. It was the last pleasant party we had; after that, all was gloom and misery.

We heard of the shocking suicides of the Commodore of the *Mary* and of General Stalker. The reason we heard assigned for this, both in the papers and by people who ought to know, was that the Indian climate so upsets people's nerves as to render them unfit for any great excitement or responsibility. Certainly, in the dreadful crisis of the mutiny much loss of life and great misery were occasioned by the incapability and vacillation of some of the superior officers: but we must not forget what we owe to others.

To the living we owe an everlasting debt of gratitude—Sir John Lawrence, Mr. Montgomery, Sir Archdale Wilson, Sir James

Outram, Sir Hope Grant, and many others; and to the dead a never-dying memory of their great deeds—Havelock, Neill, Nicholson, Lawrence, and Wheeler. England and Scotland have good cause to be proud of their chivalrous and noble sons. Who can forget Willoughby,[32] Salkeld, Home, and the other heroes of the Cashmere Gate!

We still heard very unpleasant reports; though things had been kept so quiet that we did not hear of the first disturbances at Barrackpore, which occurred on the 28th of January, till the middle of February. Then the papers began to take more notice of the gathering storm. First, we heard of a special court of inquiry being assembled at Barrackpore; next, of the determination of the *sepoys* there to rise against their officers, proceed to Calcutta, and attempt to take Fort William; then of a general parade at Berhampore; afterwards of a native court-martial taking place at Fort William, which condemned two *sepoys* to fourteen years' imprisonment for mutinous conduct; subsequently, of the mutinous behaviour of Mungul Pandy, a *sepoy* of the 34th Regiment; and, finally, of the disbanding of the 19th Regiment at Barrackpore, by General Hearsey.

Sometime in April, the Maha*rajah* returned with Major Macpherson, who brought with him his sister, Mrs. Innes; Lieutenant Innes having gone to Lucknow. The *rajah* seemed to have enjoyed himself very much, and to be pleased with the flattering impression he had made at Calcutta.

The last grand military display we had was the blowing up of a mud fort; it was a very striking sight Who could believe these suave, respectful *sepoys* were cherishing a diabolical plot! I here saw, for the first time, the *rajah*; he was plainly dressed, and did not look very kingly, or in any way striking. Of course, there was a large throng of natives come in to enjoy the "*tomascha.*"[33]

Shortly after his arrival, the Maha*rajah* gave a grand fête. We were invited; bat as I did not care to see this display of native parade, and as it was very hot, we declined the invitation.

---

32. "The hero who, with his own brand, fired the Magazine at Delhi"
33. *Tomascha*—games, amusements.

CHAPTER 4

The Mutinies

It seems surpassingly strange that so little notice was taken of the impending danger by those whose duty it was to care for the safety of a mighty empire. We had, at the beginning of the year 1857, three regiments less than before the annexation of Oude. There were no European regiments at many of the largest stations: Allahabad, Cawnpore, Benares, and Delhi, were all left to the protection of disaffected regiments. The Government at Calcutta, in serene complacency, was coolly issuing orders for the disbanding of regiments: as though that could in any way stop the evil

We now heard of the hanging of Mungul Pandy and of incendiarisms at Umballa. Many reasons were assigned for these disturbances: first, the trumpery one of the greased cartridges; and, secondly, the annexation of Oude. But neither of these were the real reason.

The heat now began to be overpowering: I was awakened one morning by the most stifling sensation in the air, and felt quite ill. The *ayah* and bearer said the hot winds had commenced. Really, I did think it was very "*arg ke mâfick*" (like fire): it made your brain feel on fire, and all the blood in your body throb and burn like liquid fire. We drove out for a short time, and I was struck with the gray, lurid look of the sky: the trees looked dry and withered.

We could no longer drive round the "course;" the only bearable place was the well-watered road between the houses. Gwalior cantonments are situated in a hollow, therefore the hot winds sweep over them unimpeded.

We felt languid and weary, and every precaution was taken to mitigate the intense heat We bathed many times in the day, and drank cooling drinks—particularly soda-water. Indeed, so much of this do the Europeans drink, the natives think it is the only water we have at home, and call it *"belathee pámee"* (foreign water).

Mr. and Mrs. Pierson arrived during the hot weather. It seems strange that in the mutiny, though Mr. Pierson was not so well known or so much liked by his men as Major Blake, Captain Stuart, and Dr. Kirke, yet they not only spared him and his wife, but assisted them to escape. A little before this, a man from Calcutta arrived to take photographs, and stayed some time. Some of these photographs were actually recovered after the mutinies, and sent into Agra. The Stuarts were taken in groups, and made very pretty pictures, which were sent home, and, I believe, arrived there safely. What a comfort they must have been! I saw several groups of *sepoys* taken also. Many photographs were found in the room of horrors at Cawnpore!

The tempest had been brewing at Meerut for some time: bungalows and houses were burnt, and no one knew who had perpetrated these flagrant acts of revolt At last eighty-five troopers, having refused to fire with the cartridges supplied them, were sentenced to six and ten years' imprisonment. In spite of the sullen, defiant looks of the *sepoys*, they were carried to a prison two miles off, in the native city, instead of being under an English guard. But for this, the terrible plot would have remained concealed till the day fixed for a simultaneous rising; when, doubtless, the consequences would have been much more terrible than they were.

All went on as usual till Sunday (the fatal day), the 10th of May.

The news, by means of the telegraph, was all over India by the 13th; but we then hoped it was not known to the natives, precautions having been taken to prevent them corresponding. It burst on us at Gwalior like a thunderclap, and paralysed us with horror. We could not help wondering how a plot, known to so many thousands, could so long remain secret, and all things

64

go on quietly as ever. We did not see the terrible details till a day or two afterwards, when we were dining with the Stuarts: I remember our gloomy forebodings, and how we talked of what had happened. Little more than a month after, out of the nine people assembled together that night, there were only three survivors.

Captain Stuart sent to the *dâk* office, at the Lushkur, for the papers, that we might see the list of killed and escaped, as many of us were in anxious suspense about friends at Meerut. Oh! what a number of people have been cut off in the full pride and vigour of youth in these fearful mutinies. What happy homes have been desolated and hearts broken! The particulars of the Delhi and Meerut mutinies are now too well known: I will not dwell on them; but think how we must have heard of them at Gwalior!

Martial law was now proclaimed in the Meerut district, and Sir Henry Lawrence sent the following telegraphic message to the Governor-General:—

All is quiet here; but affairs are critical. Get every European you can from China, Ceylon, and elsewhere; also all the Goorkas from the Hills: time is everything.

On the 17th, the whole Contingent was paraded to hear the Government proclamation, which was read by Brigadier Ramsey, who also addressed them. This he could do very well, as he knew the language perfectly. Captain Pearson and Lieutenant Cockbourn left Gwalior with half the cavalry and artillery regiments. Captain Campbell left also for Agra in command of the *rajah's* body-guard.

Major Macpherson now took uip his abode in the cantonments. We went one day to dine with him, and I was introduced to the Maharajah Scindiah, who happened to be there. I have a distinct recollection, when he shook hands with me, of his limp cold hand— just like all natives.

From that time the *rajah* used frequently to come to the cantonments to see Major Macpherson.

I can never forget the fearful gloom of that month; but as our feelings are better described in my own and my husband's letters home, I will here insert some of them.

Gwalior, Saturday, May 16th; 1857.

I write to you today, although the mail does not leave Bombay until the 28th, because there is no knowing now how long the road between this and Bombay will be open for the passage of the mails. The country, north of Agra, is in a dreadful state. You will probably have heard of mutiny and disaffection having shown itself in some native regiments near Calcutta, in consequence of which some men were hung, and one whole native regiment and part of another were disbanded: apparently the severest punishment the Government dared to inflict Well, it appears now that there has been an attempt at conspiracy for a general rising throughout the country.

It is known that it was intended to rise upon all the Europeans and murder them. And now the insurrection has broken out at Lucknow, Meerut, and Delhi, and other places, where there are no European regiments, the English are of course entirely at the mercy of the brutal, treacherous native soldiers; and, as you see, it has been only the presence of two English regiments at Meerut that has saved any of the Europeans.

Of course we are alarmed here. There are only about twenty English officers, with their wives and children, in the station, and about 5,000 native troops, so that we are entirely at their mercy. Already, half of our native cavalry and half of the artillery have been sent to Agra, and these were far more to be trusted than the infantry who remain. Even the *rajah's* bodyguard has gone to Agra.

There is an English regiment at Agra, but there are many native regiments, 3,000 cut-throats in the gaol, and a hostile population; so that they would have little chance against so many enemies. And, positively, the Governor has called up all the native regiments, and told them that if they do not like the service, they are at liberty to leave it without molestation. Fancy such a course as this when a rising is feared throughout the country!

I do not think that our lives are safe for a moment Oh, how gladly would I send off my wife to England, or even to Agra, this moment if I could. The insurgents, of course, will be increasing every day, and if they come here, the native soldiers have as good as told their officers that they will not resist them;—'they will not fight against their brethren;' and it would not be simply death to fall into their hands.

This is God's punishment upon all the weak tampering with idolatry and flattering vile superstitions. The *sepoys* have been allowed to have their own way as to this and that thing which they pretended was part of their religion, and so have been spoiled and allowed to see that we were frightened of them. And now no one can tell what will be the end of it There is no great general to put things right by a bold stroke. We shall all be cut up piecemeal.

Instead of remaining to have our throats cut, we ought to have gone to Agra long ago, or towards Bombay; and all the European regiments should have been drawn together, and every native regiment that showed the least sign of disaffection at once destroyed, or at least driven away for, as a leading article in the Agra paper of this morning observes, what native regiment can now be trusted? I would leave for Bombay at once, but it would be death to be exposed even for an hour to the sun. What to do I know not The officers of course dare not stir one step, but I wonder they do not contrive some plan for sending the ladies and children up to Agra, or to some place where there are English troops. There is gloom on the few English faces, and a scowl upon the face of every native already.

This letter will certainly make you very anxious about us. Sarah happily is all safe, being near Calcutta; but I hope you will get a more favourable account from me enclosed with this, or, at least, hear that we are in some place of safety. I would send my wife off at once if I had the chance. The possibility even of our falling into the hands of these demons is horrible

G. W. Coopland.

P. S. It is dreadfully hot here: everything is like fire.

Gwalior, May 19th, 1857.

I shall write to you some time before the mail will leave Bombay, but in the very unsettled state of the country, and the *dâk* being stopped, it is better not to lose any time. You will know what dreadful times we live in, when we cannot be rare of our lives for a day, and live in a state of constant anxiety and dread. You will perhaps have seen in the papers that there have been riots in India. The insurgents are now spreading themselves all over. Nothing has yet been heard of the officers, their wives, and families, at Delhi.

The rebels have set up a king and a judge there. They seem to have chosen the best time for rebelling, when the hot weather is commencing, and it would be dangerous for the European troops to be exposed to it. All the regiments from the Hills are being ordered down to reinforce Delhi, Meerut, and other important stations; but it will be long before anything can be done, as no reliance can be placed on the native troops.

Here the troops say they won't fight against their brethren. The artillery and cavalry have left here for Agra, together with the Maharajah's bodyguard, which Captain Campbell has the temporary command of. There are only about thirty Englishmen in this station, and the native troops are not the least to be depended upon. They would most likely take part with the insurgents, of whom there must now be a great number; and they will soon be joined by all who hate the English. The insubordination in our own servants is most remarkable. They look as if they would like to cut our throats.

The life we lead is quite miserable; the heat before was bad enough to bear, but now it is dreadful, when you live in fear of your life. Here we are in the midst of a lot of savages (for most of than are nothing better), seventy miles from any European regiment, and the insurgents are not for from us. They attacked a small station between here and Agra, and nearly murdered an officer. They murder people in the most cold-blooded way. At Agra there are 3,000 cut-throats in the gaol, very badly guarded, and if they were let out, what would be the consequences?

I wish we were safe at home. George has his rifle in readiness. All night long we are only separated by a thin piece of wood from our *coolies* who pull the *punkahs*, and who would not hesitate to cut our throats if they had the chance.

We do not know from day to day what will happen. Captain Campbell gave his wife a brace of loaded pistols before he left her, so you may fancy the state we live in. I hope we shall soon hear better news when the English troops meet the rebels; but they will never be able to stand the heat, as they are only invalided troops from the Hills. Poor Sarah Money (formerly Menteath) had to part from her husband not a month after their marriage, as his regiment was ordered against the rebels.

R. M. Coopland.

Gwalior, May 22nd, 1857.

I have already sent off a letter for you, for the mail which is to leave Bombay on May 28th, giving you an account of the dreadful rebellion that has broken out in India. I am very sorry that I have no better news to give you now; we are still in great uncertainty and danger.

Nothing of course is heard from Delhi, which is still in the hands of the rebels; and it is to be feared that many of the Europeans who were there when the rebellion broke out have been massacred. I gave you before the names of some that had been murdered there, and nothing further has been heard.

It is a dreadful time for Europeans to have to move down into the plains; but of course it was necessary to strike a blow at once.

We hear that the commander-in-chief is already on his way

to Delhi with three European regiments, cavalry and artillery, and two or three native regiments that are supposed to be yet faithful; and it is said that native troops will be found sufficiently trustworthy from stations near Delhi to help in surrounding and investing it. It will be long even before they reach it, so we shall have to wait to know our fete, and the fate, apparently, of English empire in India. It seems that the massacre at Meerut was frightful; that though there were two English regiments in the station, the natives succeeded in murdering a large number of their officers, and many women and children. But we have heard nothing certain.

The mutineers from Meerut and other places have already spread themselves over the country, and just now something terrible has happened at Etawah, a small station only about forty miles to the east of this place, for a whole regiment has been hurried away thither from here this morning. It is to be hoped that they will be faithful. They are all natives, and have only three English officers.

We get no newspapers, and as I, of course, am not admitted to military consultations here, the only news we get is by chance conversation, or by my writing to the brigade major, or some other officer, and asking what is going on.

You know that we are not in English dominions, but in those of the *Rajah* of Gwalior. Happily he remains faithful to the English, at least so far, and in appearance, though now no one can tell what native is to be trusted.

The weather is now dreadfully close and hot, though they say that the extreme heat has not yet set in.

The change in the behaviour of all servants and natives is wonderful, since the disturbances broke out All are insolent, no longer like submissive slaves, but as if they were very forbearing in not at once murdering you; and the people eye us, when we drive out, in the most sinister and malicious way.

G. W. Coopland.

Gwalior, May 23rd.

I write again, as I think you may be anxious to know how things go on.

We are all in a very anxious and dreadful position; for what must be a decisive blow to this dreadful conspiracy, is now going on at Delhi A large force of English troops have reached Delhi, and are to commence operations today. The last mail from Agra, which came in today, brought word that the rebels had taken Allyghur, where there is a treasury, and so had got possession of a large amount of money, and had stopped the communication with the Punjaub; so that now we can know nothing certain of the state of things there, and can only hope that the *sepoys* will remain faithful there; for if they join the rebels, all is lost.

The fate of India will be decided in two or three days— perhaps is deciding now. There are supposed to be 7,000 *sepoys*, all trained by the English, in possession of Delhi; and it is now believed they have a large number of English officers prisoners, whom they have not yet murdered. Our fate depends upon the result at Delhi; the slightest failure will be the signal for re-volt and massacre among all the native troops throughout the country. Of course here, as everywhere else, there is the most anxious expectation, There are now only ten English offic-ers in the station, with many ladies and children, and in the midst of native troops ready to break out at a moment's notice, and are only waiting to see what happens at Delhi.

We hope that Agra is safe, as our own lot depends, in a great measure, upon it. There is great fear, if Delhi is not taken, of the insurgents coming here, as Gwalior is on their way, and the atrocities they commit are fearful to think of. The insurgents have burnt down a railway station-house not very far from Cal-cutta, so it will be very difficult to get there now; they have also burnt down a large hospital at Agra. The rebels intend to make terms, by means of the prisoners, with the English who are now besieging Delhi.

One young officer did a very brave thing—he blew up a

71

place containing firearms of all sorts. It is supposed he blew himself up with it, as nothing has been since heard of him. You have no idea of the gloom here; people seldom go out of their houses, and all look as if they expected some dreadful calamity. We dined last night with the Stuarts. Several officers were there, and they all spoke most doubtfully of things, and said, if a decisive blow was not struck at Delhi, it would be all over with the English.

It will be dreadful work for the regiments to have forced marches in these scorching winds. We have no news from the Punjaub, as the *dâk* is stopped. Things have been in a very unsettled state at Peshawur for some time; they killed an officer who was out of cantonments lately. This is worse than the Santal rebellion, as it is amongst the Company's own troops. Some of the native regiments that left here are now at Delhi Some of the officers I met last night said they had observed the insolent manner of the *sepoys* here for sometime.

R. M. Coopland

P.S.—Before I write again, I hope to have better news for you; if not, there is no knowing if we shall be alive.

Gwalior, June 2nd.

I am very sorry to say that the aspect of things is not at all more favourable now, and we ourselves have been during the last few days in the midst of the greatest alarm and trouble. The rebellion continues to spread all around us, and has broken out, it is to be feared, even in the Punjaub; but we do not hear much, and that very irregularly, since, in many places, the post roads and telegraphs are in the possession of the rebels, and where it is open the Government keep it to themselves, and seem to hide the real state of things as much as possible from the people.

But we know that at Etawah (perhaps sixty or seventy miles from us) the houses of the officers have been pillaged and burnt down, and the treasury carried off; the same has been done at Mynpoorie, a considerable station between Agra and Cawnpore. The insurgents are all over the country, plundering and murdering as they please.

Nothing has yet been heard from Delhi, everything being in the hands of many thousands of rebels, who have got possession of treasure, it is said, to the amount of between half a million and a million of *rupees*, besides the property that they have got in Delhi, which was a very wealthy city. It was expected that the commander-in-chief would have made an attack upon Delhi a week ago, and now that nothing is heard of him, we are almost in despair; either he is panic-struck, or the native troops we trusted have turned traitors, or he has been defeated, or cholera has broken out among his troops. And everything depends upon his success; if he is defeated, we shall all go at once.

It is terrible to watch how fear has gradually come over the Government First, there was a proclamation promising speedy extermination to all rebels, saying that English troops were gathering from all quarters, and that vengeance would soon overtake their enemies. Now, to our shame and humiliation, a proclamation has appeared, declaring that every *sepoy* who has taken part in this rebellion will be allowed to go to his home in. peace on giving up his arms at the nearest station, *i.e.* offering entire impunity to the wretches that have murdered and treated with every outrage our women, and children, and devastated everything with fire and sword.

But now to come to ourselves. Two regiments and the cavalry having been lately sent off to other places, there are now here two regiments of infantry, two companies of artillery, and perhaps a hundred cavalry. The English community consists now of eleven officers, mostly with wives and children, three surgeons, the wives and families of four officers that have been sent off with their regiments, and four sergeants with wives and children.

Well, it seems that on Wednesday last, and during Thursday, the most dreadful reports kept coming in to the brigadier, the political agent, and some other officers secretly, that the whole of the troops here were to rise simultaneously on Thursday evening, at eleven o'clock, and burn down all our houses and murder us; of course none of these reports ever reached us, and about half-past five on Thursday evening Captain Murray game rushing into our house, and asked to see me alone.

He told me that he had been sent by the brigade-major to inform me that the troops were going to rise at eleven o'clock that night, and make wholesale burning and slaughtering; that every woman and child either had fled, or must at once make off to the Residency—a large house between seven and eight miles off, where the political agent at the Court of Gwalior lives; and that I must drive my wife over there in our buggy, since arrangements had been made for the occupation of all carriages in the station. It was of the utmost importance that our flight should be made unobserved; we must wait till the usual time of our evening drive, and pretending that we were going out as usual, must slip off on the road to the Residency; we must not take anything with us, for fear of exciting suspicion.

This was all said in a few moments, and the officer hurried away. You may imagine our feelings, not knowing how many had escaped, nor whether we should succeed in doing so, or should be stopped on the road. We hastily dressed, and ordered our buggy to be ready, not without many fears that perhaps the groom had run away, or the horse would be found lame; we took each a nightdress, gave a last look at our nice drawing-room, favourite books, &c, and my wife played on her piano, probably for the last time, and then about half-past six we got into our buggy and drove off, leaving our money and everything we had, just as if we were going out for our customary evening drive.

I first drove down the station, thinking to avoid suspicion, and then drove into Mrs. Campbell's compound, to ask if she had gone. We found that she had gone early that morning, and so, thinking there was no time to lose, turned down the road towards our place of refuge. We had at once to pass a long bridge guarded by soldiers, and there feared we should be stopped; but happily they let us pass, and we got clear out upon the road. The road was frightfully bad, in some places covered by gullies, and I had never been that way before, so that as darkness came on, and we were obliged to depend on the directions of any passing natives, and we were frequently passed by armed cavalry, we were not a little uncomfortable, and began at last to think (such was the wild, desolate look of the surrounding country) that we were being entrapped. At last we reached a large encampment of Mahratta horse and infantry surrounding a large stone house, which we were glad to find was to be our place of refuge.

I have not time to give you a minute description of all that occurred here. You must imagine thirteen ladies, almost all with one or two children, and four sergeants' wives with their children, crowded together, having just left their husbands, as they supposed, in the greatest danger, and expecting that their houses, and all that they had, would in a few hours be in flames, and a birth and death both expected to happen any time; no beds, no change of dress, and suffocatingly hot; and then an order that everyone should be ready to start at a moment's notice, for perhaps we might have to hurry off towards Agra.

The political agent, a son of one of our officers, and an invalid soldier, were the only white men present You must imagine what a night we passed, entirely in the hands of the *Rajah's* troops, and expecting to hear the officers that might have survived come galloping in with news that all was over.

But news came at last that the officers had gone among their men, and that the dreadful hour was passed, and no outbreak had been made; and then that the officers were sleeping among the lines, and the artillery officers and the brigadier before the guns, so that it was supposed that the storm had passed for the present—to burst out on another opportunity. Early in the morning we were told that the *rajah* had intimated that he could not afford troops to guard us at that distance; we must come down to one of his palaces.

Of course we were obliged to submit; and before long the natives of Gwalior crowded to a sight such as never had been seen in their streets before. Fifteen or sixteen carriages dashing through, surrounded by hundreds of wild Mahratta horsemen, and filled with English ladies and children. A gallop of four or five miles, through heat and dust, brought us to the *rajah's* palace.

After waiting sometime in the courtyard, we were conducted up a long flight of steps to the top of one part of the palace, which we were afterwards informed was near the *rajah's* harem. Such misery I have seldom seen—poor little children crying, ladies half dead with heat and fatigue, some in tears; nothing to defend us from the heat; one mother weeping over a child supposed to be dying, without medical aid or necessaries of any kind.

The *rajah*, however, did what he could—sent in some old English chairs and a table which he happened to possess, and two or three native beds; and even had frames, filled with thorns, put in where there were no windows, in order that water might be thrown upon them to keep us cooler. The heat, however, was terrific, and we began to think how many such days it would be possible to survive.

As night came on, a few native beds were brought in, and, as far as they went, assigned to the different ladies. The excitement in the native city below us was immense—the people crowding round the palace and gathering on the tops of the neighbouring houses to get a glimpse of the English prisoners.

An immense number of troops was brought up to guard us, and large cannon without end.

After another miserable night—I never got water to wash my face, or changed my linen, (my wife, happily for her, shared a bed with another lady this night,)—we were told a messenger had arrived from the brigadier, to the effect that we were to return at once to the station.

It appeared that the men had determined to remain faithful for the present, and that the native officers had gone to the brigadier, and explained that they were offended at the departure of the ladies and at their being placed under the care of the *rajah*; that their men would remain faithful, and we had nothing to fear.

About six a.m. we bade farewell to the *rajah's* palace, and reached our houses again about seven, finding all just as we had left it This was Saturday morning, and here we are still, Tuesday morning; but our condition is very pitiable. We are here only on sufferance; our masters are always around us: we have to be obliged to them for not burning down our houses and massacring us. How can we trust one of them, when we know that regiments just like them have been guilty of every enormity?

How gladly should I find myself with my wife on board an English steamer! but we cannot escape now, the roads are unsafe, even if the climate spared us. If a great blow is not struck soon at Delhi, all will go. The Governor of Agra is most anxious that the news of our alarm here should not reach Agra, fearing the effects of it there, though they have one English regiment Where this will end no one can tell.

The country is no longer ours, but in the hands of *sepoys*; and our lives, and all we have, too. I hope you will all compassionate us, and think about us; and if it is not too late, I hope England will not leave us to be massacred with impunity, but send troops to save us: though, perhaps, all will be over before they reach us.

G. W. Coopland.

P. S. Wednesday morning, June 3rd.—Worse news still. We

depended upon Agra, and now we hear that the European regiment there has had to set upon the two native regiments, and disarm them: what the 1,600 villains let loose will do, we cannot tell. No news from Delhi; everyone asks what the commander-in-chief can be about? There are also fears about the native troops at Allahabad; and if they took the fort there, they would get, it is said, 30,000 or 40,000 stand of arms. Enough to arm the whole country against us.

Gwalior, June 11th.

You will be anxious to hear how things are going on. Well, first of all, I must tell you that the good news of the fall of Delhi has just now come to us by telegraph from Agra. We have heard no particulars, and only know that Delhi was taken on the 8th, and that arrangements were being made for levelling the whole place to the ground. When I wrote to you last, I said that we were all wondering what had become of the commander-in-chief and his army, and hoping soon to hear of his arrival before Delhi.

Well, next morning news came that he had died of cholera at Kurnaul. Since then, up to this morning, each day has brought us intelligence of some additional disaster. First, we heard that at Lucknow, where encomiums had been delivered by the authorities on the loyalty of the troops, everything was in disorder, the city burnt down, the troops in open mutiny. Next, that the same was occurring throughout the Punjaub, at Mean Meer, Ferozepore, and other places; that even in Peshawur, it had become necessary to disarm the native troops; that at Umballa all the native troops had mutinied, and been cut up by the Europeans coming down from the hills.

Next came news of an alarm from Simla, where invalids, ladies, and children are assembled in multitudes, having gone up to escape the heat of the plains. The native troops had proposed terms to. these poor creatures, on which they were to be spared. Hundreds had been crowded for safety into some magazine, or building of the kind, without beds or any other comfort Several ladies had lost their intellects through terror; some had escaped on foot into the jungles; many had fled to Dugshai and Kussowlie, and there cholera had broken out among them.

Another day informed us that all the native troops at Bareilly had mutinied, and that the whole district of Rohilcund was up in arms. Then came word that in our own neighbourhood, at Ajmere and Nusseerabad, the whole of the native troops had risen and carried off the artillery towards Delhi, though there was a European regiment present, and that several officers of this regiment had fallen in a fight with them.

Then we heard worse news, that at Neemuch the same tragedy had been enacted, and that all the troops there had mutinied, including even one regiment of this Gwalior Contingent

This last news has been carefully kept secret, since it was feared that the troops here might be shaken when they heard of the defection of one of their own regiments. This Contingent having, up to this time, remained sound.

On Sunday night last we were alarmed by loud shouting, and on going out I found the roads full of artillery and native troops making off towards Jhansi: a neighbouring station, where the troops had risen and carried off the treasury, the officers and their families having fled into the fort They went out some distance, but were recalled the same evening, it being feared that they would not face the rebels at Jhansi.

Since then we have been in great doubt and uncertainty, not knowing that the next hour might not bring a like calamity on ourselves.

As yet the men here remain quiet, but we are altogether at their mercy. They do almost what they like: lie down while on guard; laugh at us, and seem to enjoy the consternation and looks of constraint and uneasiness that are plainly visible among us. The least hope of success at Delhi would have set all into a flame. You may imagine our peace of mind has not been very great, receiving, as we have done, every day fresh details of horrible outrages and massacres.

Some time ago we heard very bad news from Calcutta. The fort there, Fort William, the bulwark of India, with all its stores, arsenals, and magazines, was within a hair's breadth of falling into the hands of the traitors. If it had not been for the loyalty of one native officer, who divulged the plot, the fort would have been seized by mutineers, and the whole capital of India would have fallen into their hands. We afterwards heard that there had been a panic in Calcutta. Multitudes had fled on board the shipping in the river, arms had been served out to all Europeans, volunteers were being enrolled, and even the French were preparing to assist against the enemy.

But now we cannot hear what may be the fate of Calcutta, or even of Allahabad and Cawnpore; all the country towards Calcutta and the trunk road being in the possession of the traitors, and every *dâk* and telegraph being destroyed, even as far as Mynpoorie, near Agra. I hope you will have good news from Benares. I think they are as safe there as anywhere. English troops have been sent up there, and as this is completely a Mahomedan rising, there is not much to be feared from the Hindoos of Benares; who are, moreover, cowardly, unwarlike Bengalees.

However, I believe we are all in the greatest danger. The European troops in India are very few, and almost incapable of acting in weather like this, and the worst season is coming. If cholera becomes general at Delhi, no one can tell what will befall them, and it will be six months before an army can be sent out from England. There are, I think, 71 native Bengal regiments, forming an army of between 50,000 and 60,000 men.

Between twenty and thirty regiments have already mutinied, and everywhere the natives are ready to rise against us. In fact, it is the villagers that in many places have committed the worst outrages. The English officers and their families are scattered all over the country at innumerable little stations. In this weather it is almost impossible to move, and if they could move they must abandon all their houses and property. Probably, too, they are afraid to move, because on the least appearance of their abandoning the country, the whole population would rise behind them. They cannot move, either, without the orders of their superiors. Even though Delhi is taken, I do not see how the small European force that we have, will be able to stand against the daily increasing hordes of rebels. Even at Seepree, the next station to this, the regiment is insubordinate or disaffected. This, with Jhansi and Neemuch, which I spoke of before, are out-stations which I have to visit

The detailed accounts of the massacres at Meerut and Delhi are most horrible. At Delhi a large number of gentlemen (including some civilians and the chaplain) and ladies had taken refuge in the palace of the old native king. The rebels, raving like demons, tore them out one after another and murdered them deliberately, and then dragged their bodies about the streets.

The escapes of some, after wandering in the jungles and hiding there for days, are most wonderful One family escaped in a carriage, having shot down, several times, the rebels who tried to stop them. In many places the regiments have first murdered their officers, in some cases not one has survived. In one instance, the commanding officer committed suicide.

I hope now Delhi is taken things will take a turn for the better. The mail does not leave Bombay, I believe, until the 27th, so that I shall be able, all well, to send you another letter about the 20th.

G. W. Coopland.

CHAPTER 5

The Escape

The day after my husband wrote this letter (the last he ever wrote) the news came that Delhi had not been taken: it was a mistake in the telegram. What it cost us to bear this dreadful reverse and give up this last hope, I cannot tell. We were again plunged into uncertainty as to our fate; for we felt that the *sepoys* would no longer keep quiet when they heard of failure. Our last hope of escape was now cut off, as a telegram arrived from Mr. Colvin, the Lieutenant-Governor at Agra, to say that the ladies and children were not to be sent into Agra till the mutiny really broke out at Gwalior.

Before this, my husband had often wished to send me to Agra; but he would not desert his post, and I would not leave him. I have often thought since that had I done so he might have escaped, by riding off unimpeded by me; many unmarried officers having escaped in this way. When the mutinies first began, if all the ladies and children at the numerous small stations had been instantly sent away to Calcutta or some place of safety before the roads were obstructed, their husbands and fathers would probably have had a better chance of escape. Instead of which, the lives of men, women, and children were sacrificed, through the efforts to avoid arousing the suspicions of the troops.

Gwalior was one of the worst places in India to effect an escape from. The houses were in rows on each side of a long road, a mile in length; behind them, on one side, were the lines of the cavalry and artillery, and branching off from them were the lines of the infantry regiments. On the other side, behind the houses, was the *nullah*. The only people who escaped on the night of the 14th, lived on this side. On the first alarm, they instantly rushed across the *nullah*.

Had the guards of their houses resisted their escape, nothing could have saved them: had soldiers been placed there to stop them, it would have been useless to attempt it; but for the first ten minutes the *nullah* was left unguarded. Our house was some distance from the *nullah*, and we had not been long enough in Gwalior to know the locality exactly. Besides, almost immediately after the alarm, the banks of the *nullah* were lined with *sepoys*, hunting for those who had already crossed. I believe the brigadier lay hidden under the bridge while they were passing over it and searching for him.

At one end of the long street was a small bazaar, the natives of which were instantly up in arms. Our house was near this end of the street, and at the opposite end was a cemetery, a parade ground and gaol. At the back of the houses and lines were the cavalry stacks, the course, the magazine, and a small place where elephants were kept

I got a letter from one of my cousins, saying that they had all been obliged to escape by riding from Simla to Kussowlie; it was a long distance; and my uncle, who. had been very ill, was greatly exhausted by riding so far in the sun. They were also very much alarmed about their brother at Peshawur, the Punjaub being in such an unsettled state.

I was much struck with the conduct of our servants—they grew so impertinent My *ayah* evidently looked on all my property as her share of the plunder. When I opened my dressing-case, she would ask me questions about the ornaments, and inquire if the tops of the scent-bottles were real silver; and she always watched where I put my things. One evening, on returning from our drive, we heard a tremendous quarrelling going on between the *sepoys* of our guard and the *ayah* and *kitmutghar*. They were evidently disputing about the spoil; and it afterwards turned out that the *sepoys* got quite masters, and would not let the servants share any of the plunder, but kept them prisoners, and starved and ill-treated them.

They had much better have remained faithful to us, and have helped us to escape; instead of which, at the first shot, they vanished, and began to plunder what they could. My husband overheard the *punkah coolies* outside talking about us, and saying that these *Feringhis* [1] would soon have a different home, and they would then be masters; and that the *Feringhis* were quite different in the cool weather, but were now such poor creatures as to require to be *punkahed* and kept cool. I could not help fancying they might have made us *punkah* and fan them, so completely were we in their power.

During this week the *bunian*,[2] who supplied us with grain for the cattle and other things, the church-bearer and the school-master, all came to be paid at once; they said they were going to take all their property to the Lushkur. This looked as if mischief was brewing.

Letters came from home full of news about the Manchester Exhibition, tours in Scotland, and all sorts of pleasures. Of course, our friends knew nothing then of the state of misery we were in.

Our last consolation was now taken away, for the telegraph between us and Agra was destroyed, and we were dependent upon rumour for intelligence. We heard dreadful reports from Jhansi, but could not ascertain the extent of the calamity there. An order appeared for a regiment to hold itself in readiness for marching, and the guard returned from the Residency, for the *rajah* gave Major Macpherson a guard.

Major Blake was constantly consulting with the Brigadier as to what was to be done. We went to call on the Blakes, and heard from Mrs. Raikes, who was staying there (her husband being at Agra), that their house had been burnt down, at one of the out-stations; though it was thought not by the *sepoys*.

On Friday and Saturday we heard nothing; and we lived in a state of dread uncertainty. My husband seldom undressed at

---

1. *Feringhis*, English—Europeans.
2. *Bunian*, shopkeeper, trader in grain, &c.

night, and I had a dress always ready to escape in. My husband's rifle was kept loaded (I learnt to load and fire it), as we were determined not to die without a struggle. Oh! the misery of those days! None but the condemned criminal can know what it is to wait death passively; and even he is not kept in suspense, and knows he will be put to a merciful end.

I well remember one Saturday night (the last night we spent in our own house) we were kept awake by the ominous sound of the *maistree* [3] making a coffin for a poor little child that was to be buried early the following morning. My husband rose at half-past four, as the funeral was at five. The *ayah* was particularly attentive in her manner to me, and began pitying the poor "*mem sahib,*" saying, "How she will grieve now her baby is dead." She stood at the window watching, and telling me all that was going on.

When the buggy returned for me, I drove to church, and found service had begun. I passed many *sepoys* idling about the road—as is usual on Sunday. They all saluted me; but I thought I observed a treacherous look on their faces. I wondered they did not attack us when we were in church, and heard afterwards that they were very sorry they did not The church was well attended, and we afterwards received the Holy Communion. Singular that we should all meet for the last time at such a solemn service!

Whilst walking in the garden, before going to church, when my husband was at the funeral of Captain Murray's little baby, I saw about a hundred *sowars* ride past the back of our house; they rode quietly in, all wrapped in long cloaks. I cannot help thinking they were the mutinous *sowars* of Captain Alexander's party, returned to join in the outbreak.

After breakfast we bathed and dressed, and whilst my husband was resting, and I playing one of Mozart's "Masses," we heard a tremendous noise in our garden. After waiting a little time to see if it would cease, my husband went out, and found one or two *sepoys* again disputing with our servants. He ordered them to be quiet; but it was of no use, they did not now care even to keep up appearances. At last they settled the dispute among themselves;

---

3. *Maistree*, carpenter

and for two hours we had perfect silence—not a sound was heard; it was a dread, foreboding stillness. I read the lines, "While drooping sadness enfolds us here like mist," in the *Christian Tear*, and felt comforted. I afterwards recovered that very book.

My husband laid down, and tried to get a little sleep, he was so worn out. He had just before been telling me the particulars of the Jhansi massacres too frightful to be repeated; and we did not know how soon we might meet the same fate ourselves.

I hope few will know how awful it is to wait quietly for death. There was now no escape; and we waited for our death-stroke. The dread calm of apprehension was awful. We indeed drank the cup of bitterness to the dregs. The words "O death in life, the days that are no more," kept recurring to my memory like a dirge. But God helps us in all our. woes; otherwise we could not have borne the horrible suspense.

Silence still reigned, and I was again reading home letters—one from my sister on her wedding tour—when in rushed some of the servants, calling out that the little bungalow where we had formerly lived was on fire, and that the wind was blowing the flames in our direction. Something must be done, as the sparks were being blown all about: the 1st Native Infantry were very active in either putting out—or increasing —the flames. All the residents began to take the furniture out of their houses and pour water on the roofs; and my husband, at the head of our servants, instantly took similar precautions with our house. The heat was dreadful, the wind high, and the mess-house was soon also a mass of flames.

Everyone who has seen a great fire in a village may imagine what a sight it was. The road was crowded, the air filled with smoke, and I heard the crackling and roaring of the flames: it was a great contrast to the dead calm that had reigned before; but scarcely more awful. While my husband was busily assisting the men, who were running about with water, and using the fire-engine; to my astonishment I found the *ayah* making bundles of my clothes, which she had taken out of the wardrobes and spread over the floor: she came to me for my keys, saying I had better have my things packed up and she would take care of them. I ordered her to replace them in the drawers and come and *pun-kah* me, as it was fearfully hot; I wished to keep her quiet, but she was constantly running off. At last the wind fell, and the fire was extinguished; but not till the mess-house, the large bath-house adjoining, and little bungalow were burnt to the ground: my husband came in, greatly exhausted with his exertions.

After dinner the poor clerk, Collins, came in to know about service: he was dreadfully agitated, and my husband had to wait some time before he was sufficiently composed to speak. He said he was quite sure the *sepoys* intended to rise that night and murder us all. Poor man! I shall never forget his look of distress: he was the first to be shot that night. My husband advised me to put on a plain dark dress and jacket, and not to wear any ornaments or hide anything about me, that the *sepoys* might not kill me for the sake of my dress or trinkets; we then selected one or two trifles that we prized and some valuable papers, which we made into small packets, and again sat down in silent suspense.

Meanwhile my husband wrote to Captain Meade (the brigade-major) to ask if we were to have service in the church that evening, as the mess-house was destroyed; and also to inquire what he thought of things. Captain Meade replied that under present circumstances no one would be prepared to go to church, and we must expect "such things" to happen in these times. I then finished a letter for home; which never went, as it was burnt in our house.

After coffee we received a note from Major Sherriff, saying he wished to see my husband; at 5 o' clock he came, and they had a long talk together. He said it was a hard thing that we should stay to be butchered like sheep; for now there was no doubt but that such would be our fate. He also told us Mrs. Hawkins had come in from Sepree, to join her husband, and that she had been confined on Saturday.

"It is dreadful," he added, "that women and children should be exposed to such horrors: they will receive no mercy I fear."

We wished him to dine with us, but he was engaged to the brigadier; and after walking sometime in the garden he went away, having first left some money which he had forgotten to give at the holy communion that morning. A few hours after he was shot, when at the lines of his regiment.

My husband now sent for all the servants and gave them each handsome presents in money: to his bearer and my *ayah* he gave double; he also rewarded the guard of six *sepoys*, who had come to guard our house when the fire broke out. We then drove out. We saw scarcely any one about, everything looked as it had done for days past; but as we were returning we passed several parties of *sepoys*, none of whom saluted us. We met the Brigadier and Major Blake, who were just going to pass a party of *sepoys*, and I remember saying to my husband, "If the *sepoys* don't salute the brigadier the storm is nigh at hand."

They did not The brigadier and Major Blake turned and looked at them. We found our guard still at our house, but they also took no notice of us. We then had tea, and sat reading till gunfire; and at 9 we retired to rest, as my husband was much exhausted.

I hope no one will think me unfeeling in writing what follows: it must be obvious to all that I cannot do so without great pain; but I think that Englishmen ought to know what their own countrywomen have endured at the hands of the *sepoys*; and what we went through that night and the following week, hundreds of ladies suffered all over India. Only a few survived to tell the tale; which can only he faithfully told by one who has experienced the misery.

Some men may think that women are weak and only fitted to do trivial things, and endure petty troubles; and there are women who deserve no higher opinion: such as faint at the sight, of blood, are terrified at a harmless cow, or make themselves miserable by imagining terrors, and unreal sorrows; but there are many who can endure with fortitude and patience what even soldiers shrink from. Men are fitted by education and constitution to dare and to do; yet they have been surpassed, in presence of mind and in the power of endurance, by weak women.

My husband went into his dressing room, and I, after undressing and dismissing my *ayah*, arranged my dress for flight, and lay down. A single lamp shed a ghostly glimmer in the room. Soon afterwards the gun fired—instantly the alarm bugle rang out its shrill warning on the still night Our guard loaded their muskets, and I felt that our death knell had sounded when the butts went down with a muffled sound. My husband opened his door and said, "All is over with us! dress immediately."

The *ayah* and bearer rushed in, calling out, "Fly! the *sepoys* have risen, and will kill you."

The *ayah* then quickly helped me to dress. I put on a morning wrapper, cloth jacket, and bonnet, and snatched up a bottle of aromatic vinegar and another of opium from the dressing table, but left my watch and rings. My husband then came in, and we opened my bathroom door, which led into the garden, and rushed out. Fortunately it was very dark.

I said, "Let us go to the Stuarts, and see what they are doing."

We soon reached their house, and found Mrs. Stuart in great distress, as her husband had just ridden off to the lines. Poor Mrs. Hawkins lay in the next room, with a serjeant's wife attending to the little baby (only a few hours old). Mrs. Hawkins' children and the little Stuarts were crying, and the servants sobbing, thus adding to the confusion. Whilst my husband tried to soothe Mrs. Stuart, I went in to talk to Mrs. Hawkins, whose husband had also gone to the lines.

Suddenly a horse dashed into the compound, and Mrs. Stuart cried out, "Oh! they have killed my husband!" I returned to her, as my husband went out to speak to the *syce*. I held her hand, and never can I forget her agonised clasp! The *syce* told my husband that the *sepoys* had shot Captain Stuart; that he thought the captain was not dead, but had been taken to the artillery lines: he also brought a message from Major Hawkins, directing his wife and children to go to the lines.

So Mrs. Hawkins was carried out on a bed, followed by the nurse with the infant, and a large party of servants carrying the other four children. They all went to the artillery lines, as the

89

artillery had promised to remain faithful.

Mrs. Stuart also set off in her carriage with her children; my husband helped her in, and tried to comfort her. Mrs. Stuart had before told me that when she returned from her former flight to the Residency, a sepoy had said to her, "Why did you leave your husband, *Mem-sahib?* That was not brave; but you women, are so weak and faint-hearted, you take flight at nothing. See! the *Sahib* trusted us; we will always be faithful, whatever happens."

Our *syce* now appeared with the buggy, accompanied by our *kitmutghar*, the latter appeared very much excited, and had a *tulwah* [4] in each hand. He advised us to cross the bridge leading to the Lushkur; but the *syce* said it was guarded with guns and sentries. At first we thought we would follow Mrs. Stuart and Mrs. Hawkins to the artillery lines, as the artillery were thought to be better inclined towards us; it was the 4th we dreaded, for they had often let fall suspicious and mutinous words. It is believed that they committed, that night and the following morning, most of the murders at the station.

Just as we were going to turn towards the artillery lines, a young sepoy came running from them towards us, weeping and sobbing. He called out, "They have shot the *Sahib*," and though my husband spoke to him, he ran past without answering. All this time we heard volleys of musketry, bugles, shots, and terrible shrieks, and saw some of the houses burning. We drove to the Blakes' bungalow, where we found Mrs. Blake, Mrs. Raikes, and Dr. and Mrs. Kirke; none of them knowing what to do. Major Blake from had ridden off to the lines the instant the alarm bugle had sounded; and things were rather quieter here.

It was now 10 o'clock. Dr. Kirke said the guard had promised to stay by us, and that now it was utterly impossible to escape, as every road was guarded and planted with guns, and cavalry were riding about. After a short time, passed in terrible suspense, the guard of the house suggested that we had better hide in the garden, as the *sepoys* would soon be coming to "loot" [5] the

---

4. *Tulwah*, sword, scimitar.
5. Loot, to rob, to plunder.

house, and would kill us. It was only postponing our deaths, as we knew that escape was now hopeless; but as life is dear to all, we did what we could to save it.

I shall not attempt to describe my feelings; but leave readers to imagine them—if they can. I will only relate the simple facts.

We followed the advice of the guard, and went into the garden, where we remained for some time. Mrs. Raikes with her baby was taken by her servant to hide elsewhere, and the Kirkes, with their little boy, went back to their own house. My husband had his rifle, which was afterwards lost. I was told afterwards by several natives that he killed two *sepoys* with it: I know not if he did.

Mrs. Blake's *kitmutghar*, Muza, who remained faithful, now took us to a shady place in the garden, where we lay concealed behind a bank, well covered with trees. He told us to lie down and not to move, and then brought a large dark shawl for my husband, who was in a white suit. It was now about 11. The guard (composed of men of the 1st) still remained faithful; though they took no active part in helping us. They kept coming to us with reports that Mrs. Campbell was lying dead in her compound; that the brigadier was shot on the bridge, and Dr. Mackeller near one of the hospitals, and (worst of all) that poor Major Blake was killed. This last report was only too true.

At last about a hundred *sepoys* came to attack Mrs. Campbell's house, which was close to our hiding place. We heard them tearing down the doors and windows, and smashing the glass and furniture; they even brought carts into the garden to carry off the plunder; then they set fire to it, and the flames shot up into the clear night air. They seemed to take pleasure in their mad work, for their wild shouts of laughter mingled with the crackling of the flames.

The moon (which had now risen) looked calmly down on our misery, and lighted the heavens, which were flecked with myriads of stars, only occasionally obscured by the smoke of the burning houses. Oh the sight of that moon! how I longed that she would hide her brightness behind some cloud, and not seem to look so serenely down upon our misery.

At last, when the mutineers had wreaked their vengeance on Mrs. Campbell's house, and only a heap of smouldering and blackened ruins remained, they commenced their attack on the Blakes' house.

We heard them looking for us; but not finding their victims there, they came into the garden and made a diligent search for us. I saw the moonlight glancing on their bayonets, as they thrust aside the bushes, and they passed so close by us that we might have touched them. But God baffled their malice for a time; though they sought us with a deadly hatred, they were unsuccessful, and we were again left to wait a little longer in bitter suspense. When they were burning the Blakes' house, the flames and smoke swept over us. Gradually the fury of the *sepoys* died away, and they seemed to be gone in search of fresh plunder, or other victims; for we heard them shouting and firing in the distance.

Our faithful Muza now crept to us, and said we were no longer safe where we were, but that he might hide us in his house, and perhaps get us some native dresses to disguise ourselves in; and gratefully we hurried after him during a lull in the storm. His house was a low, small hut, close to the garden, where the other houses of the Blakes' servants were; and we rushed past so quickly that, though we saw a number of *sepoys*, yet they, in the excitement, did not see us. Mrs. Blake, in her hurry, fell, and hurt her head and shoulder. We crouched down in the hut, not daring to move, and scarcely to breathe.

I remember asking Mrs. Blake to take off her silk cape, as it rustled, which she did. In the dark I fell backward over a small bed and hurt myself. Muza then barred the door, and fastened it with a chain. After half an hour the *sepoys* returned, more furious than before; they evidently knew we were somewhere about We heard them disputing, and the clang of their guns sounded as though they were loading them.

They entered the kitchen of the house, which was only separated from the room we were in by a thin wooden partition.

Muza then went out; we did not know what for. Had he deserted us? The *sepoys* talked and argued with him; we heard them count over the cooking vessels and dishes, and distinctly say *"do, tien, char, aur eck nai hai?"* [6]

After dividing the spoil, we heard them again ask Muza if we were in his house, and say they must search; but he replied that his mother was ill, and that they might frighten her. They asked him, "Have you no *Feringhis* concealed?" and he swore the most sacred oath on the Koran, that there were none in his house: but this did not appear to satisfy them, and we heard them coming in; they forced open the door with the butts of their muskets, the chain fell with a clang, and as the door burst open, we saw the moon glistening on their fixed bayonets. We thought they were going to charge in upon us: but no; the hut was so dark that they could not see us.

They called for a light; but Muza stopped them, and said, "You see they are not here: come, and I will show you where they are." He then shut and fastened the door, and they again went away.

There was again a dead silence, followed by the dying shrieks of a horse, as it rushed past our hiding place; so we supposed they had gone to the stables.

After a time Muza returned and said: "They will be here again soon, and will kill me for concealing you, when I swore you were not here; so I will take you to the bearer's hut: he will not betray you."

He then opened the door and we went out. Day was beginning to dawn, and the air felt cool, after the close atmosphere of the house we had been in for so many hours; it was the bearer's hut we were taken to; one of a cluster of huts built of mud, and very low and small I again fell and hurt myself, as it was not yet light, and we again lay on the ground, quite worn out with watching, and terror; our lips were parched, and we listened intently to hear the least sound: but a brooding silence prevailed. We were soon joined by Mrs. Raikes, with her baby and *ayah*;

6. Two, three, four; is there not another?

93

the poor baby crying and fretting.

It was now nearly six o' clock, and grew gradually lighter, when the *sepoys* again returned howling and raging like wild beasts. They came round the hut, the baby cried, and we heard them ask, "Whose child is that?"

One of the women replied they did not know; they called "Bring it out;" when Mrs. Raikes exclaimed in an agony of fear, "Oh! they will kill my child! "

When the woman carried it out, the *sepoys* yelled, "*Feringhi, hi:* [7] kill them!" and I saw through the doorway a great number of them loading their muskets. They then ordered the woman to bring out a large quantity of plunder that lay on the floor of the hut, pictures, plate, &c; she took them out slowly, one by one, and gave them to the *sepoys*.

We all stood up close together in a corner of the hut; each of us took up one of the logs of wood that lay on the ground, as some means of defence. I did not know if my husband had his gun, as it was too dark in the hut to see even our faces. The *sepoys* then began to pull off the roof: the cowardly wretches dared not come in, as they thought we had weapons. When they had unroofed the hut, they fired in upon us.

At the first shot we dropped our pieces of wood, and my husband said, "We will not die here, let us go outside."

We all rushed out; and Mrs. Blake, Mrs. Raikes, and I, clasped our hands and cried, "*Mut maro, mut maro*" (do not kill us).

The *sepoys* said, "We will not kill the *mem-sahibs*, only the *sahib*."

We were surrounded by a crowd of them, and as soon as they distinguished my husband, they fired at him. Instantly they dragged Mrs. Blake, Mrs. Raikes, and me back; but not into the bearer's hut; the *mehter's* was good enough for us, they said. I saw no more; but volley after volley soon told me that all was over.

Here we again lay crouched on the ground; and the stillness was such, that a little mouse crept out and looked at us with its bright eyes, and was not afraid. Mrs. Campbell came rushing in

7. *Feringhi, hi,* there are English there.

with her hair hanging about; she wore a native's dress, her own having been torn off her: she had been left alone the whole night.

Then poor Mrs. Kirke, with her little boy, joined us: she had that instant seen her husband [8] shot before her eyes; and on her crying "Kill me too!"

They answered, "No, we have killed you in killing him."

Her arms were bruised and swollen; they had torn off her bracelets so roughly: even her wedding ring was gone. They spared her little boy; saying; "Don't kill the *bûtcha* [9]; it is a *missie baba*." [10] Poor child! his long curls and girlish face saved his life! He was only four years of age.

I was very thankful to see Mrs, Campbell, after the frightful report we had heard; for till then we had thought her to be safe under Major Macpherson's protection. The *sepoys* soon returned, and crowded in to stare at us. They made the most insulting remarks, and then said, "Let us carry them to our lines;" whereupon they seized our hands, and dragged us along very fast. It was a beautiful morning, and the birds were singing. Oh! how could the bright sun and clear blue sky look on such a scene of cruelty! It seemed as if God had forgotten us, and that hell reigned on earth.

No words can describe the hellish looks of these human fiends, or picture their horrid appearance: they had rifled all the stores,

---

8. Dr. Winlow Kirke, who had for nearly twenty years been a medical officer of the company, first with the Bundelcund Legion in Scinde, then as a medical adviser to Sir Charles Napier, afterwards with the Bengal troops at Bareilly, subsequently with the European artillery at Ferozepore, and, lastly, as superintending surgeon to the Gwalior contingent. He was much beloved, both by his brother officers, and by the *sepoys* under his care, for his benevolent disposition and goodness of heart: his kindness to the *sepoys* in sickness has been much commended; and it was generally thought, that if a rising took place, he would escape, being so much liked by the natives; but his death proved how delusive was the confidence to be placed in these black-hearted wretches. The doctor who had ministered to their necessities and comfort when in hospital, who had cured them when sick, and tended them when convalescent, these miscreants shot before his wife, and beat out his brains with the butts of that muskets.

9. *Bûtcha*, little one, child.

10. *Missie baba*, little girl

and drank brandy and beer to excess, besides being intoxicated with *bhang*.[11] They were all armed, and dressed in their fatigue uniform. I noticed the number on them; it was the 4th—that dreaded regiment Some were evidently the prisoners who had been let out from the gaol the night before; and they were, if possible, more furious than the rest. Several mounted *sowars* (the same, I believe, whom I had seen ride in the day before) were riding about the roads and keeping guard, and wished to fire at us, but the infantry would not let them. The road was crowded with *sepoys* laden with plunder, some of which I recognised as our own.

After they had dragged us to their lines, they took us from house to house, and at last placed us on a *charpoy* [12] under some trees. Mrs. Gilbert and her child now arrived, and poor Mrs. Procter; the latter in a dreadful state, having just seen her husband killed. All our horses and carriages were drawn up in a line under some trees, and I saw a beautiful Arab of Mrs. Raikes' lying shot. Hundreds of *sepoys* now came to stare at us, and thronged round us so densely we could scarcely breathe.

They mocked and laughed at us, and reviled us with the most bitter language, saying: "Why don't you go home to your houses? Don't you think it is very hot here? Would you like to see your *sahibs now?*"

We said we wished to go to Agra; they replied, "Oh! Agra is burnt to the ground, and all the *Feringhis* are killed."

They then struck the native gong. I think it was about eight o' clock.

After keeping us for some time, as a spectacle on which to wreak their contempt, when they had tired themselves with using insulting language, they said we might go where we liked; but when we asked how? they demurred at giving us one of the carriages, till some, more merciful than the rest, at last said we might have one. They gave us Mrs. Blake's—a large *landau*. The horses were very spirited and plunged a good deal: the morn-

---

11. *Bhang*, an intoxicating liquor made of hemp.
12. *Charpoy*, native bed.

ing before, they had broken the traces. How we all got in I can't say: there were Mrs. Blake, Mrs. Raikes, her baby and *ayah*, Mrs. Kirke and her little boy, Mrs. Campbell and myself; and some sergeants' wives clung to the carriage: how they hung on I don't know. The *sepoys* threw into the carriage one or two bottles of beer, and a bottle of camphor-water. The first thing the horses did, was to run down a bank and across a small *nullah*.

Muza drove; and a *syce* went with us a little way, but soon grew tired, and fell back. When we got a little way from the station, we came up with some more sergeants' wives and children; some of them nearly naked, and in great distress, having seen their husbands shot, and dragged about, and others not knowing the fate of their husbands. Poor things, their distress was very pitiable; their feelings being less under control than ours.

I never can remember how it was we were separated from Mrs. Proctor and Mrs. Gilbert, with her nurse and child; but think the Grenadiers carried them off to their lines, as they afterwards rejoined us. The horses now grew very restless and tried to run away, and Muza did not know how to manage them. We came up to a *chowki* [13] and were afraid the mutineers would stop us: they did not; but they. told us that Mrs. Hennessy and Captain Murray had been killed in escaping.

We here debated where we should go, and at last agreed to go to the *rajah* and entreat him for protection.

The Lushkur was five or six miles from the Mori and we reached it about noon. We passed crowds of natives, whom we expected to stop us every instant. When we reached the palace, we asked to see the *rajah*.

The palace was surrounded by a crowd of horsemen, soldiers and natives, all most insolent in their manner to us, calling out "your Raj [14] is over now."

The Maharajah refused to see us: though we entreated some of the *rajah's* servants to be allowed to speak to him, we were roughly refused. Some say he was looking at us from a balcony

---

13. *Chowki*, stage.
14. *Raj*, rule.

97

all the time. Why were we so heartlessly treated by him, when he had been so kind to Major Macpherson and his party, even lending them carriages and a guard, and facilitating their escape in every way? Did he shelter Major Macpherson in his political capacity, and the brigadier as a man of importance? Perhaps he thought that helpless women could never be of any use to him. This is a mystery that no one can explain to the *rajah's* credit. We felt it keenly, to be thus driven from his palace gate with contempt.

We proceeded on our way, the people yelling and shouting after us, and we expecting every instant to be stopped and torn out of our carriage and given up to be killed by them; for nothing could exceed their savage looks and language. At the outskirts of the Lushkur we were obliged to stop, as the horses kept breaking the traces as fast as we tied them together again; moreover they were much exhausted, having been in harness the whole night before, for Mrs. Blake's escape.

A *chuprassi* [15]of the *rajah's* took the carriage from us, and made us get out and wait by the road side till he sent us two or three native carts; they were miserable things without springs, had no covers to protect us from the sun, and were drawn by wretchedly weak bullocks. We got in and were taken to a large *pucka* house in a garden, where some great bullocks were munching grain in a room; and there we stayed. It was now about one o' clock, I think. We here found an European belonging to the telegraph, and his wife with her little baby: she was a half-caste, and they were disguised in native dresses. The weak childish conduct of this man was sickening; he almost cried, and kept saying, "Oh we shall all be killed:" instead of trying to help, he only proved a burden to us.

We had now almost lost the power of thinking and acting, for we had been from nine the preceding evening without food, water, or rest; and our minds were on the rack, tortured by grief and suspense. Here we were, about eight miserable women, alone and unprotected, without food or proper clothing, exhausted by

15. *Chuprassi*, messenger.

fatigue, and not knowing what to do; some had no shoes or covering for their heads. At last Muza said we had better get into our carts and push on; for the natives of the Lushkur, hearing we were here, would follow and kill us. The bullocks went very slowly, and we could not make them move faster. The sensation of horror and helplessness oppressed us like a night-mare: for all this time we were only a few miles from Gwalior, and could even hear the shouting and crying there.

Mrs. Campbell having broken one of the bottles of beer, we had each drank a little, which greatly refreshed us.

We toiled slowly onwards the whole of that long, hot afternoon; the dust rising in clouds, and the hot wind parching us. The men who drove the bullocks could hardly make them move. We mixed a few drops of the camphor-water with the water Muza occasionally brought us from the wells we passed, and found it support us a little.

The shades of evening were drawing on, and we were as yet only a few miles on our weary way, when Muza said we were pursued by some *sowars*, who were coming to kill us, and he feared he could not save us, as we were on a flat sandy plain with no shelter. We reached, at last, a small *chowki* by the road side, where the horses for the mail and the *dâk gharries* were kept, and the *syces* who attended to them. There were some wild, savage-looking men cooking food round a fire. Muza spoke to them, and then told us to get out of our carts and hide here.

We all sat on the ground, and Muza said, "Only pretend to go to sleep: but I fear I cannot save you, as they are bent on killing you."

We waited, with our carts drawn up. It was nearly dark, and we heard the horsemen coming quickly on. At last five *sowars* appeared, armed with matchlocks and *tulwahs*, and as soon as they saw the carts they stopped and dismounted, Muza went towards them and began talking to them.

We heard him say, " See how tired they are; they have had no rest. Let them sleep tonight; you can kill them tomorrow: only let them sleep now."

This they consented to do, and went a little way from us; but when it grew darker they crept near us, and began loading their matchlocks and unsheathing their *tulwahs*. Muza came to us, and said he feared they would not spare us. He then asked us for all the ornaments we had. Mrs. Blake was the only one who had any, Mrs. Campbell and Mrs. Kirke having been stripped of theirs, and I had left mine behind. I instantly took off my wedding ring and tied it round my waist, as I was determined to save it if possible. Mrs. Blake had several valuable rings, other ornaments, and money about her; these she gave to Muza, who handed them to the *sowars*. We heard them quarrelling together, and I believe they held a loaded pistol to his breast and made him swear that we had no more.

Muza then said we must speak to them, as they would not believe him. So Mrs. Blake and Mrs. Campbell, who spoke Hindoostanee fluently, spoke to them, and offered them 40*l.* if they would take a note to Captain Campbell at Agra, asking for a guard.

At first they said they would, and went to one of the *syces* to ask for paper; but presently returned and said we meant to betray them; and again they threatened to kill us. Just then we heard in the distance the tramp of a large body of horse and the clang of arms: this rather startled the *sowars*, and gave us some hope. When the cavalry came nearer, we saw that they were part of the *rajah's* bodyguard, returning from escorting Major Macpherson and his party.

They stopped, and we all ran towards them; and Mrs. Campbell whose husband had had the temporary command of them, entreated their native officer (who was dressed in an English officer's uniform) to guard us, and let some of his men go with us. She offered them a large sum of money if they would. The Maharajah owed Captain Campbell long arrears of pay, and this also I believe she offered them; but to no purpose. She then entreated for the protection of only one or two of his men. As they had escorted Major Macpherson, why could they not escort us? The *rajah* might have given orders for them to protect any helpless refugees from Gwalior. They refused, saying they had not the

100

Maharajah's "*hukum*." [16] So we had the bitter disappointment of watching them ride off. Whether the *sowars* were frightened, I know not; but, so far as I remember, they did not again molest us. We then lay down, and some of us went to sleep: the poor children did, at least.

Very early next morning we again set out Muza got us some "*gram*" for food, like vetch, which the animals live on; it was very dry, and this, with a little water mixed with the camphor-water, was all we had to eat. About noon on Tuesday we reached the second *dâk* bungalow on the way to Agra (when we had before come to Gwalior, we had come by another bye road, this not being then finished). Here we halted for an hour or two, as we heard frightful reports about Major Macpherson and his party; we were told that as soon as they had reached the Chumbul, the *rajah's* bodyguard had left them, and that they had been attacked by the villagers, who had killed them.

They even told us the names of those who had been killed, and so circumstantially that we could not doubt The Rajah of Dhalpore, they said, had taken possession of the ford and would not allow anyone to cross. We did not know what to do, whether to go on, not crediting what they said, or, believing them, stay where we were. The servants at the bungalow pressed us to stay, saying, we should all be killed if we went on; but we thought they wanted to entrap us, and would only wait till they were joined by others, and then kill us.

We sent for the *dâk*-book, in which travellers write their names, but only saw "Major Macpherson and party;" there was no list of names. This we much regretted, as we were anxious to see who had escaped; and I most earnestly wished to know if Mrs. Stuart, Mrs. Hawkins, Mrs. Hennessy, and several others, had escaped, as we had heard such frightful reports. Mrs. Campbell wrote all our names in the book, that others who might escape should see them.

We then partook of a little "*dhâl*" [18] and rice, the first food

---

17. *Hukum*, order, command.
18. *Dhâl*, pulse, split peas.

we had tasted since Sunday night, excepting the *gram*. The poor children were very glad of it, but we could eat little, being so weak with exposure to the sun: afterwards, however, the doctors told us, it was well we had eaten so little, as our weak state alone saved us from sunstrokes.

On looking at my foot, which was very painful, and inflamed, I found that I had cut it, as my boots were very thin; so I tied my pocket handkerchief round it. We were all covered with "prickly heat," a very painful and irritable eruption; and we could not rest, as crowds of natives would continue thronging in to stare at us; even looking through the windows of all the rooms. They all had firearms, which they brandished, and they looked so ferocious that we did not feel at all safe. Here we were joined by Mrs. Gilbert, poor Mrs. Proctor, and Mrs. Quick, a sergeant's wife; they had been very ill-treated at the Lushkur: Mrs. Proctor had even had a *tulwah* held to her throat.

In the evening we proceeded on our journey in the carts. Our faithful Muza had procured us some *chuddars* [19] in which we wrapped our heads, and disguised ourselves as well as we could, so as to appear like a party of natives travelling. The oxen slowly dragged their weary limbs along, hanging their heads and stopping every instant When we started we were surrounded by natives; but strange to say, they let us depart, thinking probably that we should never reach Agra, and that we should only die a lingering death on the way; or that if we did reach Agra we should only find it in ruins.

We met five or six large carriages returning from conveying Major Macpherson and his party to Agra. We stopped them and vainly entreated the drivers to take us only as far as the Chumbul; but this they scornfully refused to do, saying they had not the *rajah's* "*hukum*." Oh, how our hearts swelled with indignation at this second refusal! It was very hard to see them drive past our miserable carts. Mrs. Quick was a very large woman—for corpulency becomes a disease in India, and her weight was such she had already broken down one cart, a small frail one, and now, toiling slowly along on foot, she implored us to take her in or she should die: her expressions and language were

---

19. *Chuddars*, large veils, sheet.

violent and dreadful, but we felt for her, and she was at last taken into one of the carts.

At night we reached a large village, but met with no sympathy: when we asked the natives for some water, they said we might get it for ourselves. Muza got us some, at last. We were then obliged to get out of the carts, and lie on the ground, in the middle of a dusty road, huddled together, whilst the villagers collected to stare at us: they even brought torches to aid their scrutiny, as it was now getting dark. The drivers of the carts made a fire and cooked some food they had got for themselves. The natives were very insolent; they looked at us all in succession, and said, "Well, they are not worth a *pice* each;" but to Mrs. Campbell they said, "You are worth an *anna:*" [20] they said she was (*burra kubsoorut*) very handsome. She was a very beautiful woman, and had formerly been called the "Rose of Gibraltar," when she was there with her father.

They pulled aside her *chudda*, with which she tried to conceal her face, and said, "We will look at you." At last, worn out with fatigue, we slept, and the next morning (Wednesday) continued our journey.

We passed through the town of Dholepore, which is built on each side of the Chumbul. The natives are a rude, fierce set, find when we reached the ford they would not let us cross, and said they would kill us. A large party of men well armed assembled together on a bank, and seemed to watch us. Muza advised us not to stir out of the carts, as they belonged to the Rajah of Gwalior, and as long as they thought we were under his protection they dared not touch us. He then left us, in order to try if he could get a boat for us to cross in; and crowds of natives collected to gaze at us.

It will be evident to all, from the behaviour of the villagers to us, that the disaffection was not confined to *sepoys*, as is sometimes asserted: indeed, the villagers always flocked into the stations after the mutinies to murder and loot. Of course there are some exceptions like Muza; and some of the *sepoys* even re-

---

20. *Anna*, copper coin worth three halfpence.

mained faithful, and helped their officers to escape.

It was the afternoon, and oppressively hot, when Muza returned, saying he had got a boat for us. We left our carts and descended the hill to the ford, where we saw a sort of raft, or rough native boat, at some distance from the shore; we had to wade the stream before we reached it, and then we scrambled into it wet as we were. Just as the boat began to move, Muza piloting, some natives dashed into the water, and, as if vexed that they had let us depart, tore a piece of wood out of the side, so that the water rushed in. The sergeants' wives and children began shrieking out, "They are going to drown us: they are pulling the boat to pieces."

I don't know whether this stopped them: but they then gave over; though some of them continued swimming after the boat. The river was very broad, and the boat began to fill with water; so as soon as we neared the opposite shore, we jumped out, and again waded a short distance. The Chumbul, like all Indian rivers, during the rains, swells, and floods a large space beyond its banks, sweeping all before it; but during the dry season it shrinks up, leaving a large margin of sand and debris: through this we had now to drag ourselves, the sand sticking to our wet dresses. Having left our carts on the other side, we entered a small *chowki* near the river bank, into which we were followed by at least twenty horrid savage-looking men, armed with rusty old matchlocks and *tulwahs*.

I shall never forget the expression of their faces; we could see well now, as it was light, and we were neither agitated nor excited, many of us having almost lost all longing for life. We sat here for more than an hour, surrounded by these men, who every now and then drew out their *tulwahs*, and slowly polished them with their fingers, seeming to whet and sharpen them. They watched us closely: one man especially, with only one eye, and that had a horrid basilisk expression in it, watched me the whole time. They appeared to consult how they should kill us, and I kept thinking what a dreadful death they would put us to with their rusty weapons: a bullet would have been a merciful death

104

in comparison. They would occasionally leave us, and then return, as if purposely keeping us in suspense.

At last a camel *sowar* rode up, and gave Mrs. Campbell a note. It was one written by Captain Campbell to the Maharajah, requesting him to have all the bodies of the killed at Gwalior buried, and particularly his own wife. This she herself read. The *sowar* said he would take her to Captain Campbell, who had come a few miles out of Agra, and was at the *dâk* bungalow at Munnia, not daring to come further, fearing an ambush; but Mrs. Campbell was unwilling to leave us, and moreover, she did not like to trust herself alone with the *sowar*, who agreed, instead, to take a note to Captain Campbell.

Mrs. Campbell (I think) pricked with a pin on the back of the note, "We are here, more than a dozen women and children: send us help."

The *sowar* departed, and Captain Campbell actually received the note.

Muza now said we had better walk on a little way, till he could procure us some more carts; so we walked on under the burning sun, our wet clothes clinging to us. Some of the women had no shoes or stockings; and one tore off pieces of her dress to wrap round her bleeding feet. Mrs. Kirke and Mrs. Campbell, who had no bonnets, put part of their dresses over their heads, to protect them from the burning rays of the sun. Mrs. Gilbert could hardly walk; but some of the women helped her along, and others carried the children.

At last Mrs. Quick fell down in an apoplectic fit, and became black in the face; some of the ladies kindly stayed with her, but in a quarter of an hour she died. The natives crowded round, laughing at her immense size, and mocked her. We asked them to bury her; but I don't know whether they did; as we left her body lying on the road.

We sat for a long time waiting for carts, in a lane with high banks on each side, which sheltered us a little from the sun; at last, to our grant delight, a native mounted policeman, riding Captain Campbell's own "*Blacky*," came up and told us that

Captain Campbell was at the first *dâk* bungalow from Agra; not daring to come any further, and uncertain if we had escaped, as Major Macpherson and all who had escaped knew nothing about us. Captain Campbell had sent him with instructions to us to rest at the next *dâk* bungalow, where he would provide us with food. The man then rode off to ask the Rajah of Dholepore for some carts for us. It seemed strange to see this man, and hear him speak so kindly to us. He alone remained faithful when all the other mounted policemen afterwards mutinied at Agra.

The horse too was an old friend which we had often driven, and Mrs. Campbell was delighted to see it again. The man soon returned; and when the carts and an elephant, which the *rajah* allowed us to have, came, we went to the bungalow. It was the same at which I had rested on our way to Gwalior nearly six months before; and I shall never forget the feeling with which I now entered that house under such different circumstances.

It was quite dark when we reached the bungalow, and our kind messenger gave us some biscuits, bread and beer, which Captain Campbell had sent. Then we lay down, some on the floor—and slept. In the morning (Thursday) at about 4 a. m. we set out in our carts, which were very uncomfortable, though drawn by fine large bullocks. Some of the sergeants' wives had tried the night before to sit on the elephant; but as it had no *howdah* [21], and they were too exhausted to hold on, we took them into our carts.

About noon we came in sight of the bungalow at Munnia where Captain Campbell was: he had sent on his buggy for his wife, so she and Mrs. Gilbert preceded us in it. We soon arrived, and never shall I forget Captain Campbell's kindness: he was truly a good Samaritan; he bathed our heads, fanned us, and procured us fowls and rice; for we were by this time utterly worn out with fatigue and exhaustion. Here Mrs. Gilbert's baby was born, and we halted till evening. Captain Campbell had a small *charpoy* [22] covered with some carpet belonging to the bungalow,

---

21. *Howdah*, seat for four people on an elephant>
22. *Charpoy*, a native bedstead.

for Mrs. Gilbert and the infant to be carried on. He had twenty horsemen with him, but could not trust them. We started about 4 p.m., and travelled all night, through bye lanes; and thus, it being dark, we avoided an ambush, as the rebels were collecting to attack us. Poor Sergeant Quick now joined us, and was told of the death of his wife.

At 6 the next morning (Friday) we reached Agra. It seemed so strange to see faces not haggard and sorrowful. We went to the house of Captain Stevenson, Captain Campbell's cousin, and were refreshed with tea; afterwards Mrs. Blake, accompanied by her ever faithful Muza, went to her friend Mrs. Griffin; Mrs. Kirke went to another kind friend, and Mrs. Raikes to her uncle Mr. Raikes; I went to Major Macpherson and Mrs. Innes, who were in a large house appointed for the Gwalior refugees. Mrs. Gilbert now heard that her husband had either arrived or was expected; which must indeed have cheered her.

Captain Murray drove me to Major Macpherson's, where Mrs. Innes met me very kindly; she took me to a room, where, after I had bathed, I laid down and fell asleep; never awakening till evening. Mrs. Innes arranged for us to sleep in the garden; as in case of an alarm we might more easily escape to the barracks. Major Macpherson and Dr. Mackeller were also to sleep in the garden with their fire-arms ready. We could now foresee danger, and plan how to avoid it; having been taught by bitter experience.

I lay awake that night, gratefully enjoying the tranquillity and comparative security: all was calm and still; the air gently stirred by a soft breeze, and the silence only broken by the chirp of a cicala. These lines recurred to my memory—

Why are we weighed upon with heaviness
And utterly consumed with sharp distress
While all things else have rest from weariness?

CHAPTER 6

The Fort

Life was a blank to me for many days; therefore I know little of the events that happened between the time of our arrival in Agra and our going into the fort about ten days after. I lay all day in a room with a wet towel wrapped round my head, utterly. stunned: everything seemed like a fearful dream. I could not believe that what had passed was real. My head felt throbbing and painful: we must all have suffered from partial *coup-de-soleil*—the exhaustion produced by want of proper food and rest, and distress of mind left me without the power of doing anything. The weather was oppressively hot, and we had not the proper appliances to mitigate the heat: there was no one to pull the *punkhas*, as the servants no longer cared to attend to us.

I had nothing in the world but what I had escaped in; and though the Agra ladies sent us a few clothes, there were so many for them to be divided amongst, that few fell to my share. Mrs. Innes was very kind in getting some clothes made for me; but there was great difficulty in procuring any materials, as the native shopkeepers and bazaar people had buried all their property, and no *kupra-wallahs* [1] or *box-wallahs* [2] now ventured to sell their goods; some went off to Calcutta, or Bombay, and others, securing their own goods, made themselves ready to plunder others, and take an active part in the rebellion. However, Mrs. Innes did manage, by sending a servant out, to get us a few coarse things. I

1. *Kaprah-wallah*, man who sells cloth or calico.
2. *Box-wallah*, pedler.

had a miserable black print. We had great difficulty in procuring a little flannel, which was now very necessary.

It is a common practice with natives, when there is an alarm, to bury their property; and in this way most of the Delhi loot was found. When a native suspects treasure has been buried, he searches for the place where he thinks it has been concealed, and throws water on it; if it sinks rapidly in, he knows the earth has been recently stirred, and then begins digging; and if he is lucky, he may light on some earthen vessel filled with gold *mohurs* [3] or *rupees*. I was told that Major Hodson, of Delhi renown, once, on a foraging expedition, came to a wall which his keen eye perceived to be the depository of treasure. He instantly went in search of assistance; but on his return, to his great disappointment, be found nothing but empty vessels: someone having been too quick for him had carried off the golden store.

After sleeping the first night in the garden, it was thought safer that we should go to the barracks to sleep; as they were in a central position and well guarded. Our beds were placed under the veranda surrounding the barracks. The Campbells, Stevensons and several others slept here. The crickets, frogs, and jackals kept up a dismal concert all night, and cockroaches, two or three inches long, swarmed all around us.

We had a long drive every night; often through pouring rain (for the rainy season was just commencing); the nights were pitch dark, and we were occasionally startled by seeing some native skulking about. We had to pass several sentries, whose challenges Major Macpherson answered; but sometimes he forgot the password, and we had to wait till Mrs. Innes remembered it. The first night it was "Oxford," and the next "Putney." The poor soldiers, many of whom were very young, looked quite worn out with patrolling and extra work.

One night the sentry close to us was fired at; instantly all the gentlemen were up, but it was not found out who had caused the alarm. Several people were thus fired at during that week. Every morning we returned from the barracks, and I again lay

---

3. *Mohurs*, a gold coin worth thirty shillings

in my room. Mrs. Innes borrowed a Bible for me, which afforded me much consolation. I had 10*l.* given me from Government, which was to last me three months, as I could not get any money from Calcutta.

The weather became daily more oppressive, and affairs looked more gloomy. Life really seemed a burden; it was only one long struggle to preserve it No one dared look forward a single day. Rumours were spread that a large force was collecting in the vicinity of Agra, against which our small force could do little good; but the fort stood us in good stead, and our deepest gratitude is due for its good service. We heard bad news from the surrounding country of Lucknow and Cawnpore, and no tidings of help coming from England then.

Major Macpherson, at my request, sent as trustworthy a native as could then be found to Gwalior to find out all particulars. Just afterwards my *kitmutghar* came in from Gwalior on the 24th, the first anniversary of my wedding day, and from him I learnt all, and more than I wished to know; and thus my last faint hope vanished. He told me that all the bodies of the killed had been thrown into a dry *nullah.* [4] He also said that the day after the mutiny the Maharajah had come down to cantonments, and been received by the mutinous troops as their king, and had held a parade. I hardly believed this at the time; but I afterwards remembered seeing in the paper that the mutiny of the 34th N.I, at Barrackpore, was to have taken place the very day the *rajah* had fixed for his grand fête at Calcutta. His sudden departure put a stop to it.

Perhaps he thought thus to avoid suspicion; but who can find out the motives of "a doubly-dyed traitorous Mahratta"? Another mysterious matter connected with the Maharajah, and which many people have commented on is, that he in some way prevented the women from being killed at Gwalior. It is said that he knew of the mutiny, and extracted a promise from the *sepoys* to spare the women: else

---

4. The Maharajah of Gwalior ordered all the bodies of those killed on the 14th and 15th to be buried a few days after the mutiny. Some months later the bodies were disinterred and buried in the Gwalior churchyard. Since the retaking of Gwalior, in June 1858, I have been able to have a tomb erected over my husband's grave.

why, it is urged, did they not kill us when we were so completely in their power, and they were drunk with *bhang* and brandy? Gwalior is the only station where the women were not killed.

If the *rajah* could so far protect us, and give a guard and carriages to take some of the fugitives to Agra,—thus showing the *sepoys* he was not wholly on their side,—why did he not warn us, and send the women and children to Agra? We should all have gone on Sunday, the instant the fires broke out Why did he not, instead of taking us to his palace, let us go to Agra, when we first made our escape to the residency, and the carriages were all ready waiting and only wanting a guard from him? for then we were not prohibited from going by Mr. Colvin's order. I am afraid it is impossible to explain these mysterious circumstances. It is also said that the *sepoys* at Gwalior were communicating long before the 14th of June—and that the *rajah* knew of it—with the regiments' of the Contingent which had left (the 1st Grenadiers and the Cavalry), and sending lists of those they particularly wished to kill.

The *kitmutghar* pretended to be very sorry for what had happened, and "wept crocodile's tears." I found out, as I had anticipated, that he had got our plate and 50*l*. in *rupees*, left in our house, for his share, and that the *ayah* had got my dresses, &c; but he complained that the *sepoys* had treated them very badly, and made them give them up the plunder, and that even the villagers, on his way to Agra, had robbed him of the little he had left. The man looked dirty and forlorn; very different to his gay clean appearance little more than a week before. He, however, brought me my poor little puppy "Jack."

Poor Mrs. Blake now heard of the murder of her brother, Mr. Bicketts, at Shahjehanpore. The mutiny there had taken place before the Gwalior mutiny, whilst the people were in church. Sunday seems to have been the chosen day for the *sepoys'* rising: whether they had some idea connected with religion, or whether they thought we were less on our guard on that day, can only be conjectured. I refrain from giving any details of the horrible mutinies, accounts of which daily poured in; for the papers have teemed with graphic accounts of every mutiny, and the massacres of Cawnpore, Jhansi, Delhi, and Meerut are seared on the hearts of many in burning characters.

I was very glad to hear from Mrs. Innes that many had escaped from Gwalior on Sunday, night. During the first ten minutes after the alarm bugle sounded, they had all crossed the *nullah*, which in some places was very shallow, though in others they were obliged to swim: they had then met at the Lushkur, where the *Maharajah* very kindly received them and, as I have mentioned, gave them a guard and carriages. They gave up for lost all those left behind. They accomplished their journey to Agra in about two days without much difficulty, excepting once, when they were nearly betrayed into an ambush at Dholepore; this it was which gave rise to the fearful reports we had heard there.

Those who thus escaped were the Meades, Murrays, Hennessys, Piersons, Mrs. Ferris, Mrs. Christison, Captain Longville Clarke, Mr. Smalley, Dr. Sheitz, Brigadier Ramsay, Dr. Mackellar, and Captain Ryves: the two last rode the whole way to Agra on horseback. Lieutenant Pierson, Captain Longville Clarke, Captain Ryves (who had escaped from Jhansi), and Dr. Mackellar, were the only officers who escaped, after having ridden down to the lines. They were in imminent danger of being fired at: Captain Longville Clarke was wounded, and Lieutenant Pierson rejoined his wife, whom the *sepoys* actually brought to him, and carried some miles in a horse cloth, slung between their muskets. It seems very strange that the *sepoys* should have treated him with such kindness, when he had only arrived about six weeks before the mutiny broke out: he was adjutant in the same regiment as poor Major Blake.

Mrs. Hennessy lived in a large *pucka*-house, which, being not so liable to take fire, Mrs. Christison and her child took refuge in before the mutiny broke out Mrs. Ferris, wife of a commanding officer at one of the out-stations, and her children, were also staying with her. As soon as the alarm bugle sounded, Mrs. Hennessy's son, a youth of about seventeen, urged them to fly: he helped them, and took care of these ladies and children, and of his own little sister, and protected them all the way to the

Lushkur.

Mrs. Ferris and Mrs. Christison escaped without shoes or bonnets, as they were just going to bed. There were at that time six ladies and eight children at Gwalior, their husbands and fathers having left with their regiments, with no one to protect them, or even to be responsible for their safety. Lieutenant and Mrs. Procter stayed all night with Mrs. Gilbert at her earnest entreaty; she could not ride, and her servants would not let her have her carriage. Perhaps had Mr. Procter ridden off with his wife, as they had planned, he might have escaped; but he would not leave an unprotected woman.

The Meades' house was on the banks of the *nullah*. Mrs. Murray, whose child had been buried that morning, had gone to her sister, so they were all together. They were just retiring to rest, I believe, when the alarm bugle sounded; they instantly snatched up their children, and with some servants, ran out and crossed the *nullah*, which was fortunately shallow there. They hid in a small guardhouse for some time, till their husbands joined them.

The guard of their own house hid them, and even advised them to go to the *rajah's*; so they walked as fast as they could to his palace, where they found Major Macpherson and Mrs. Innes, who had driven from the Residency to the palace, in a great state of alarm about those left behind. Seeing the *sepoys* hunting about on the banks of the *nullah*, hearing the shouts and firing, and seeing the houses blazing, they thought all was over with those left behind. All those who escaped in this manner knew the surrounding country well, and some had been born at Gwalior.

I still was very anxious to know the fate of poor Mrs. Stuart and Mrs. Hawkins; and at last heard that Mrs. Hawkins had arrived in Agra with her remaining three children and little Charlotte Stuart. She had seen her husband, her two children, Mrs. Stuart, and her child, and her nurse, a European, all killed! She afterwards described to me the horrid scene.

On Monday morning the *sepoys* rushed into the hut where they were hiding, and fired at Captain Hawkins; the same bullet killed Mrs. Stuart, who was clinging to his arm; they then killed the nurse, and it was supposed the infant was killed by falling with her. A blow with a *tulwah* killed Mrs. Stuart's little boy, two years old, and Mrs. Hawkins's other child. It seems very wonderful why they spared Mrs. Hawkins's three remaining children; for two of them were boys, and they had sworn to kill all the *sahibs*: poor little Kirke was only spared because they thought he was a girl.

Mrs. Stuart's bearer remained faithful to Mrs. Hawkins, and hid her three children and Charlotte Stuart on the top of a hut Mrs. Hawkins was too weak to move, and the *sepoys* would not let her have any water; at last she crept down to the *nullah* to get some water for her children, when one, more merciful than the rest gave her some. She also got a note conveyed by some means to Colonel Filose, who lived in the Lushkur. He and his brother are descendants of the famous French officer who trained the Mahratta troops in former days; and ever since a descendant of his his had the command of the *rajah's* forces. Colonel Filose lived in a handsome house in the Lushkur, and was treated with great respect by the *rajah*. He sent a cart for Mrs. Hawkins and her children, to whom the *sepoys* at last gave some clothes, which she sadly needed, and let them go, accompanied by the faithful bearer.

Captain Stuart lay all Sunday night in a hut, wounded, but not mortally. The faithful bearer attended to him and gave him some milk and water. In the morning he asked after his wife, and on hearing she was killed said he no longer cared to live. The *sepoys* then took him to the place where the elephants were kept, some distance off, and there shot him. Captain Stuart and his wife were both young; but perhaps it was better they should die together. Poor Mrs. Hawkins was very ill for some time, and as soon as it was safe went up to her brother in the hills. I shall never forget her patient endurance; though sorely tried, she never murmured.

Little Charlotte Stuart, who was about six years old, remained in the fort under the care of some kind friends; but the poor little thing, from being the merriest child in Gwalior, became quite grave and melancholy. The bearer never deserted her. One day, on meeting Mrs. Blake in the fort, she asked her if she had any pictures of Gwalior.

There was one other woman killed at Gwalior; I forget her name, but she was the widow of the conductor, who had something to do with the commissariat at Gwalior: he had risen from the ranks, and had saved a great deal of money. He died a short time before the mutiny, and his wife buried his boxes of treasure, thinking they would be safe; and on the *sepoys* demanding the treasure, she refused to show them where it was hid, whereupon they shot her.

Poor Mrs. Ferris, shortly after her arrival, heard of the death of her husband. He was coming in to Gwalior from one of the outstations, to join his wife, who had been sent there for safety, when he and a young officer who was with him were stopped and dragged out of their *gharry* by the villagers, tied to a tree and flogged. Major Ferris soon died; but the young officer survived the flogging: perhaps his youth and good constitution sustained him; at all events, he came into Agra and brought the report of Major Ferris's fate; but he was ill for a long time after. I must now return to the events at the fort

It was now feared that the Gwalior Contingent, which had all collected at Gwalior, on finding that Agra was not destroyed and all the *Feringhees* killed, as they had said, would join the Neemuch mutineers, who were collecting in our neighbourhood, and march on Agra; but, strange to say, they did not, being too much occupied in plundering and quarrelling among themselves to care for further conquest. Had they marched on the fort, they would certainly have taken it, and the same tragedy might have happened as at Cawnpore; for they were well disciplined, and had a heavy siege train. It was thought prudent to issue an order that all the women and children should go into the fort At first the order was not peremptory; but many who lived at a distance from the fort took advantage of it

The gentlemen were not included in this order, as they were to remain, and do what they could to protect the city; and many were enrolled in the militia commanded by Lieutenant Greathed. All the force we now had to depend upon, since disbanding the native regiments, was the 3rd Europeans, about six hundred strong, Captain D' Oyley's field battery of six guns, and a corps of European volunteer cavalry under Lieutenant Greathed, about two hundred in number.

The stations at Allyghur had been held, since the mutiny there on the 19th of May, by a detachment of the Gwalior Contingent; but when they heard of the mutiny at Gwalior, they would no longer remain faithful even in appearance, though they told their officers to escape. On the 23rd of June the guard at the gaol mutinied, so that it had to be guarded by some of the 3rd Europeans, commanded inside by Dr. Walker, superintendent.

Hearing there was a chance of a mail reaching Bombay, I wrote to my father and to my husband's father; and I afterwards heard that mine were almost the only letters sent by that mail which reached England. They had unfortunately heard at home of the mutiny at Gwalior before the arrival of my letters.

It was finally arranged that Dr. Mackellar should take Mrs. Innes and myself to the fort. We started about 5 o' clock p.m. of the 29th, and I took my last look of the house and garden where some of the most miserable days of my life had been passed—days never to be forgotten. I only saw it again as a mass of blackened ruins: one of the many proofs of the natives' bitter hatred for us. We had a very unpleasant drive, having to pass through one of the crowded bazaars. The throng and noise was overwhelming, the numbers being increased by the villagers, who had flocked in ostensibly for safety, but no doubt in anticipation of the events that soon followed, when they joined in plundering and sacking the cantonments.

They had brought all their household goods in *hackeries*[5]; and the growling camels, bellowing bullocks, and barking pariah dogs seemed to be trying to outdo one another in noise. We had some distance to drive, as the fort was further from cantonments than the city, and the nearer we approached it the denser became the crowd; it was now increased by carriages full of ladies

5. *Hackery*, native cart drawn by bullocks.

and children, on their way to the fort, by carts, *hackeries*, mud camels loaded with boxes, tables, chairs, and bedding; now and then officers on horseback, galloping along with some order, or a native chief, or *sowar*, glittering with arms, and showing off their horsemanship on prancing steeds, dashed through the crowd.

The native population seemed to be in a state of great excitement, evidently enjoying our retreat; but beneath this outward excitement of demeanour lurked deep and treacherous designs, only waiting an opportunity to develop themselves.

We descended a steep hill, and the fort then loomed upon us in all its massive strength, with its walls and battlements of dark red stone, and its formidable looking entrance guarded by some of the 3rd Europeans. We had not time then to estimate its merits and defects; and though its massive walls and loopholes, from which frowned the cannon, and the gateway with its drawbridge spanning the wide and deep moat surrounding the fort, were assuring, still we could not help shuddering at the possibility of its being besieged.

Indeed, had the enemy then attacked it, our small force would have been quite insufficient to defend its immense extent of walls and ramparts in such an exposed position; and there were afterwards found to be numerous underground passages, leading from the city immediately into the fort. We can now look back with thankfulness that we were not exposed to a siege.

Here we had to walk, as carriages were not admitted across the drawbridge; and it was very fatiguing to force our way through the crowd that now thronged the entrance. At last we entered the barbican, and passed through the large massive doors clamped with iron, the wicket of which was only open: we had to wait sometime in the outer court till the first door was shut, as only one was allowed to be open at once.

We walked up a steep inclined plane, paved with rough stones, which was commanded by the walls and guns, and by a guard-house on each side the archway, leading from the outer court; we then passed through another gateway into the armoury square, filled with cannon and piles of ball and shell arranged on each side of the centre road. The crowd and pressure was so great here that I had only time for a passing glance; but I now remembered where I was, for when I first saw the fort a *mali* [6] had run after me to give me a beautiful bouquet gathered from the palace garden.

How we ever reached our quarters I know not; for no one seemed to know where to go, and the officers from whom Dr. Mackellar asked the way were quite as much in the dark as himself; however, by dint of struggling and pushing, we found the place appointed for the Gwalior refugees by the authorities: our locality was the palace garden, afterwards denominated "Trafalgar Square," or "Block F." After passing through several small courts and alleys we entered a large square and ascended a flight of steps on to an extensive plateau, or terrace, whence we had a beautiful view of the Jumma flowing beneath the walk, and the country stretching far away, with the Taj gleaming softly and fairy like in the gathering darkness; but I did not notice all this at the time, being utterly dazed and bewildered at quitting my quiet room for the confusion of a crowd of excited and alarmed people. The first glance of our future dwelling-place was discouraging and disheartening in the extreme.

Before proceeding with my narrative I will attempt to give some description of the fort, which may be interesting to some, it having been the dwelling-place of many of their countrymen for six months.

The fort, which is called the key of Hindoostan, was taken, in 1803, by the English, under Lord Lake; this and the victory of Laswarie put into our hands all Scindiah's possessions on this side the Chumbul. The fort yet bears marks of the siege, in the fractures of the marble and ornaments by the cannon shot.

This fort was one of the few places which remained in our possession in that part of India. Agra first came into notice in the beginning of the sixteenth century: before that it was an inconsiderable village. It was chosen by the son of Belloli, in 1501, for his residence. Sultan Baber, in 1518, defeated the emperor, and put an end to the dynasty of Lodi.

Half a century later it was further enlarged by the Emperor Akbar the Great, who built an extensive palace and again changed its name

---

6. *Mali*, gardener.

to Akbaradad; he built an entirely new city on the right bank of the Junma and was also the founder of the fort at Allahabad. Agra continued to be the seat of the Mogul government until the year 1647, when Delhi was declared the capital of the Emperor Shah Jehan; from which time the decline of Agra may be dated.

During his residence at Agra, Shah Jehan, son of Jehanguire, whom he succeeded in 1605, erected the Taj Mahal. His reign was the epoch of the greatest splendour and prosperity of the Mogul dynasty; though its territory was afterwards greatly extended by Aurunzebe, the magnificence of whose court was unequalled, even by the tales of oriental pomp. Jehanguire's wife, Noor Jehan, was celebrated for her beauty and wit, and has been the fertile theme of many oriental poems and romances.

Shah Jehan was overthrown by the united forces of Aurunzebe and Morad, who deposed and imprisoned him in 1658. Though imprisoned in the fort of Agra he was treated with great respect, and allowed an ample establishment. He died in 1666, in the seventy-fourth year of his age, and was buried in the Taj by the side of his wife.[7] Aurunzebe died in 1707, and was the Great Mogul of Hindoostan.

It is no easy task to attempt a description of the fort. It is situated so as to command the town and river, and covers an immense extent of ground. Within the walls is a strange mixture of buildings, some for pomp and others for defence. In former days it must have fully realised the most extravagant ideas of oriental luxury and splendour; as it contained sumptuous palaces, lofty marble halls of audience, pavilions, towers and kiosks, terraces and balconies, labyrinths of small grottoes, like cells and passages, *tyrconnels*[8], and subterranean passages. In more modern times, barracks, magazines, storehouses, and hospitals were added, and every nook and corner crammed with people.

The palace built by Akbar, entirely of marble, and the two large halls—the "*Dewan-i-khas*," or hall of nobles, the place where the

---

7. Múmtaz Begum; she is frequently mistaken for the beautiful wife of Jehanguire, the Nourmahal of "Lalla Rookh." Nourjehan was buried at Lahore.
8. *Tyrconnels*, underground vaults.

durbars were held, and the "*Dewan-i-Amor*," hall of audience—are all very splendid. These halls are raised above the terraces on which they stand, by a platform several feet high, which is surrounded by a low carved marble balustrade. Another hall is called the "*Shish Mahal*" or looking-glass palace. These halls, all of white marble, though falling into decay, retain much of their ancient grandeur. The walls, like those of the Taj, are of formed slabs of marble, profusely decorated with mosaics of precious stones. The natives pick out these stones—many of which are very valuable, and make chess-tables, boxes, trays, and ornaments of the marble, which they inlay with the gems; such articles, as well as models of the Taj, are frequently bought by travellers.

The *Zenáná* [9] is a very curious building of two stories; the upper one used for all common purposes, and the lower being divided into cool grottoes, where, in the hot weather, the *houris* used to retire to bathe, and whiled away the monotony by games of play: it is a strange medley of passages, stairs, and grottoes. Down a narrow passage there is a deep well, which you can quite imagine has been the death place of many a fair and frail beauty; the offender was dragged here, and hung from a beam which stretches above the deep dark gulf yawning to receive her dead body.

This well is now nearly filled up; but formerly it was of great depth, and looked an awful depository of such dread secrets. The "*Motee Musjid*," or pearl mosque, also within the walls of the fort, and next the armoury square, is considered one of the most beautiful specimens of Moslem architecture. It is built entirely of a beautiful creamy white marble, said to be what was left after building the Taj. Ascending a flight of steps of red sandstone, and passing through a vestibule richly decorated with carving, mosaic, and cupolas, you enter a large court paved with slabs of marble; in the centre is a large tank, and the court is surrounded by a row of cloisters, or cells, formerly inhabited by priests and devotees, and now by invalid officers. The Mosque itself is open to the court, and consists of three aisles of arches supported on

9. *Zenana*, the ladies' apartments..

massive pillars. The polish of the marble is so fine, that it glistens like a mirror. Like other Mahomedan buildings, the *Motee Musjid* is raised on a *chabudra* [10] and ascended by two or three low steps. This place was used as a hospital during our occupation of the fort. Near the *Dewan-i-khas* there was a beautiful garden laid out, much like that of the Taj; but shortly after our arrival it was rooted up, being considered unhealthy, on account of its dense foliage and trees absorbing the damp; and it was only inhabited by cows, goats, fowls, and a young donkey.

Around three sides of this garden was a row of small apartments, thought to have been occupied formerly by the king's ministers and *vakeels*. These rooms were allotted to the Agra civilians.

Our quarters, which were much less comfortable, were near the *Dewan-i-Am:* that, I think, was the name of the large marble hall, the court of which was entered, as I have said, by a gateway closed by handsome bronzed doors. Round this court ran a wide balcony or gallery twelve feet wide, the roof supported on arches; and from this balcony projected a narrow stone walk, guarded by a low parapet This gallery, in former days, was occupied by the king's servants; and the remains of rings are now visible, from which they used to hang *purdahs* or thick curtains, to divide the veranda into compartments: our "dens," or "kennels," as the officers used to call them, because they reminded them of their former quarters at Addiscombe and Sandhurst, only they were not so large and comfortable. We divided them by *jamp*-screens, made of grass and bamboo poles. The grass grows in the jungle to the height of six or eight feet; it is silky, but strong and flexible, and the natives use it for thatch and to divide their huts.

The officers who had the allotting of the quarters (a task that was no sinecure) had appointed to us each one arch, which we divided as I have before described. The temporary partitions of grass were so thin, you could hear every word uttered in the next division; and in the morning interchanges of inquiries took

10. *Chabudra*, terrace, plateau.

place, and it was amusing to hear the conspirator-like whispers people used to converse in when they did not wish to be over-heard.

But to return to our first night. Dr. Mackellar was soon obliged to leave us, as he had hospital duty to perform, so we were left alone: only Mrs. Meade, Mrs. Murray and their children, Mrs. Proctor, Mrs. Innes, and myself, occupied our square; the rest had not come. The fort being so large, we were quite sepa-rated from the crowd of people that had come in that day; though afterwards the veranda below us was occupied by half-castes. We vainly tried to put things in order; for our few articles of fur-niture lay scattered about in hopeless confusion. It was growing darker, the poor children were hungry and tired, and their la-ments and the officiousness of our native servants added to our troubles: the servants, though ostentatiously attentive, seemed to enjoy our perplexity and bewilderment; but they at last got us some tea. After taking it, we found it quite hopeless to attempt putting our "dens" in order, so we had our beds put outside on the projecting stone walk, which was about four feet wide.

The children were then put to sleep, and we set out to explore some part of our future dwelling-place. First we walked on the large terrace near our quarters, and fronting the *Diwan-i-Am*; it is raised from the terrace on a *chabudra*, and we ascended into it by two or three steps. It consisted of a large outer hall, separated from an inner one by arches; and from the outer hall, which was open on two sides, we had a beautiful view of the river and Taj; the full radiance of the moon making the river shine like silver, and giving a look of unearthly whiteness to the Taj.

The silence was so intense that the only sounds we heard were the rippling of the water and the hooting of the owls. We passed through the inner marble hall, ascending some more steps on to a still higher but smaller terrace, whence we had a bird's-eye view of all the buildings of the fort and of the palace garden near us, which was not then occupied. Here was a beautiful kiosk [11], octagonal in shape, the walls of fretted marble, and the

---

11. Kiosk, pavilion open on all sides.

circular roof of copper gilt. This kiosk, which was formerly used by the emperors as a summer-house, we afterwards called "The Tower." The dead stillness made us feel like intruders in these ancient halls and terraces, which seemed fitted only for the habitation of the shades of their former kings. After wandering about some time, we returned to our own balcony, where our servants, rolled in their white *chuddars*, lay about asleep.

The next day all my friends went to pass their day in cantonments, so I had a dreary day alone; and having no books I occupied myself in watching die people coming to take possession of their allotted "quarters." The noise and confusion was deafening; coolies running backwards and forwards with furniture, boxes, &c, bringing large supplies of wood and other useful things, removing old things from their places to make room for the future occupants, and piling things on the roof of our balcony, which surrounded the courtyard on three sides.

Some were making the *jamps*, and all were screaming and shouting without intermission; for a native thinks no work can be done without a great amount of gesticulation and shouting. At last came a lull in the storm, when they were all occupied in eating or sleeping; but this silence, after the terrible noise, only lasted for an hour.

I overheard the natives in the next compartment to mine talking of the Gwalior mutiny; one of the servants who had come in from Gwalior was giving his companions a detailed account of all that had happened on that fatal day: how this "*sahib* was killed" and where another was shot. It was harrowing to my feelings to hear all this, for I now knew quite enough of Hindoostanee to understand what they said, and I distinctly heard them go over the whole account with minute exactness, gloating and dilating on the horrible facts, and then laughing with savage glee over the number that had been killed: I heard them repeatedly speak of the "*padre sahib*"—my dear husband.

Strange to say they had actually placed a guard over the cemetery on that night (the 14th) to prevent the graves being desecrated, for fear the spirits should haunt them; but afterwards they grew more hardy and reckless, and it is said they frequently opened the graves. I believe they opened the grave of one of the former lieutenant-governors of the north-west provinces; and that is the reason why, when Mr. Colvin died, he was buried within the fort walls.

Shortly after our occupation of the fort it was divided into "blocks;" our quarters, as I have before said, were in " block F," and each compartment was numbered: thus letters were directed to Captain M——, Block F, No. 3, or whatever letter and number it might be. On every gateway, arch, and conspicuous place, were painted large stars, as landmarks; so that with a little questioning you could find your way all over the fort: for so large was it and provided with such a heterogeneous mixture of passages, buildings, gateways, and arches, that I have heard people say it was impossible to find your way through it without a clue.

After we had been settled there, and had learnt to look on it as our home for some time to come, everything was arranged. A staff of sweepers to keep the interior clean were paid by the authorities, and *bheesties, coolies,* and other satellites necessary for order and comfort, were hired; butchers, bakers, *dhobies,* and others carried on their trades within the fort; walls were built and others thrown down; gardens were laid out, and all the daily offices of life were attended to and thought of; nor was death forgotten, for even coffins were made. The fort was divided as follows:—

The Agra civilians occupied comparatively comfortable quartos in the palace gardens; the large marble ball then being employed by the head civilians as a "*cutchery,*"[12] and on Sundays for service: one officer's marriage even was celebrated in it. The officers and their families lived in tents, pitched on a large green opposite the Delhi Grate, and near the *Motee Musjid.* Here also was a row of small tiled houses, formerly the officers' quarters when the fort was garrisoned, and now occupied by some of the head military officers, Colonel Grassford, Colonel Fraser, and others, with their families.

There were also some other houses, in one of which Lady Outram lived, and the rest were inhabited by officers and their

---

12. *Cutchery,* business-room; civil office.

wives. The place where formerly the gun-carriages had stood was occupied by the nuns, and their large school; they turned one large room or storehouse into a chapel, and fitted it up marvellously well with crucifixes, altars, and candlesticks.

The Roman Catholic archbishop and his ecclesiastical staff lived in some large tents on the green, near the officers. The chaplains, Mr. Hind and Mr. Murray, had comfortable quarters, and Mr. French and the other missionaries lived in the palace garden. The unmarried soldiers lived in one set of barracks, and the married with their families occupied another set. The latter were much more comfortably off than we were, and had brought in some of their furniture; indeed some of the married soldiers' quarters were really very snug. The places where the shopkeepers and merchants lived were very wretched.

On the archways and tops of buildings they made small thatched huts, of the same grass our *jamps* were made of. But it would be a waste of words to describe all the extraordinary places people inhabited: sufficient to say, every available place was crammed, either with sheds of *chopperwork* [13], or rude sorts of shanties, huts, and tents.; and the casemates and barracks were all crowded with occupants, almost as closely packed as bees in a hive. The confusion of tongues was such as to give one some idea of the confusion at the Tower of Babel The half-castes, or "*Kala-Ferin-ghis*," as the natives call them, who are uncharitably said to have the vices of both different races, and the virtues of neither, were in immense swarms, and had to accommodate themselves anywhere. A large number of them lived in our "square," just beneath our balcony: the rest lived in holes, *tyrconnels*, or on the tops of the buildings all over the fort.

Poor creatures! they must have had a miserable time of it; for their habitations were very wretched. The census of all the persons in the fort, which was taken on the 26th of July, amounted to no less than 5845; of which 1989 were Europeans, consisting of 1065 men and 924 women and children: the whole of the rest being natives and half-castes.

---

13. *Chopperwork*, thatching.

The walls of the fort are three-quarters of a mile in circumference, and it was victualled for a six months' siege; but I am very glad we were never obliged to depend on the fort for defence against a heavy siege-train, or on the supplies of the commissariat officers; for in either case we should have been very ill off. The defences of the fort were, however, much strengthened: sixty guns of heavy calibre were mounted on the bastions, mortars were placed in position, and the powder magazines were secured from accidental explosion. The external defences also were much improved by levelling some houses near; and preparations were completed for blowing up the superb Junna Musjid, if needful: for if we had been attacked, the enemy might have occupied it, and so have commanded the interior of the fort

There were several large archways or vestibules within the fort, besides those for egress and ingress. Two of these were in the armoury square; that at the top of the inclined plane, being used as a shop by one or two of the Agra shop people, who had saved a few of their wares: inside, you ascended into a gallery up a narrow flight of steps, where was arranged, on hastily put up shelves, bottles of wine and beer, canisters of preserved meat, biscuits, and a few drugs, and some stationery. The gallery on .the opposite side of the vestibule was occupied by the owners, who had made it into a comfortable little sitting-room; and beneath the galleries were piles of boxes and goods. The vestibule at the opposite end of the armoury square was used as the *dâk* office, or post-office; and before it in the morning and evening, were generally seen one or two mail-carts and *shigrams*.[14]

Now to describe "block F." Our quarters, as I have before mentioned, were on a *piazza*, supported on pillars, and we not only had to divide it, but to screw the front with *jamps*, so as to form small rooms. The floor was of *kunka*,[15] and the doorways were closed by *chicks*[16], or screens made of thin split reeds, which admitted light and air; but as the *jamps* did not reach to the roof,

---

14. *Shigram*, travelling carriage used in Bombay.
15. *Kunka*, beaten earth.
16. *Chick*, screen.

which was formed of massive blocks of sandstone, the partitions had the appearance of a long range of stalls. Our quarters were characterised "stables above, and pigsties below;" the half-castes being beneath us.

Our furniture consisted of two narrow soldier's cribs, with very hard mattresses and but scanty bedclothes, a small camp table, two or three chairs, and boxes to contain our stores and meagre wardrobe; and in one corner were the cooking vessels, and earthen pots for water. Our *toilette* apparatus consisted of a small *chillumchie*, [17] and a cracked looking-glass. A lamp, a few cups and saucers, plates, knives and forks, completed the *ménage*. This "den" and its furniture I shared with Mrs. Innes; and it is a sample of all the others.

In these "dens" we performed all the necessary acts of life: cooking and eating, dressing and undressing, sleeping and sitting up; but occasionally we went into the marble hall, where we sometimes carried our *rezais* [18] and lay down, as the breeze from the river made it cooler than our heated and crowded quarters; Many of the gentlemen and some of the ladies also, had their *charpoys* carried into the marble hall, and passed the night there, for the sake of the coolness; indeed some of the Agra people. who were richer in furniture than we, took all their meals there. One almost wondered that the ghosts of the ancient moguls and *sultanas* did not start from their graves in horror and amazement at the desecration of all their sacred temples and beautiful halls and palaces, which were defiled by being turned into cooking and sleeping places by the "cursed *Kaffir.*" indeed, no pen can adequately describe the metamorphosis.

I must now recur to the evening of the second day in the fort, when all my friends returned, bringing fresh and alarming reports: not only was the Gwalior Contingent expected, but the Neemuch mutineers were close to Agra. An order was now is-sued that every man capable of bearing arms, was to be armed and take part in garrison duty. Of course this was not very cheering,

---

17. *Chillumchie*, brass bason.
18. *Rezais*, quilted coverlet

for at Gwalior alone there were four regiments, besides two batteries, and guns of heavy calibre. I cannot well remember what passed the first week we were in the fort, such was the bustle and confusion of people daily arriving, who had not before thought it necessary to come into the fort; some having the barracks to sleep in, while others had houses near the fort.

The authorities had given orders that no one was to bring in more than one box each, and a few articles of furniture; this order was not literally obeyed in every case, it being thought a very severe one; and many continued to smuggle in, not only a fair quantity of necessaries, but luxuries in the shape of champagne, plate, &c. It must have been very trying to leave beautiful houses, filled with books, pictures, plate, and other valuables, the collection of years, to the mercy of *budmashes*,[19] and released prisoners, especially as the necessity was not apparently urgent.

The destruction of property was very great; all the houses, both of the military and civil lines, were burnt, and even the barracks, which were quite new (the soldiers had never even occupied them); the handsome Roman Catholic cathedral, and our churches and colleges shared the same fate. It was afterwards said, that the cantonments ought not to have been abandoned; and certainly had a little more foresight been used, much property might have been stowed in the *tyrconnels*, which were very extensive; this was the opinion of many of the Agra people, who had lost upwards of 4000*l*. or 5000*l*. worth of property, including furniture brought expressly from England at a great expense.

On the evening of the 4th of July, the Kotah Contingent mutinied, 700 strong. It was thought to be staunch; and their officers had declared them quite safe, notwithstanding the many proofs they had had of the base treachery of the *sepoys*. This Contingent had been brought into the vicinity of Agra, where. it was encamped between the barracks and the lieutenant-governor's house; and a detachment of them had been sent to replace the European guard of the gaol, which contained more than 3000 prisoners of the worst character.

---

19. *Budmashes*, rascals.

Cannon had been planted before the doors of the goal to fire upon the prisoners should they escape in case of a rising; but all these well planned schemes were frustrated by the unexpected mutiny of the Kotah Contingent. A detachment of 350 foot and two guns had been ordered out, to form an advance guard to repel the body of insurgents; but on the approach of the other rebels, they mutinied, as perhaps they had intended, and attempted to shoot their officers, but only succeeded in killing their sergeant-major.

They then quietly marched out of Agra, and joined the other mutineers, but left their guns. Directly after this mutiny, a peremptory order was issued for every woman and child to go into the fort, and a portion of the 3rd Europeans was appointed to protect it; the rest of the 3rd, and the militia, remained in cantonments.

Early on Sunday morning Dr. Christison came into the fort, much to the relief and joy of his wife, who had not seen him since he left Gwalior with his regiment on the 14th of May; during which time she had heard frightful reports of the regiment mutinying and killing Dr. Christison, Captain Alexander, and Lieutenant Cockburrn. These reports afterwards proved untrue: Dr. Christison, with several other officers, had escaped from some out-stations on Saturday evening; but they could not then get into the fort, on account of the uproar and confusion attending the mutiny of the Kotah rebels.

The same morning (the 5th of July), Brigadier Polwhele gave orders that the troops commanded by Colonel Riddel and himself, and consisting of 650 of the 3rd Europeans, one battery, commanded by Captain D'Oyley, and 200 of the volunteer European cavalry, commanded by Lieutenant Greathed, should march out of cantonments at 11 o'clock a. m. towards the village of Shahgunge, beyond Government House, three miles from cantonments, and four from the fort.

The enemy, consisting of 7000 infantry, 1500 cavalry, and 8 guns of heavy calibre, were encamped on a large plain near the village of Sussia, on the road to Futteypore Sicri, the fourth milestone from Agra. When our troops entered the large sandy plain which lies to the right of the road, the line of battle was formed, and the enemy were seen in strong position behind the village of Shahgunge, their guns flanking the village, and the cavalry flanking the guns.

Our force now formed into line, with three guns on each flank; those on the right commanded by Captain D'Oyley, and those on the left by Captain Pearson of the artillery of the Gwalior Contingent; the infantry being in the middle, and the mounted militia somewhat in the rear. When about 600 yards from the village, the enemy opened fire on our right battery; which was responded to with such good effect, that after two rounds from each gun, the enemy were seen retreating in great numbers. The 3rd Europeans got the order to lie down, the guns were unlimbered, and then the fight commenced in earnest.

It was evident that our guns took no effect on the high mud walls of the village, which siege guns could alone touch; the consequence was that the enemy became emboldened, their cavalry in great numbers harassed our right, and the skirmishing of their infantry gave us great annoyance with their rifle firing, which we, from want of cavalry, were powerless to repel. After a while, the 3rd Europeans got the order to advance, which they did gallantly, under a heavy fire. A rifle company of the mutinied 72nd did great execution on our force.

The village was stormed and taken; but another tumbril blowing up, we had only four guns serviceable, and no ammunition for the artillery. Poor Captain D'Oyley now received his mortal wound; but still continued to give orders supported on a gun-carriage. Want of cavalry prevented our following up the victory; we had carried the village, driven the enemy from their position, but for want of ammunition and cavalry were obliged to retreat. Immediately that the rebels perceived that their artillery was not answered, they knew there was something wrong with us; they therefore advanced upon their former position with their guns, and pursued us the whole way to Agra; firing round shot at us, and harassing us with their cavalry. The Civil Line's infantry militia, met our troops coming in, and formed across the road a rear-guard; maintaining this position till the whole force reached the fort at 6 p. m., having been actively engaged for full three hours.

The total killed, including those who afterwards died, was 49; wounded, 91: of the officers, Captain D'Oyley was mortally wounded, and Lieutenant Lambe afterwards died of his wounds. The officers wounded not mortally were Major Thomas, who afterwards died, Lieutenants Pond and Fellows, and five of the Civil Line's infantry militia. Of the unattached officers six were wounded: Captain Alexander, of the Gwalior Contingent Cavalry, was wounded in the wrist by a spent-ball, and Lieutenant Cockburn, of the same regiment, had a horse killed under him by a round shot, and the concussion of the air was so great that it severely injured the sinews of his leg. The result was a total of 141 killed and wounded out of a force of about 800.

Poor Captain D'Oyley's death was a great loss, for he was a most gallant officer. An officer afterwards told me that when he fell, overcome by pain, be said, "Ah! they have done for me now: put a stone over my grave, and say I died at my guns."

On being asked if he would like to be moved to a place of greater safety, he said it would be of no use, as he felt he was mortally wounded: but he told them to try what they could do for the other poor fellows. I believe he lived till the next day.

Another instance of bravery deserves notice. Young Hennessey, whom I have before mentioned as behaving so coolly in the mutiny at Gwalior, and who had never received any military education, or had been beyond Gwalior, except to a school in the hills, went out with his father into the battle, by his own wish; and his gallant and plucky conduct received universal admiration. Only a soldier who has been in action can thoroughly appreciate his conduct, as everyone who was in the fight, even those who had been through the Punjab and Seik campaigns, said it was a very severe one; the shrapnel shell, round-shot, and grape flew about like hail. Young Hennessey gave us a most enthusiastic account of this his first battle, and the number of *pandies* he had killed and wounded. Some months afterwards he was severely wounded in his sword-arm, in an engagement near Allyghur, and he has lately received a commission in H. M.'s 24th Foot.

All within the fort were for some hours in a state of anxiety and doubt as to our own fate and that of those gone out against such fearful odds; and our suspense was painfully increased by hearing the firing and booming of the cannon for three hours. The distress and anxiety of the poor wives of those in action was dreadful to witness; the chance of their ever seeing their husbands again seemed small, as we could not help fearing that many lives would be lost.

I was too ill to go out of my "den," having taken a dose of opium; but some of the ladies went to the flag-staff on the Delhi Gate, which being very high, commanded an extensive view, and plainly saw our force retreating, pursued by the enemy's cavalry. The confusion and distress that ensued on our troops rushing in was terrible. The servants instantly commenced running away to join in sacking the cantonments, crying "*Sahib logue ke rajh hoguier!*" (The English rule is over!).

All the killed and wounded were brought in in *dhoolies*; and some of the officers told us they never beheld such a heartrending scene as that near the gate, where the poor wives were waiting, asking the fate of their husbands, many of whom they met dead or mortally wounded. One poor woman, who had been waiting a long time for tidings of her husband, at last lifted up the curtain of a *dhoolie*, and saw his dead body. She had only been married to him the day the women were ordered into the fort; so immediately after the ceremony they had parted.

She was a very nice young woman, who had only lately come from England with an officer's family; her husband was a young sergeant in the 3rd Europeans, and much respected: I had known her before in Calcutta, and frequently saw her afterwards; but she was then sadly altered. No sooner were our troops within the walls of the fort, than the *budmashes* released the prisoners, and they, together with the *sowars*, set to work to destroy and burn the cantonments. Poor Mr. Hubbard, whose brother we had met at Benares, was killed that night: he had very rashly gone out of the fort to see after his college. Major Jacob, who had formerly commanded the Maharajah of Gwalior's troops, and more than thirty native Christians were also killed.

All the non-combatant Europeans were safe in the fort by 7

o'clock; some had absolutely not come in till after the battle. The uproar in the city baffles description. The sky was lighted up for miles round by the blazing of the houses, and the natives were rushing about "drunk with enthusiasm, drunk with *bhang*," setting fire to, looting, and destroying everything, and firing at and killing all the poor creatures who professed Christianity. Everyone in the fort was in a state of excitement, for we did not know what might happen; and people were running about to look at the burning cantonments from different parts of the fort.

The Agra people must have felt very much enraged while thus quietly looking on at the wanton destruction of their houses and property: a good deal of furniture was thrown into the river, but the natives carried away a great quantity, which they hid in the neighbouring villages, where it was afterwards discovered by our troops in a ruined condition; and for days afterwards we had the aggravation of seeing chairs and tables floating down the river, or sticking in the sandbanks. The soldiers fired at every black face that showed itself within range; and they even threw two shells (by way of bravado, I suppose, as they did no harm) into the midst of the chaos.

The enemy never came into Agra, though they were expected: in fact, many thought it was they who were plundering the cantonments; but their forces hovered in our neighbourhood for some time, keeping us in a state of alarm and apprehension, and eventually left for Delhi, *via* Muttra.

I hardly remember anything of the week following the battle, everyone was in such a state of excitement. The heat was frightful, and in consequence of our servants' desertion, we had to do everything for ourselves: this was particularly trying to us, as the climate tends to enervate people, and make them less active and energetic; and the hosts of servants everyone keeps, render people dependent on them. A lady's life in India, however, though very luxurious, is not so useless and frivolous as some imagine. We had to cook, wash our clothes, and clean out our "dens," and those who had children had the double task of attending to them and keeping them inside the "dens," as it was dangerous to let them be outside on the stone walk alone, the parapet was so low:

little Archie Murray did fall over into the court below, a distance of twelve or fourteen feet, but happily escaped uninjured.

We had little food this week; *dhâl* and rice, neither of which were very good, composed our fare; and if we had been besieged, that was all the food we should have had to depend on. However, it said we had enough of both to last a ten months'siege. Our rations were served out to us by the commissariat officers; but often we had great difficulty in getting them, and when we did, the difficulty of cooking them almost took away our appetites: particularly when we had the disgusting process to go through of washing the dishes.

The *dhâl* and rice looked a very uninviting mixture; something like a pease-pudding, only not so good. Some people like it; but I suppose that must be when it is better cooked, and eaten under more favourable circumstances; as it was, I could not bear it, and lived on *chupaties* (cakes made of flour and water—the staff of life to the Hindoos). I never enjoyed anything in the way of eating so much in my life as a *chupatty* cooked by our brigadier, and eaten after fasting nearly all day.

The want of water was a great trouble to us, as it is such a necessary in India, for bathing and wetting the *tatties* with, as well as for drinking. What we had was not good, as it was drawn from a well inside the fort; the officers brought it for us in buckets. No one but bodies of armed men now dared leave the fort; and even they ran great risks, and were shot at; but afterwards we managed to get water from the wells outside, when things were more settled, and a staff of *bheesties* was kept.

The want of beer, too, which is so necessary, on account of the exhaustion caused by the climate, was a great privation to us. Afterwards, however, the commissariat officers allowed the officers and others to purchase some of the soldiers' beer, but we had great difficulty to prevent it going sour after it was tapped, as it was not at all good: some of my friends used to put raisins, sugar, and herbs, into the barrels, which were kept in the inner marble hall. Such difficulties as these, however, I believe the Agra people did not go through, as many had brought in their own supplies; but as I did not go beyond our own quarters for the first two months, I cannot say much of the others.

The officers sometimes made parties to go into the city and loot; but so great was the devastation, that they never brought us back anything, except a few cups and saucers and a coffee-pot They told us it was the most wretched and forlorn sight they had ever seen; nothing but the charred walls of houses, with furniture, books, and pictures, utterly destroyed, lying about the streets.

The weather now began to be very unhealthy; July being the worst month for the rains. It is difficult to describe the effect the atmosphere has on you at that time; the damp and stifling sensation of the air is dreadfully oppressive. Cholera also began slightly to show itself: it kills so rapidly in India, that many die in a few hours; I have been told of people taking *tiffin* together, and of one of them being buried next day at gunfire. It is a strange but accredited fact that, in India, if a person in dying state lives over gun-fire at sunrise he will linger till gunfire at sunset. The first case of cholera in the fort was that of an officer.

On Sunday, the 12th of July, Captain Burlton, of the Gwalior Contingent, was talking to us just after morning service, discussing the sad events of the last few weeks, the hard life we were leading, and the extra duty he had to perform, and hoping his wife was safe, as he had not heard from her for some time. (She afterwards escaped from Goonah with the rest of the fugitives.)

After talking for some time, he said, "I must try and get a little sleep; I feel so worn out with last night's work."

As he was wet through, one lady told him he ought to change his clothes, and he replied, "I would, if I had any to change."

In the afternoon we heard that he was ill, and later that he was seized with cholera. Several doctors did all they could to save him, and as his quarters were very damp (just beneath the marble hall), they tried to carry him up a narrow flight of steps, but found it impossible. He died shortly after midnight, and was buried the following evening at gunfire.

About this time we had violent thunderstorms, which generally come on after midnight, or early in the morning; they occurred every night for more than a week. They commenced with terrific peals of thunder and vivid flashes of lightning, lighting up for an instant the white marble hall, and brilliantly flashing on the river and opposite bank, with a weird and ghost-like effect: then all was black darkness again, and you heard nothing but the rushing torrents of rain, and the peculiar whirring, droning sound which always accompanies a tropical storm.

After a time, some of the servants began to return, and it was now found necessary to give each native a "pass," without which they could not be admitted into the fort These passes were cards with the bearer's description, name, and occupation written on them. We had very few clothes, and these were diminished, as often the *dhobies* would not bring them back after washing them, but would say they had been stolen. The manners of the servants were most insolent and contemptuous; they often said our "*rajh*" was over, and considered us doomed; fully expecting that when their brethren had defeated us at Delhi, which they never doubted would be the case, they would march to Agra and cut us all to pieces with little trouble.

Formerly they used to address us as "your Excellency, protector of the poor," and say, "Will it please your highness to let your slave do such a thing? " and use such hyperbolical expressions, but now they dropped even the customary "*Sahib*" and "*Mem sahib*," and often addressed us as "*Tum*" [20] instead of, as formerly, "*Ap*."[21] "*Tum*" in Hindoostanee is considered as familiar as "*tu*" in French. They would also often lie down in our rooms, and when we spoke to them, did not get up.

The *budmashes* used to sing scurrilous songs under the walls, and draw pictures on them of the *Feringhis* being blown up, with their legs and heads flying into the air; they also stuck up placards, saying on such a day we should all be massacred or poisoned. One baker was really hanged for planning a scheme for poisoning all the bread; and it was feared they might poison the wells. It is said they dug up the dead bodies and exposed them in the churches before the Communion Tables, and then

20. *Tum*, thou.
21. *Ap*, your honour.

burnt them; and in the Roman Catholic cathedral they tore from the walls the pictures of our Saviour, cut holes in them, and thrusting their prophet's green flag through, paraded them about the streets: they also mounted the pulpits in our churches, and preached the extermination of the *Feringhis*; saying we were the "*Mashriks*"[22] of the Koran.

Rumours of a depressing nature from Delhi, news of fresh mutinies, and massacres of men, women, and children, daily poured in; and the tidings from England were that, instead of sending out troops "overland" instantly, the parliament and ministers were disputing and squabbling among themselves over the Causes of the mutiny, and weighing the comparative merits of greased cartridges and cow's fat, forgetting the fearful loss of life going on in the meantime.

At Delhi alone, since the 8th of June, 100 officers had been lost, and more than 1000 men. We used to drop the English papers in despair, when we saw the troops were coming round by the Cape, and our hearts sank at the thought of how long it would be before help could come to us. I will only mention one instance of the length of time before help from England could be of use: the 7th Fusiliers, which left England early in June, did not reach Kurrachee till December, and were just coming up the country when I was leaving in March.

The Gwalior mutineers were still at Gwalior, their numbers increased by the Indore and Mhow troops, reckoned at nearly 5000 infantry and 900 cavalry, with thirty guns.

Scindiah kept them quiet, first with one false promise and then another; but we fully expected, when they were tired of this game, they would all march to attack us. Our conduct must have seemed strangely apathetic to the natives at this time, to be thus apparently yielding up to them the country which had cost us so much to gain; and our servants would constantly ask us whether troops were really coming from England? and when we replied by giving an account of the ample reinforcements on their way, they would smile incredulously and say, "why did we not take

---

22. *Mashriks*, heretics.

Delhi? and why did we allow the cantonments to be destroyed at Agra?"

These and hundreds of like questions they would ask, and our replies seemed to them idle tales. The natives have no regard for truth; they seem to take an absolute pleasure in lying: I have frequently seen them shed tears over a pathetic tale that they were making up to us as they went along. On our asking questions, they would often tell us things that could never have happened, and when we charged them with it, they would say, "You asked me: what could I say?" This was the more trying, as we often wished to find out what had happened at Gwalior, and to know particulars of those who had been killed.

On Sunday the 20th of July, we received intelligence of the hideous massacre at Cawnpore, We had previously heard some bazaar rumours, but did not believe them. I shall never forget the effect this awful news had on us. We were gathered in the marble hall after service, when we first heard it. We could only think with silent horror of the fearful fate of our poor countrymen, and picture to ourselves that such might soon be our fate; for we were surrounded by swarms of enemies, and the force at Gwalior was alone sufficient to take the fort.

It was a sickening task to read the long list of victims who had been massacred, just when help was at hand. But who can describe the unutterably revolting indignities our poor countrymen endured, and their harassing trials; first in the agonising suspense before they were obliged to retreat into the entrenchments, then in the days of suffering and misery endured there? What must have been their feelings when their provisions decreased day by day, and even a drop of water was frequently purchased by the death of the volunteer who went for it? Then the base and cruel butchery of the cold-blooded monster Nana Sahib! One cannot imagine how such a diabolical plot could be disguised for years under the mask of friendship.

I used often to wonder how such awful news was received at home. Our daily life was only varied by accounts of fresh disasters, mutinies, and massacres; India seemed to be rapidly gliding into the hands of its original possessors. In the north-western provinces, Agra, Allahabad, and Meerut were all we could now call our own. We heard of Havelock crossing the Ganges, and being obliged to retire; of the enemy occupying a strong position near Bithoor; and heard of the mutinies at Indore, Mhow, and Dinapore. At Seegowlie, when the 12th Irregular Cavalry mutinied, they shot the commanding officer, his wife and child, and cut off their heads, and burnt the doctor, his wife, and child to death, in their bungalow: she was a cousin of Mrs. Campbell's. One poor officer in the fort, who had lost his wife and all his children in the mutiny at Jhansi, used to wander about looking like a ghost

We now got our letters again; but it was very trying to read letters addressed to those who would never read them. I heard of my uncle's death at Simla; his regiment had been disarmed. I wished to go up to my aunt, but that was impossible. Our daily life dragged on very wearily. We rose early in order to get a little air "on the tower," which was free from the noise and disorder of the half-castes. Our fare began to be a little better now, for some of the natives ventured in, by means of passes, to sell eggs, butter, fowls, &c. After breathing a little fresh air from the river, we returned to breakfast on tea, *kidgeri*, [23] and *chupatttes* which the servants had brought from the bazaar. We often sat several hours on "the tower" and took our chairs into the kiosk for shade. The pontoon bridge across the Jumna was now removed, for fear of the insurgents crossing the river. It was an amusing sight to see the natives throwing themselves from the *ghâts* [24] into the river, or washing their clothes, and saying their prayers, kneeling with their faces towards the east, and no doubt praying most fervently for the annihilation of the "*Feringhis.*"

From hence also we could see the ramparts, and watch the soldiers being drilled for the artillery; and just beneath us was a small courtyard, in which was a guard house, where the soldiers used to sit on a "*charpoy*" or swing themselves in a swing they had contrived to put up, (all but the one on duty). We used often to hear them saying to their servants, "*Jildy* [25] *jow* and fetch my *khana.*" [26] Their attempts

23. *Kidgeri*, rice boiled with spices, raogar, &c
24. *Ghât*, landing-place.
25. *Jildy*, mispronounced for *Juldi*, quick.
26. *Khana*, dinner.

at Hindostanee were rather absurd; but strange to say, the natives always understood them. We used also to see the nuns, with their long train of pupils, taking their daily walk on the ramparts.

When the sun got hot we either sat in the marble hall or lay in our own "dens." The weather was still intensely hot, and the glare on the white marble and red sandstone was very painful to the eyes. We contrived to put up some rude *punkahs*, by fastening coarse native cloth to bamboo poles; but the difficulty was to get the *punkah coolies* to stay, as they were always running away. We dined about three o' clock and in the evening again sat in the "tower."

The only variety in our day was the arrival of *cossids*,[27] from Delhi, with news. These men were paid as much as forty or fifty pounds for taking a message, as it was a most difficult and dangerous task; for the natives always examined them, and killed them if they found they had messages: they used to hide these despatches in their hair, shoes, and "hubble bubbles." One man hid his in a piece of stick and when he was attacked threw the stick away, but afterwards recovered it.

In July we heard of the lamented death of the brave and noble defender of Lucknow, Sir Henry Lawrence. He was wounded by a shell on the 1st of July, and died on the 3rd, to the deep distress of everyone; before his death he appointed Brigadier Inglis his successor in military matters, and Major Banks his successor as Chief Commissioner in Oude. All in the fort received the news of his death with feelings of consternation and alarm; for in him we regretted not only an able officer, but one fitted to act in such a crisis. His courage and heroism had endeared him to everyone, and we all mourned his loss. One enduring mark of his beneficence is the Lawrence Asylum, in the Hills, for educating soldiers' children.

No one, whom I knew, kept a journal in the fort; for the confusion and noise rendered it impossible: we found it quite sufficient to write letters home. We were only allowed a certain weight, and were obliged to be guarded in our expressions about Delhi and the state of the country; as it was discovered that the

27. *Cossids*, especial messengers.
28. *Baboo*, clerk, writer in an office.

natives used to open our letters and read them; the *baboos* [28]can, most of them, read and translate English. In the Punjab all the letters of the *sepoys* were opened, and they were found to be keeping up a regular correspondence with the rebels at Delhi, and other places.

Mr. Colvin used to send letters in Greek, Hebrew, and cypher, to Colonel Greathed and the Government at Calcutta, vainly imploring aid; for we were in great dread of the Gwalior mutineers, now amounting to about 12,000, with fifty guns. The servants who came in from Gwalior told us the *sepoys* had regular parades, and their officers used to dress themselves in the English officers' uniforms, and call themselves brigadier, brigade major, &c, and drive about in our carriages. They had taken the pianos down to their lines, and, after playing on them, had torn out the wires and keys.

Mrs. Campbell gave me a Bible and Prayer Book: as a few had now been brought into the fort, and were sold. I used constantly to read over the beautiful lamentations of *Job 4* for now I could better understand them. We also shared amongst us a volume of *Melville's Sermons*; but we had few other books of a religious nature. Some of the Psalms now we read with a different feeling. The 79th had a fresh meaning for us. A few of my friends had other books, *Dynevor Terrace* and some others, which were greatly sought after, we lent about.

Some of the costumes worn in the fort were rather peculiar: Captain Campbell used to dress in a scarlet *sallû* jerkin,[29] with a black belt, in which was stuck a brace of pistols, white trowsers, and either a little Scotch cap, or a *solar-topee* [30] and *pugri*.[31] His assistant, a half-caste who was very tall and muscular, used to follow his master about arrayed in quite a small arsenal of firearms, and other offensive weapons. He had formerly been a pirate, and looked so ruffianish, that I called him "Dirk Hatteraick." He died of fever in the fort, and was a great loss to Captain Campbell, as

---

29. *Sallû*, native calico generally bright red.
30. *Solar-topee*, hat made of piths in various shapes.
31. *Pugri*, a turban.

he used to train the men to the gun exercise, of which Captain Campbell had the management in our part of the fort.

Mrs. Blake now came to live in our quarters: she had formerly lived with some friends in tents on the green near the Delhi Gate. In our "row" the Meades, Murrays, and Mrs. Procter, had the three first arches; Mrs. Blake had No. 4; Mrs. Innes and I occupied Nos. 5 and 6; and the Christisons No. 8. After them came some of the Agra people, and Mr. Nichols, a missionary who had escaped from Mynpoorie. In the opposite gallery of the court lived the Piersons, and some others. The officers had a small place where they contrived to have a bath, and perform their toilettes.

Dr. Mackellar had his meals with the Christisons, and slept in the marble hall. Mrs. Hawkins, Mrs. Ferris, and Mrs. Kirke, the Hennessys and the Campbells, had quarters in the Palace Garden. Major Macpherson, who was very kind to me all the time I was in the fort, had a little place under "the Tower," which he employed as an office; he had also the next arch to us, No. 7. Mrs. Innes used to be with her brother in his office the-best part of the day, and I believe assisted him very much in writing; for no native secretary could be trusted now.

The *baboos* or clerks understand English perfectly, and are well educated; they read Shakespeare, Byron, and Milton for amusement The Maharajah of Gwalior used constantly to send his *vakeel* [32] to transact business with Major Macpherson, and I was told the *chuprassis* who were waiting outside, used to lie down, and put their ears to the "*chicks*" to hear the conversation, which was carried on in Hindostanee.

The poor children had a weary life of it; accustomed, as they were, to airy rooms and plenty of attendants, the confinement was very trying to them. They suffered much from the heat, bad food, and a troublesome sort of fever and eruption. The servants used to tell them to play at *sepoys*, and call one side the *sepoys* and the other "*Gora Logue*" (European soldiers). In the evening, when the weather grew cooler, swarms of half-castes and Euro-

32. *Vakeel*, envoy, ambassador.

pean children collected on the large terrace fronting our marble hall, and had sham fights with wooden swords: little Jungy Meade went about with a cartouche-box, and a small toy sword strapped round his waist.

Some of the children had not recovered their fright at Gwalior:Archie Murray and Jungy Meade used to awake at night, and scream out that the *sepoys* were coming with swords to kill them: they often asked after their little playmates killed at Gwalior.The *kuppra-wallahs*[33] now ventured into the fort and sold their wares; they invariably asked us if we did not want *kala kuppra* (black cloth), and there were few who did not want it. I got a black dress, cloak, and bonnet, made by one of the milliners.

Many of these European milliners were entirely ruined. One I went to told me it was very hard she was obliged to leave all her goods behind, when she came into the fort; she also said she had had 300*l.* worth of millinery "looted" on its way up the country when the mutiny broke out. She had several *dirzies* sitting at work making some wedding garments on the ground in a little courtyard full of fowls and puddles of dirty water.

Shortly after, a young lady was married to a gentleman in the Uncovenanted Service, in our hall (the *dewan-i-am*). It was a very gay wedding considering the circumstances: the bride was in a veil and lace dress, attended by brides' maids in pretty bridal attire; and after the ceremony, they pitched a tent on the terrace, and had a dance and supper, to which they invited all the officers.

In the cold weather, when people had become more reconciled to their confinement, they had balls and musical parties in the arsenal; but in our square the days passed on so monotonously that, as we had no almanac, we forgot the days, except when the Baptists held their meetings, every Wednesday and Friday, in a place in our square.

Our great pleasure, when the weather got cooler, was all meeting on "the tower" (which I ought to have explained was the small terrace on which the "kiosk" stood). Six of us were widows, owing to the Gwalior mutiny!

Aching heart,

---

33. *Kuppra-wallahs,* men who sell cloth, &c.

143

Breaking part,
Through this dark world driven;
Meeting bright,
Endless light,
Waiteth us in heaven.

CHAPTER 7

The Fort (continued)

I had now an additional source of care and anxiety in my baby, though it was of course a great comfort. Owing to the great difficulty in getting a *Dhye*[1] for him, he suffered very much, and one doctor told me if I did not get a good *Dhye* for him, he would not live twenty-four hours, so Major Macpherson kindly allowed his chuprassistogo out and search in the neighbouring villages for one; for the *Choudrini*, or woman who has the monopoly of hiring out *Dhyes*, had set her face against their coming into the fort.

Everyone had been very kind to me; a room had been lent me, quieter and more comfortable than my own; Mrs. Longden and Mrs. Fraser also gave me some baby clothes, otherwise my little boy would have been almost destitute, as few of the *kuppra wallahs* had ventured into the fort until after he was born. Mrs. Innes was most kind to me, and Mrs. Campbell often came from the palace garden to see me, bringing *eau de Cologne* and other little luxuries.

A soldier's wife attended to the baby; she was a most kind-hearted Irish woman. Her husband had gone with a party to Allyghur, consisting of 150 of the 3rd Europeans, under Captain Stevenson, three guns, and 30 of the mounted militia; the whole commanded by Major Montgomery: Dr. Mackellar also went out with this party; They were intended to march against the insurgents at Hattras, but afterwards went on to Allyghur, then in the possession of the Insurgents, who had set up a king under orders of the King of Delhi.

---

1. *Dhye*, native wet nurse.

The result of the engagement there on the 24th of August was most successful. Our loss, however, was five killed and twenty-five wounded. Captain Longville Clarke was severely wounded, Captain Murray had a horse killed under him, and Mr. Tandy one of the managers of the Agra Bank, and Ensign H. L. Marsh of the 16th Grenadiers were killed. Lieutenant Lambe, who had been wounded on the 5th of July, now died, after lingering more than a month. It was very saddening to hear the "Dead March in Saul" played by the band of the 3rd Europeans, for one brave soldier after another. Wounds and fever were now diminishing our small force rapidly.

My quarters were now transferred to a small temple, in a court yard paved with white marble, near the Palace-garden Marble Hall, the *Dewan-i-khas*. The walls of my apartment were of yellowish marble, in which were innumerable small niches, in which formerly lamps were placed for illuminations: these were of great use for stowing away things in. From the window I had a pleasant view of the river beneath, and between the walls and the river was quite an encampment of horses and their attendants: the carriages which had been rescued from the "*Budmashes*" were secured under "chopper" sheds.

My Irish nurse, Mrs Cameron, was a cheery companion to me; she used to tell me long stories, and as she could not read I read the newspapers to her, and gave her all my home papers to send to her husband. One day, after I had been reading some of the particulars of the Cawnpore massacre, which related that the soldiers swore they would kill a *sepoy* for every hair of Miss Wheeler's head, she said, "I think Hell will be almost full now."

I asked "Why?"

She replied, "Because there has been such a lot of them brutes of *sepoys* sent there."

This conversation took place after hearing of Havelock's victory at Cawnpore, when he captured fifteen guns, and another engagement near Bithoor, making his 9th victory.

Another soldier's wife said to a lady who had remarked that the *sepoys* were like devils, "I think it is a bad compliment to the devil to say the *sepoys* are like him."

The *Mofussilite* was printed in the fort, the printing press being now in use, so we received detailed accounts of what was going on. About this time I had given me the great luxury of a bath, in the shape of half a beer barrel.

I used to amuse myself by watching the people going about on the river in boats; people being now permitted to go out of the fort These boats were like those formerly employed for coming up the river; they had each a "chopper" roof and were divided into two rooms. The Meades, Murrays, and some others took the small quantity of furniture that they had recovered and lived in these boats for change of air. This mode of life was thought by the doctors to be so healthy that they sent the wounded soldiers to live in boats anchored near the shore.

It was a pitiable sight to see the emaciated forms of the poor men, carried in *dhoolies* down to the boats, then placed on *charpoys*, and carried back to the hospital at night. I could also see the road winding towards the Taj, and people driving and riding on it; for now they could safely leave the fort during the day: though sometimes they were fired at I had also the amusement of watching the encampment of horses and their *syces*; the latter had their wives and families in small huts, making quite a colony. The horses were picquetted in rows, and it was amusing to see the *syces*, who were most of them tall fine looking men, grooming the horses very carefully, and sometimes washing them. They were a very savage set, however, not much encumbered with clothes, having only a *cummerbund* round the waist; some had not even turbans, and they were always fighting and quarrelling.

One day I saw a native woman beating her own infant of about a year old, in the most horrible manner, first with her hands, then with a thick stick, till tired of this she threw it on the ground and kicked it; the poor child of course screamed terribly the whole time, and I felt miserable at being quite powerless to prevent it When it grew dark I could see no more till the next morning, when I saw the child lying on a *charpoy*, its father trying to force something down its throat, and its cruel mother lying near asleep.

147

The poor little creature gave one convulsive shudder and died; its father then washed it, went to the Bazaar to buy a piece of cloth, wrapped the corpse in it and then walked off with the still warm body, followed by the other children; then with a spade he dug a hole and cast in the body of his child. The mother in the meantime threw herself on the very *charpoy* from which her dead child had just been carried, and finished her sleep. I told Captain Campbell and Major Macpherson of the circumstance, but they said nothing could be done, as we dare not now contradict or thwart the natives.

The scene by moonlight had a strange effect; the light shimmering on the ripples of the broad river, and glancing on the groups of natives, rolled up in their white *chuddars* on the ground; and the horses standing like statues in rows, looked spectre-like, or as if turned into stone. On the opposite bank of the river there always glowed a bright fire at night; and I afterwards found out it was the natives burning their dead. One of my *Dhyes* lost her husband and came crying to me for money to buy wood with to burn her husband's body; and at night she showed me the fire and said "Look, *Mem Sahib*, they burn my husband there."

My mother had sent me out a box of clothes from home; but the country was in such a disturbed state, I could get neither them nor my money from Calcutta. Letters from England, however, came regularly now, and I received one addressed to my husband, telling him of the death of his cousin in the Austrian service, who died of consumption at Venice. This brought to my mind the happy days that my husband and I had spent with poor Captain Coopland only the year before at Vienna:—

A sorrow's crown of sorrow is remembering happier things.

On the 9th of September, Mr. Colvin died. He had been in a bad state of health ever since his coming into the fort; and seemed utterly powerless to act in such a momentous crisis, being both mentally and physically worn out. After lingering some days in an almost insensible state, he died, and was buried in the Armoury Square. I have before given the reasons why he was buried within the fort walk. We watched his funeral from the

"Tower," as his quarters were in the palace near the *Dewan-i-khas*.

Sometime in the middle of September I went out for my first drive; until then, since June 29th, I had never been beyond our square ("Block F.") and my only walk had been on "the tower." I shall never forget my sensations: I felt like one in a dream.

Major Macpherson and Mrs. Innes had often been out driving, but I had not been able till now.

This morning I was awoke by the welcome message, "Mrs. Innes' *'salaam'* and would I like a drive?" I dressed quickly, and leaving baby to the care of Mrs. Cameron (who was delighted that I should have a change), got into the *tonjon*, and was borne along through the palace garden—where a number of other people were preparing for walking or driving—down the inclined plain, and out at the Delhi gate. The gateway was crowded with natives carrying in things to sell, *bheesties* with water, *coolies* with bags of sand for the fortifications, and people hurrying out for their drives.

At last I was fairly outside the gates, and the bearers setting the *tonjon* down at the other side of the drawbridge, politely assisted me into Major Macpherson's carriage, which was standing with a lot of others, waiting for their owners, the *syces* meanwhile whisking off the flies with *chowries*.[2]

When the coachman asked me which way I should like to go, I chose the Taj road. Oh, how delightfully the fresh air blew on my face, when free from the walls of the fort! Quickly we wound by the side of the river, on which was anchored quite a little fleet of boats, awaiting the rising of the river to continue their journey to Allahabad; and there were large boats, gay with flags, and occupied by people wearied of fort life. We passed under a hill which the *coolies* were digging away, and by some ruins they were preparing to blast.

The country looked delightfully fresh and blooming after the late rains, the breeze was cool and refreshing, and the air sweet with delicious scents. At last I passed the Taj, its white marble and golden

---

2. *Chowries*, whisks, for driving off flies.

149

tipped minarets sparkling in the bright son against the blue sky. It was a painful contrast on approaching the cantonments, utterly destroyed and desolate; and around their blackened walls and ruined houses seemed yet to linger a sickening smell of burning: I passed the racket court, the mess house, and other public buildings all more or less ruined; the disgusting vultures, either sitting on the blackened walls, or prowling about amongst the ruins, were not scared at the approach of the carriage, and even the jackals stopped and looked at me, as if they had a right now to despise us.

On my way back I passed a bazaar, the natives of which looked so maliciously at me that I felt quite frightened; for had they chosen to drag me out of the carriage, there was nothing to prevent them. This rather took away from the pleasure of the drive, and I was very thankful to return to the protection of the gloomy walls of the Fort I passed many equestrians, some of them grotesquely attired, and soldiers returning from their walk.

I was glad to find myself in my own little room again, and baby all well.

The next day I went for the first time to see my friends in "Block F.," whom I had only seen when they had been kind enough to come and sit an hour or two with me in my little temple. I was quite startled when I entered our marble hall; it was completely metamorphosed. The inner hall, which was separated from the outer hall by arches, across which were hung *chicks*, looked like a drawing-room. At one end a window had been broken through the thick wall, giving a beautiful view of the river and country beyond, and having something of the effect of a camera *lucida*.

The floor was covered with handsome native carpets, there were two drawing-room tables, on which were placed work-boxes, desks, and despatch-boxes; sofas, armchairs, a piano, guitar, and flute-case, completed the effect; and, above all, to my great delight, I beheld a bookshelf: but on inspection the books were ragged and incomplete, not one set being perfect.

However, hearing that they were public property, I selected for my own reading, *The Heir of Redclyffe*, an odd volume of

Friends in Council, and one or two other old favourites. Some servants were preparing breakfast, and the white tablecloth and the china cups looked quite luxurious.

I was also quite astonished to see the transformation our little kiosk on "the tower" had undergone, Captain Campbell having just had it given him for his "quarters," as it was more convenient for fain than living in the Palace garden. Round the circular kiosk a veranda of "chopper work," supported on bamboo poles, had been put up, to keep off the glare of the sun. Mrs. Campbell had carpeted the inside with a thick Mirzapore carpet, and furnished it with a charpoy covered with a scarlet *rezai*, chairs, a table, and chests.

The proceeds of Captain Campbell's and "Dirk Hatteraick's" looting expeditions were ranged on shelves; and outside, under the veranda, were also suspended little shelves, which were used for a temporary larder. I was amused to see strings of black ants ascending and descending the wall, and looking like moving bell-ropes; the scent of the provisions attracting them.

I often used to breakfast with the Campbells. Captain Campbell had bought a nice little posy for his wife, and they used to ride out every morning and evening.

The Christisons, whom I went to see, had also made many improvements. Dr. Christison, having a taste for pictures, had decorated the bare blank *jambs* of his den with prints which he had collected from the *Illustrated London News*: one was "Town and Country," and another a portrait of "Madeleine Smith." He afterwards bought, at Mr. Raikes's sale, some books and a chest of drawers. Poor Mrs. Christison had been very ill; and I pitied her very much, being confined in such an uncomfortable little place; for these dens were only twelve feet by six.

Little May Christison, who was a most amusing, clever little child, and could make herself understood in English and Hindostanee, though but two years old, had also been ill with fever. I was astonished to see how much better the children were dressed than formerly. Little May was dressed in a pretty silk bonnet, and checked *pelisse*; Jungy (Jungy was a pet name the servants gave him, and means little prince) and Archie were also arrayed in new suits, and they were taken for walks all round the ramparts, and twice a week to hear the band, which played on the Green near the Motee Musjid,

We still often sat on "the tower," watching the sun set, and the flames rising from the villages round Agra which our troops burnt. One village which they destroyed in this way, was not gained without a sharp fight with the villagers, who offered resistance. Sixty villagers were slain, amongst whom were two women, accidentally killed, who were loading guns, and otherwise assisting their party. From this tower we could see the burial-ground, which lay on the slope of a hill not far from the fort, and looked dreary and mournful.

The graves were mere heaps of sand, occasionally varied by a tombstone, and scarcely an evening passed without some burial going on: either a little child, followed by its mourning parents, or some poor soldier, who had no relative to mourn his loss, and who was placed in the ground with as much speed as was consistent with due respect to the dead; after which the few soldiers who had followed him to his last resting-place returned, the band playing some lively march.

A little distance from the graveyard was a row of gibbets, on which some wretch daily paid the just penalty of his crimes, by a death which they despised: one culprit even adjusted the rope round his own neck, and joked about it. At first the bodies of the criminals were given to their friends; but afterwards this was put a stop to, for they carried them round the walls, decked in garlands of flowers, and excited the people by the sight of these "martyrs."

One day, in returning from a drive, I met a cart loaded with these ghastly burdens. A great many of the villagers in revolt, were brought in and hanged, and also some mutinous *sepoys* who were found lurking in the neighbourhood. When they were being tried, some used to feign madness, and act in the most absurd way, catching flies and jabbering; others would say the most insolent and revolting things to the officers on the court-martial.

Mr. French now went out daily to teach his students in an old ruined school-house near the fort The midsummer holidays had commenced just after the battle on the 5th of July, and Mr. French had given them an extra fortnight in consideration of the state of things; Mr. Leighton and Mr. Cann also went to the college buildings in the city afterwards. Mr. French sometimes came to see us and was very kind: he lent us *Henry Martyn's Life*; but told us that he had lost nearly all his books. The books of the Agra bank and other valuable documents, had also been destroyed.

Previously to this, Mr. Longden had gone out with a party to Secundra, a few miles from Agra, where there was formerly an establishment for native Christians who were taught different trades, also a printing press and church. Mr. Cana of the Agra College and others had gone out soon after the battle to see if they could rescue anything: they dragged the tanks and ponds, and recovered some astronomical instruments and other things. We often amused ourselves by looking through a large telescope, belonging to the Agra College, at the Southern Cross and other constellations which Mr. Longden and Mr. Cann explained to us, and were better seen in the southern latitudes.

We were now in daily expectation of being besieged by the Gwalior mutineers: we heard from the Maharajah's *vakeel*, and by the mails which now ran between Agra and Gwalior, that on the 3rd of September the Gwalior mutineers quarrelled with those at Indore, who wished to march to Delhi, while the Gwalior wished to march to Cawnpore and Agra; that they then all marched to the residency, and there the Indore troops persuaded 600 of the *rajah's* 2nd Cavalry Corps to join them. The *rajah* consequently discharged many of the *sowars*, and having paid them, sent them out of Gwalior.

The Indore troops were supplied with ammunition by the Mora mutineers, in spite of their disagreements. The whole of them, consisting of the 23rd Native Infantry, three troops of the 1st Light Calvary, seven guns, and 600 of the *rajah's* mutinous *sowars*, joined by a great number of *Budmashes*, set out on the 7th for the Chumbul, on their way to Agra. The rains had so swollen the Chumbul, it had been previously imppassable for artillery; but now that the river was sinking they were able to cross. The native officers of the Mora mutineers quarrelled with the Maharajah because he would not give them conveyance and grab, and reproached him for having detained them for months with false promises; and, in spite of the Maharajah, they forced the villagers all around to give up to them their cattle and what conveyances they had, sad afterwards planted a battery of twelve guns on the road to the Phool Bagh and the Lushkur.

The Maharajah was kept for some time in great suspense; but at last he came to an agreement with them, and for the present prevented them going to Agra and joining the Indore troops, who had now crossed the Chumbul, and were hovering in the neighbourhood of Agra.

The Gwalior contingent finally marched to Cawnpore, and after defeating General Windham were themselves defeated by Sir Colin Campbell on the 7th of December. They were 14,000 in number, and lost 16 guns and their baggage.

As the Indore troops were expected, a large place in the fort was prepared underground, and made shot and bomb-proof; and here, in case of a siege, all the women and children were to be put. I believe it was planned amongst the officers that, in case it became inevitable that the women would fall into the hands of the rebels, they should all be blown up in the powder magazine: even the soldiers said they would themselves shoot us rather than that we should be treated like the poor Cawnpore ladies.

The guns were frequently loaded, as we had so many alarms. Captain Campbell, who had often to sleep all night near his guns, said "His friends gave him more trouble than his enemies." The walls were now planted with sixty guns, and 150 trained gunners from the militia were appointed to assist the regular artillery men. I could recognise the officers voices when they went the grand rounds and visiting rounds at night, along the rampart below my quarters.

My *kitmutghar*, who had often been to see me when I was unable to see him, again came and brought my little dog "Jack," who was delighted to see me; but as I was not allowed to keep a dog inside the fort, I gave him to Captain Campbell to give to some of the European soldiers, who are always glad to have a thoroughbred dog instead of the pariah ones, good sort of dogs being very scarce. I kept his collar as a little memento of Gwalior. The *kitmutghar* cried over the "*chota sahib*,"[3] and gave him a pretty fan.

We were now most anxious for news from Delhi, as we had heard of the arrival there of a siege train, and reinforcements, and the assault was expected to take place on the 14th. Until now we had been very desponding about the taking of Delhi, and had expected we should have been obliged to stay in the fort a year.

At last, news came that on the 14th, four columns of British troops, each one thousand strong, had entered the Cashmere gate and taken possession of the whole line of defences from the Water Bastion to the Caubul gate, including the Moree Bastion, the English Church, and Skinner's house; that Brigadier Nicholson had been wounded, and 61 officers killed, and 1178 rank and file killed and wounded. That on the 15th they shelled the Palace and Selimghur, and other strong places, and effected a breach in the magazine, and finally took it with 125 cannons, and that they then attacked the palace, and on the 20th the whole of the city was in our possession.

On receipt of the joyful news, a salute of fifty guns was fired; it ought to have been 101. We heard that the reason of our loss being so very great, was the defection of a native regiment which was to have covered one of ours. We soon after heard of the death of General Nicholson, who was much lamented as a brave and able officer.

About the end of September, Lieutenant Pond of the 3rd, was married to the sister of another officer in the palace-garden marble hall, the Dewan-i-khas. It was a very gay affair; Mrs. Innes, Mrs. Campbell and many others were present at the ceremony; the officers being in full regimentals and the ladies in gay attire.

We were much troubled by that terrible annoyance, bugs; they swarmed in the old woodwork of the fort. Europeans can form no idea of the extent of this disgusting nuisance, which is

---

3. *Chota sahib*, little master.

so bad in this part of India that whole villages are deserted by the natives to escape these pests.

My baby was now christened in our marble hall, Mrs. Campbell presenting him with a robe, and Major Macpherson a hood and cloak; and I now occasionally drove out with my friends as the weather was getting pleasantly cool. We used also to take regular walks, morning and evening, round the ramparts. Mrs. Murray and Mrs. Christison, who played very well, often had musical parties in our marble hall, when Captain Campbell accompanied them on his violin. Mrs. Kirke, having had a carriage lent her for a few days by an Agra civilian, she and Mrs. Christison one evening went down to the Delhi gate, where the carriages stood drawn up in lines on each side of the road; and having been told that the carriage was lined with white and drawn by bay horses, they took possession of one of this description, and went for their drive.

The next evening Mrs. Christison and I went out in the same carriage, and on returning from a long drive we were surprised to see an elderly gentleman waiting at the gate, and looking very irate. As soon as we drew up, he asked the *syce* by whose orders he had taken his carriage out. The *syce* replied looking at us, "By these *Mem-Sahibs* here."

We now found out that we had taken the wrong carriage, and with many apologies, we alighted. The angry owner told us that for two evenings he had been down at the Delhi gate with some ladies ready for a drive, and found his carriage gone.

It was certainly provoking, though Mrs. Christison thought it a good joke; but her husband west next day to make proper explanations and apologies. We had still very few servants, and were obliged to share them amongst ourselves, in consequence of which they got very high wages.

They invariably melted down their *rupees*, and made them into bangles and all kinds of ornaments; and after each fresh acquisition the *ayahs* used to come and show themselves, loaded with ornaments, and say, "Are they not pretty? where are *your* ornaments?"

Their necks, arms, ears, and ankles, were covered with chains, and bangles,[4] &c; some of them were beautifully dressed: one *ayah* wore a bright blue velvet jacket, a coloured muslin shirt, and a white *chuddar*, beautifully worked.

We now heard more details from Delhi. When first our troops entered the city, most of the mutineers had sent off their baggage and then followed. The townspeople at first took refuge in the palace, but finding things were hopeless, they and their animals poured in stream out of the Ajmere gate, unmolested by our troops, who watched them from our camp; and in a few days the city was totally deserted. A column then set off to pursue the flying rebels towards Allyghur and Muttra; some of them, it was supposed, had fled into Rohilcund, Muttra, and towards Oude. We heard that Mr. Hervey Greathed, Commissioner and Political Agent, died of cholera, on the 19th of September, and was succeeded by Mr. Saunders, who had escaped from Moradabad.

The conduct of Major Hodson, who shot the princes, and guaranteed the king his life, was much commented on in the fort; and we were sorry that he had spared the king, who, though old in years, was still older in cruelty and wickedness, [5] The gallantry of the 60th Rifles who, with the plucky little Ghoorkahs, had kept the mosque near Hindoo Rao's house during the whole siege, was the theme of admiration; and the noble daring of Lieutenant Salkeld, and Home, and Sergeants Carmichael, Burgess, and Smith (the last of whom is the only survivor) was eulogised with the greatest enthusiasm by all in the fort. We deeply regretted the death of Brigadier Nicholson; he was only thirty-six. "The Lion of the Punjâb," as he was called, could ill be spared. His brother also was killed.

On the 21st all the officers breakfasted in the Delhi Dewan-i-khas. A few mornings before they had breakfasted in the Church, which was now turned into a hospital.

A salute of 101 guns was fired for the next joyful and cheering news of the relief of the gallant little band at Lucknow. We had

---

4. Bangles; silver bracelets, generally soldered on the wearers arms or ankles.
5. We afterwards learnt that Major Hodson had General Wilson's express orders to spare the king's life.

all admired the patient and Christian behaviour of many who had relations at Lucknow, during the wearing suspense of many months; especially Lady Outram and Mrs. Innes: the husband of the latter had been in Lucknow during the whole siege.

On the 19th of September, Havelock had crossed the river at Cawnpore with 2700 men; Sir James Outram, with noble generosity, surrendering the command to his able and skilful coadjutor, General Havelock, who marched twenty miles the first day, and fourteen the next, leaving Outram at Cawnpore, which was threatened by the Gwalior contingent General Havelock drove the rebels back to Lucknow, with the loss of their guns; and on the 24th, a salute announced to the garrison of Lucknow the welcome news that relief was near.

On the 25th, the Presidency was relieved, only just in time, for the enemy had mined under it, and were intending to blow up the buildings and all in them. General Neill, who was killed, added to the long list of irreparable losses—600 being killed and wounded; and we had to mourn the loss of many a brave officer. No one can tell how eagerly the list was looked for, as we heard so much of the frightful losses sustained by the garrison. Mrs. Kirke saw there the death of her brother-in-law, but was relieved by learning of the safety of her sister and her children, the Ommaneys. Mrs. Innes was overjoyed to hear of her husband's safety; she had not heard of him since May. He has since been presented with the 'Victoria Cross,' for some act of signal bravery performed in one of General Frank's engagements. Others, too, were filled with joy and thankfulness, and we began now to hope that God was prospering our arms.

The *Dewalee*, or feast of lamps, which had been much dreaded, as the natives get so excited during its continuance, now commenced all over the country. The excitement in the city of Agra was prodigious, and we heard nothing but *tom-toming* and explosions of gunpowder: the great delight of the natives is to put the gunpowder into earthen pots, which they then blow up. They lighted up the city at night, and it was a very pretty sight; the bridge and all the houses sloping down to the river being brilliantly illuminated.

They also lighted up the bridge of boats, which had now been reconstructed, and placed a little booth on it for their *Nâtch* girls; and they let off fireworks representing snakes and all sorts of animals. They kept this up for many nights, and invited the officers to see the illumination, and a *"Nâtch,"* held in the booth. As this feast happened just after the taking of Delhi and Lucknow, the hypocritical wretches pretended it was in honour of these great events.

We watched these sights from "the tower," and tracked the fairy-like lights floating down the broad river, and looking like fire-flies in the darkness. It is a custom of the natives to send down the river a little lamp (a small saucer in which a wick is placed) or *chirage*; if it sinks, or the light dies out before reaching a certain point, the owner of the lamp thinks he will be unfortunate, or die soon.

We hoped now, after the taking of Delhi and Lucknow—which showed the natives our *"Rajh"* was not over, as they had fondly expected, and that now their green flag no longer waved over these cities—that the column which had left Delhi would come to Agra on its way to Cawnpore, and take m there *en route* to Calcutta: we even made preparations, and bought a camp-table each, some cooking vessels, and provisions; for we were weary of our long imprisonment, and wanted to get home to oar friends. Our stock of English provisions was ebbing very low; we had no brandy in the fort, very little wine, and no sugar but the native sugar, which is either like sugar candy, or quite moist; we had but little medicine, either, and that of a bad kind; and worst of all, we had nearly come to an end of the quinine, which is so necessary in India.

But we now heard that our old enemies, the Indore mutineers, were coming on: tired, we supposed, of their cowardly inactivity, and disappointed of their intention of going to Delhi, they had determined to strike a blow at Agra. They had all this time been waiting at Dholepore, only thirty-six miles from Agra, and were now joined by the Neemuch and some of the Delhi mutineers; consequently all the people wore now ordered in from the boats, the guns were kept loaded, and double sentries placed.

159

We heard that Colonel Greathed had defeated the flying Delhi rebels at Malaghur, taken the fort there, and blown up the defences: unfortunately this blowing up cost the life of Lieutenant Home of the Engineers, one of the Cashmere-gate heroes. After this victory the column halted a day or two to send their sick and wounded to Meerut, reaching Allyghur on the 4th of October, and Hattras, about forty miles from Agra, on the 9th.

The Indore mutineers were actually now within a mile of Agra; but no notice was taken by the authorities, who were so supinely indifferent that they even did not take the trouble of sending out spies, though our own servants told us the rebels were very near. Colonel Fraser, the temporary lieutenant-governor of the northwest provinces, and Mr. Read, the head civilian, sent urgent messages to Colonel Greathed, who only just arrived in time by forced marches. Early on the morning of the 10th we got up to see the column cross the river by the bridge of boats; many people went on to the battlements and the Delhi gate, but we went to our old post of observation, "the tower."

Oh, how our hearts swelled with pride and thankfulness as we watched this gallant band of heroes cross the bridge. A soldier can never be sufficiently valued, thought of, and honoured; and yet how little is he cared for! Coarse food and small pay is thought good enough for one who is generally exiled from his home and friends for years, often for life; who endures untold hardships, has few pleasures, and frequently sacrifices his life for his ungrateful country, which grudges the taxes paid for his support. People who sit at home surrounded by comforts and luxuries, forget what the soldier goes through.

They can admire and honour a Havelock, a Neill, a Wilson, and other great generals who have made themselves names by their great deeds; but the poor private, who in his capacity is equally deserving, is overlooked: a medal or a small pension is considered sufficient reward for deeds which are utterly unrequitable. Even in the case of the blowing up of the Cashmere gate, few remember the names of the brave sergeants. The sufferings of the soldiers during the Crimean war, and now in the arduous work of regaining India—when men were struggling against the climate, contending against numbers, and suffering from want of proper food and necessaries—ought to open the eyes of those British people, who perversely close them, to the deep debt of gratitude they owe their noble defenders.

But to return to the 10th of October. The column that was now marching across the bridge consisted of the Queen's 8th Foot, part of the 9th Lancers, two troops of Horse Artillery, two corps of the Punjâb Sappers and Miners; one field battery, the 2nd and 4th Punjâb Infantry, 125 of the Punjâb Cavalry, and 200 of Hodson's Horse, making altogether about 3000. We watched them till the sun grew hot, and it was a most cheering sight; their bayonets glittering in the sun and their brilliant array followed by long lines of camels, elephants, and *dhoolies* (the latter filled with sick and wounded), and the crowd of camp followers and baggage which always attend a march in India.

Many of the men looked haggard and worn out with their long campaign: most of them wore the khakee, or dust-coloured uniform, which had been adopted at Delhi, as the bright scarlet and white uniforms made the men conspicuous marks for the enemies' guns. This khakee uniform is considered good, both for this reason and because it prevents a body of men looking so remarkable when marching. As the column passed below the walls of the fort, our men gave them a hearty English cheer. The Seiks looked very picturesque on their wild and strangely-caparisoned horses. Some of the officers came to breakfast with their friends in the fort, and one who visited Major Macpherson, gave a most interesting account of the siege of Delhi.

All remained quiet till about ten o'clock, when suddenly, to the astonishment of every one, firing was heard in the direction of the "Brigade Parade" ground, where the lately arrived force had encamped.

Some thought it at first an irregular salute; but no one knew what it really was till some of the officers rushed out to see what was going on. Strange to say, the Agra authorities had not taken the precaution of investigating where the enemy was; though the night before the whole of the militia had been encamped in Cantonments, and might have been cut to pieces, the enemy being only a mile off.

The battle now began in earnest, and the booming of the cannon sounded fearfully near. Our camp, being surprised, was in great confusion: the men were resting after their long march; some were bathing, and others breakfasting. The onset of the mutineers was made in the following manner: A soldier was quietly sitting outside his tent, eating his breakfast, when a native dressed as a *faquir* came dancing up towards him, playing on a *tom-tom* [6], and, on drawing near, he whipped out a *tulwâh*, and in an instant cut off the poor soldier's head.

Immediately a force appeared which had been hidden behind the cemetery, and their guns, which were behind the ice pits, instantly opened fire on our disordered camp. Many men and horses were killed and wounded ere we were aware of what was going on: and had they charged on us with their cavalry the consequences might have been most disastrous to us; as it was, they did take one of our guns, but it was subsequently retaken. The 9th Lancers were soon in their saddles, and Lieutenant French was killed, and Lieutenant Jones dangerously wounded, in retaking our gun.

As soon as our troops could be formed, they charged the enemy, who soon retreated, pursued by our men down the road towards Dholepore, and we took some of their guns. Our force was there joined by Colonel Cotton (known to many by his soubriquet of "Gun Cotton"), in command of the 3rd Europeans. The enemy's camp was two miles in advance, and their baggage and carts strewed the road. Our infantry were then ordered to halt, and the cavalry and artillery pursued the rebels to the Kharee Nuddee, where the latter crossed the river, about ten miles from Agra. Our troops, after firing upon them grape and round shot with good effect, returned to the camp with the guns the enemy had left on this side the river; both men and horses being too tired, after their forced march, to pursue the enemy

6. *Tom-tom*, native drum.

further.

The engagement had been most brilliant, and we took the enemy's camp, guns, and treasure.

All this time the fort had been in great confusion; reports coming in that the rebels were victorious, and our forces were retreating. Our servants, as usual all scampered off, saying our "*Rajh*" was over. They must have gnashed their teeth with disappointment when they found we were not defeated. At one time a report was spread that the enemy's cavalry were sweeping round to attack the fort, and all the officers not on duty in the fort went out to join in pursuing the retreating enemy: Major Macpherson and Captains Meade and Murray also went; but Captain Campbell and others of the Engineers were obliged to stay by their guns.

At last, so many officers rushed out, that an order was issued that some were to stay to protect the fort. Gradually, towards evening, they began to return, bringing glowing accounts of the engagement; saying that it was a "splendid victory, and 1000 of the rebels had been killed:" but afterwards this number came down to between 300 and 500, the horses having been too tired to continue the pursuit, and the rebels having spread themselves all over the country, hiding in the jungle, in the long grass, and in ditches. It was discovered that the Nusserabad and Neemuch mutineers, the 16th Grenadiers, and some of the Gwalior contingent, had joined the Indore troops some of the buttons of the 4th Native Infantry of the Gwalior contingent were found.

The officers remarked how strange it was to see the dead *sepoys* and Seiks lying side by side; many of the former with their breasts covered with medals received in the campaign against the Seiks. The Seiks behaved most bravely, and took many prisoners. No "loot" of any great value was found in the rebels' camp, except a little jewellery and all their cooking vessels and uniforms: the rebels fighting in their native dress; but a Seik, who knew where to look for treasure, found a saddle and holster stuffed with gold *mohurs*.

Many of the officers complained bitterly of the carelessness of the Agra authorities, saying it was "too bad that they could not rest and have their breakfasts in peace, after a march of forty-one miles in thirty hours."

The Seiks brought their prisoners into the fort most triumphantly. One Seik was dragging in a *sepoy*, who was struggling: "You won't struggle long," said the Seik, " for you will soon be hanged."

The *sepoy* replied, "I don't care; for I have just killed two of your brothers."

" Have you, you pig?" cried the Seik, "then I will take you no further;" and with that he cut off his head. Captain Meade told us he saw the head the next morning lying near the Delhi gate, with a ghastly grin of defiance on its face.

A day or two after the battle, Colonel Greathed left: not very well pleased, I believe, with his over warm welcome; but covered with fresh glory. We were all dreadfully disappointed at not being allowed to go with the column to Cawnpore. Mr. and Mrs. Drummond, and Mr. Harrington, however, were allowed to go; the latter being thus favoured as he had lately been made a Member of Council at Calcutta. They were not, however, allowed to set out with the column, but drove a little way on the road, and then joined it. We were sadly disappointed at having our hopes of getting home thus dashed to the ground; for now there seemed no chance of our quitting our dreary prison for a long time. I often thought of a song I used to sing at Gwalior, and which was a great favourite with my husband.

There's a hope for every woe,
And a balm for every pain,
But the first joys of our heart
Come never back again.

There's a track upon the deep,
And a path across the sea,
But the weary ne'er return
To their ain countrie.

Our force only had thirteen killed and fifty-four wounded in the battle. Some people may imagine that *lâks* of *rupees* and heaps of treasure are taken, and multitudes of the rebels are killed; but generally the numbers come down to half the first, calculation. The natives are too quick for us: they don't wait to be shot at; and by their knowledge of the country and quick marches, have great advantages over us. There is little doubt that, had they been better led, we should not have regained India so easily, for our training had made good soldiers of them.

It appeared, from documents found in the palace at Delhi, that a sort of monarchical government was established, of a military character. The English terms were used, instead of the Persian or Arabic; and the great authority to which all matters, both civil and military, were referred, was the "Court," a body composed of a number of colonels, a brigade-major, and *seketur*, or secretary. All the colonels were *sepoys*, who either made their mark or signed in Hindoo characters. Muster-rolls of the revolted regiments were kept. One *sepoy* colonel seems to have presented to the king a kind of memorandum on the best mode of governing the country, after getting rid of the *Feringhis*; and stating that, with all its faults, as the English Government was the best which Hindostan had ever had, he advised the new government to be formed on that model.

Colonel Greathed left us a guard of 200 Seiks, wild, savage-looking men, and so ragged and dirty, they reminded me of gipsies. They had most curiously shaped swords, and wore queer sort of headgear. They said it was very hard they were not allowed to "loot" Agra, as it was such a rich city. We afterwards heard that the natives of Agra had sent fifty pounds' worth of sweetmeats to the Indore mutineers as a present, these children of the East being fond of such childish luxuries. We heard of a Seik finding some jewels of great value; but I don't know whether the report was true, Many said the Seiks found a heap of plunder; but not so much as was expected, the *sepoys* having taken a great part of the "loot" with them when they fled,

We saw a great deal of the Seiks in our quarters; for on the terrace fronting the *Dewan-i-Am* stood a large block of black marble, on which, in the palmy days of the Mogul Empire, the emperors used to sit and hold audiences; and opposite it was a white marble block, on which the *Wuzeer* (or prime-minister) used to sit The natives hold the black marble seat in great reverence, and ought never to approach it without "*salaaming*."

It is said that when Agra was taken, in 1784, by the Mahratta chief Madagee, he attempted to seat himself on this black marble seat; but, as such an indignity could not be submitted to, the marble split almost asunder: certainly a fissure is now to be seen. The Seiks hold this stone in great veneration, and, after the battle, they kept coming in parties, "*salaaming*" and saying prayers to it. They never approached it without taking off their shoes. A Seik having spoken to little Jungy Meade, who was playing in the Marble Hall, Jungy began talking to him, till his bearer snatched him away and told him not to talk to "that man." The Seik instantly drew his sword and said to the bearer, in a loud angry voice, "It is you who kill women and children; we come to protect them."

On hearing the dispute, we all ran out, and the Seik began explaining to Mrs. Meade that he meant no harm to Jungy, who was a "very nice *chota sahib*."

Many prisoners were hanged after the battle, and as it was discovered they did not care for hanging, four were tried and sentenced to be blown from guns; accordingly one day we were startled by hearing a gun go off, with an indescribably horrid muffled sound. We all rushed out of our "dens" to know what was the matter; and heard that some *sepoys* were being blown from the guns. All our servants hurried away to see the sight; and then was heard, at short intervals, three other guns go off. The sound was horrible, knowing as we did that a fellow creature (whatever he may have done) was being blown into fragments and his soul launched into eternity at each report of the cannon; and we felt quite ill for the rest of the day. An officer told us it was a most sickening sight. The four guns, taken out of the fort, were placed near the river. One gun was overcharged, and the poor wretch was literally blown into atoms, the lookers on being covered with blood and fragments of flesh: the head of one poor wretch fell upon a bystander and hurt him.

It was a long process, fastening them to the guns; and an officer having said to a *sepoy*, as the latter was being tied on, "It is your turn, now,"

The *sepoy* replied calmly, " In one moment I shall be happy in Paradise."

The *sepoys* dislike this mode of death more than any other; for the Mahomedan likes to be buried, and the Hindoo thinks he cannot be saved unless his body is burnt: but who can pity these wretches, who have spared no torture or cruelty to man, woman, or child, and who are even known to have blown a lady from a gun!

A short time afterwards, as Mrs. Kirke was passing in her *ton-jon* near the place of execution, her little boy. who was playing about, went to the spot where the bodies had fallen; when the *chuprassie* said, "Don't go there: that is the place where the poor martyrs were killed;" and he looked at the spot with the greatest reverence.

An officer, when trying the prisoners, asked a *sepoy* why they killed women and children. The man replied, "When you kill a snake, you kill its young."

The day after the battle the doctors sent to ask some of the ladies to help to nurse the sick and wounded soldiers in the hospital. Mrs. Blake went that night, and I would gladly have accompanied her to do what I could for the poor soldiers, but I dare not leave my baby at night, and during the day there was an abundance of volunteer nurses. Mrs. Raikes, of Gwalior, who had recently lost her baby, was a very kind excellent nurse. After this, the ladies attended the hospital regularly; watching the soldiers at night in turns, giving them their medicines and cooling drinks, and moistening their bandages. The men were very grateful, and said it was worth while being wounded, to be waited on by ladies.

Poor Lieutenant Jones was dreadfully injured: he was hacked all over, and had twenty-one wounds; many a one of them the doctors said enough to kill him. He bore his sufferings without complaining, though they were intense. He lay in one of the small rooms, separated from the "*Motee Musjid*," where the common soldiers lay, by a marble lattice now stuffed with *jamps*. Formerly these small rooms were used by the ladies of the Mogul court, to hear the service from without being seen. Mr. Ma-claine was also wounded, but some kind friends took care of him. He belonged to the 3rd Europeans; and had been through the whole Delhi campaign.

I once or twice accompanied Mrs. Blake to the Motee Mus-jid; and standing at one end, and looking down the marble arched aisles, filled with rows of *charpoys* on which the wounded soldiers lay, dressed in flannel suits made by the ladies in the fort. Some of the sufferers looked dreadfully ill: one poor drummer-boy had been crushed by an elephant and afterwards died; but others looked quite jolly and cheerful.

One Irish sergeant was a very amusing character; he made poetry on the kindness of the ladies in nursing the sick soldiers. Government had provided the hospitals with small tin mugs for their tea; but as they did not like them, some of the ladies brought them cups and saucers, and gave them *chota hazerai* (tea and bread) themselves.

In the court round the "Motee Musjid" the wounded of-ficers were sometimes carried out on their charpoys for air. I went once with Dr. and Mrs. Christison to see one of them, Lieutenant Glubb of the 9th Lancers, who told us all about his escape from Delhi. He said that when they all were waiting near the flagstaff, some coolies dragged up a cartful of dead bodies of the poor English who had been killed, and that afterwards when they encamped near there, on the 9th of June, he again saw the same cart, but then filled with bleached skeletons! In this court the Seiks had their quarters, and the prisoners were kept manacled.

We heard of the murder of Major Burton, resident at Kotah, and, his two sons, by the Kotah Contingent, part of which had mutinied at Agra in July. Even at the eleventh hour they con-tinued insatiable in their rage. The *Rajah* of Gwalior's English teacher, who was a native, told us that the Contingent had left Gwalior for Cawnpore, intending to attack Outram; and that on their way they stopped at Dholepore, and took three brass guns from the Rajah of Dholepore to add to their artillery.

This man also told us that the Maharajah Scindiah had got possession of all our carriages, horses, dogs, and pictures. Our Brigadier (Ramsay) managed, through this teacher, to buy back two of his horses; but when they came to Agra they looked so thin and ill-treated, he regretted the purchase. The teacher, who went backwards and forwards between Gwalior and Agra, promised to send us some of our property, which, however, we were to pay for; and one day a box came, but it only contained odd books from the library, and some music. But the latter much delighted the musical inhabitants of "Block F.," and, to my great joy, I found amongst the books the very *Christian Year* I had been reading on that Sunday the mutiny broke out at Gwalior.

Inside the books were written, in English, impertinent things against the *Feringhis*, and their parade movements and drill. In one was written, "Captain Campbell, first-class mutineer." When the English teacher again came to Agra, we all besieged him with earnest requests that he would try and recover some of our property; and hearing that the *rajah* had bought 30*l*. or 40*l*. worth of books for his school, hoping some of mine would be among them, I promised a large reward to the teacher, as well as paying for the books, if he would get me some back; most of them being my husband's college books, with the college arms stamped on them, which I described to him.

Colonel Filose and his brother, with their families, had all this time been living in their houses at the Lushkur, though in much terror; as the natives constantly threatened them, and searched their houses to see if they had any other *Feringhis* concealed The colonel offered large rewards if a body of men would come from Agra and escort them back there; but it was not considered safe to venture beyond range of the fort guns, which had a salutary effect on the natives. Colonel Filose was very kind in buying back many of our things; though it was rather hard to pay full price for our own property. He said that many of our goods were sold at bazaars at the Lushkur, and people were buying them and taking then off to Indore and Bombay.

At last he sent a box of things, and we all rushed to see it opened. Mrs. Campbell found her watch, without the chain, and a velvet "Church Service;" Mrs. Murray, a Scotch shawl, and dress; Mrs. Blake, a picture and a lace shawl; the Christisons, a book of poetry; the Piearsons, a guitar; Mrs. Gilbert, a baby's cloak; Lieutenant Cockburn, some photographs, and Captain L. Clarke, a turquoise shirt-pin. I afterwards recovered a cameo brooch with the gold setting carefully picked off; this, and the *Christian Year*, were all I ever got back of my property at Gwalior. The box contained a slip of paper with the price of everything noted down.

Some of the servants now came in from Gwalior: they all looked dirty and miserable, and complained of the treatment of the *sepoys*, who had starved them and taken away their plunder. Had they remained faithful to us and warned us, it would have saved me much trouble. Mrs. Murray's *ayah, gora* and bearer brought in her dogs, and the tail of one, called "Ginger," which had died on the way; to prove the truth of what they said, they cut off its tail and brought it to show. Captain Campbell's dog "Bob" also came in, looking very wretched and starved; and Captain Longville Clarke got back some of his and Captain Casserets dogs: the latter having left the fort for Lucknow, Captain Clarke took care of them.

The servants told us that the *sepoys* had rooted up our pretty gardens, and turned the houses not burnt down into cattle sheds; they had also destroyed the furniture, and scattered the dresses and ribbons about the street; emptying preserves and pickle-jars over them, to spoil them: they had also burnt the books kept by the officers, with the name and description of each *sepoy*, to prevent their being recognised if taken; forgetting that there were duplicates of those books kept at Calcutta.

We were often much alarmed by hearing strange sounds underground, as if someone was mining under the fort; and we knew there were underground passages leading from the city to the fort. These mysterious sounds always began at night, and appeared to be just under the palace, where Mr. Colvin had formerly lived, but which was now occupied by Mr. Read. Many

170

of the officers sat up all night, but could make nothing of these sounds; and as we remembered the warnings we had often had, and the pictures of the *Feringhis* being blown into the air, stuck by the natives on the walls, we feared they were preparing to blow up some part of the fort.

One night the sentry caught a native prowling about near the powder magazine, with matches and other combustible matters concealed about him; the wretch was tried, and confessed that he was going to blow up the magazine. Another night, we were told, by our spies, that the Gwalior mutineers, with fifty guns, were going to attack the fort that night, and the natives said they could take it in three hours; but it turned out to be a false alarm, as the Contingent was on its way to Cawnpore.

We heard that Colonel Greathed had reached Cawnpore on the 28th of October, and that Brigadier Hope Grant had taken the command; also, that the column had been reinforced by 5000, and a large supply of provisions, and was to proceed to the Alumbagh, to await the arrival of the commander-in-chief. Later on, we heard that General Havelock was besieged in Lucknow, and had only food left for twenty days, and that Outram dared not leave Cawnpore on account of the Gwalior Contingent. We hoped affairs would now begin to brighten, as some thousand troops of the tardy help from England had arrived, and above 20,000 more were on their way.

November was a very dull, dreary month for us; we could no longer walk on the terrace at night, on account of the cold, which was very bitter. We felt it more from having been exposed to such great heat. Our quarters were very cold; for I had now returned to my old "den," No. 6. which I separated by *jamps* from Mrs. Innes's, on account of baby. We tried all manner of devices to keep out the cold: the Meades and Murrays had their *jamps* plastered outside with mud, which gave them a very ugly look; but we found double *jamps* the best protection. The wind blew through the *chicks* and starved us; so we put a *jamp* before them at night: not during the day, as they were the only means of admitting light into our "dens."

171

We bought some coarse native cloth, and hung it round the inside, like tapestry; also some common native carpets for the floor, which was *kunkur*, and, consequently, very cold and damp. We also whitewashed the wall inside our "dens," and the roof, to keep off our old enemies: they used to keep us awake most of the night. Poor baby was a martyr to the bugs, and I have often had to pick them off him.

As we could not get any English blankets, we substituted *rezais*, which are made of quilted cotton wool covered with chintz. But we were fortunate enough to procure some warmer clothing: *lebadoes*, or quilted garments, something like a dressing-gown, to wear in our "dens;" and in the bazaar we found some black and brown "shag," which made the children warm coats and jackets. The 3rd Europeans now turned out in *Khaki* coloured uniforms; and the children used to shout out "Quakers" after them.

At last it was considered safe to go to the hills. Captain Alexander, Lieutenant Cockburn, and another officer, went on sick leave up to the hills: they were well armed however. Little Charlotte Stuart, also, was taken by some friends, as she was to go home with Lady John Lawrence's party: she came to say good-bye to us, and looked very pale and sorrowful, poor little thing! Some of the officers also ventured to go to Delhi; and poor Mrs. Hawkins and her children went to the hills with a guard of *sowars*. We heard of the murder of poor Lieutenant Neville, of H.M.'s 81st, near Pakputton on the Sutlej, on his way to England: his intended bride arrived at Bombay in the *Windsor Castle* on the very day the news of his murder reached there!

The Meades and Murrays now went out to live in tents. Some people lived in the mosques near the Taj, and others constantly made parties to go there. Mrs. Christison and I went, one day, to feast our eyes on the beauties of the Taj; we wandered in the lovely gardens, where "the flowers of earth vie with the stars of heaven," and gathered oranges, which were now ripe. I left my baby under Mrs. Cameron's charge, who now had the care of Mrs. Proctor's baby: she was very proud of my little boy, saying she had saved his life; which she certainly had, by her kind care and attention. On our way back, we passed through the native city of Agra, where I had never been before. The principal street is paved with flags, and was crowded with natives, who looked at us with an "evil eye."

A Jew pedlar having returned from Delhi, laden with cashmere shawls, caps, scarfs, and slippers, I bought some, as they were now difficult to get, the looms at Delhi being destroyed.

Captain Longville Clarke, just before he went with the party to Futtypore Sikri, heard of the murder of his brother at one of the outstations; which made him more furious than ever against the *sepoys*.

Colonel Cotton headed the party which went to Futtypore Sikri to attack some of the rebels whom Colonel Greathed had defeated. They took a great many prisoners, and made them clean out the church; but as it was contrary to their "caste," they were obliged to be forced to do it at the point of the bayonet: some did it with alacrity, thinking they would be spared hanging; but they were mistaken, for they were all hung.

We were now rejoiced to hear of the final relief of Lucknow, by Sir Colin Campbell, on the 17th of November, and of the arrival at Cawnpore of the poor Lucknow ladies and children. We were thankful that these poor sufferers were at last safe on their way home, after the long trial which they had so heroically and patiently borne; out we were disappointed at not being able to join them at Cawnpore as we had hoped.

Our joy was also sadly damped by hearing soon afterwards of the greatest loss that had yet happened to us: for Havelock was not only a brave and chivalrous soldier, but a good Christian, and beloved by both his officers and men. It was very sad that so many brave generals should have died in the first flush of victory, and, without seeing the results of their great deeds, leave their laurels to be worn by others.

In the beginning of December we heard that a column had left Delhi for Cawnpore, and would take us on its way. It was said the line of march extended fifteen miles; that we were to travel in carts, and sleep at night in tents; and on arriving at

Cawnpore we were to proceed to Calcutta, either from Alla-habad by steamer, or by *dâk gharry*. After making arrangements, our hopes of release from our dreary imprisonment were again deferred, to our great disappointment; the column coming no further than Allyghur, on account of a fight it had had on the 25th of November, with the Joudpore Legion near Kurnaul, in which Colonel Gerard was killed.

The *cossids* told us there had been hard fighting between Colonel Wyndham and the Gwalior rebels at Cawnpore; so, as there was little hope of our getting to Calcutta, I thought of go-ing to my aunt Monteath at Simla, and after staying there a short time, returning home *via* Moultan and Bombay.

In the second week in December, the wounded soldiers, who had now recovered, gave a grand fête at the Taj, in honour of the ladies who had attended them. Regular cards of invitation and programmes were printed; the *tiffin* was to be spread in one of the mosques, and nearly everyone went to it. We left the fort about noon; Mrs. Christison and I drove in Major Macpherson's carriage, and he and Mrs. Innes came after. The road was crowded with soldiers and carriages, and the river with boats, all on their way to the Taj. It was a very gay scene.

In one of the mosques of the Taj, all the ladies, children, offic-ers, and soldiers were gathered; and here and there might be seen a native, looking green with rage at their sacred building be-ing thus desecrated. The mosque was beautifully decorated with flowers, and a table was spread with all the dainties that could be procured. Almost everyone looked happy and cheerful, and the ladies went from one soldier to another saying kind words, and congratulating them on their recovery.

We staid here and had some *tiffin*; and I remember one man of the 9th Lancers offering me some milk punch, that being the only beverage they could procure, as the wine in the fort was drunk. After *tiffin* they had a dance, in which some of the ladies joined; but there were others whose deep mourning garments showed that, with them, it was a time of heavy sorrow.

After watching the dancers for a short time, Mrs. Blake and

I, with some others, walked in the garden. We here met Major
Raikes of Gwalior, who said that he and his wife were going up
to the Punjab; and his uncle, Mr. Raikes, one of the Agra judges, was
also leaving for England. He told us that it would be long before
we could get to Calcutta; and if we went further up the country,
we might have a chance of going to Bombay with the invalids, who
were going by the Sutlej, *via* Ferozepore.

After walking for some time in the garden, we returned to the fort.
Mrs. Blake agreed to go to some friends at Umballa, Mrs. Proctor to
the Punjâb to her mother, and I to my aunt at Simla: Lieutenant Fitzgerald, of the artillery, Mrs. Blake's nephew, who had just come from
Delhi, was to go with us; so we all spent the next two days in hurried
preparations for our emancipation. I had some difficulty in persuading
my *dhye* to accompany me, as I had only had her a short time; but she
at last agreed to go with me, if I would take her husband and child also,
give her some clothes, and pay her 2*l*. a month, and "caste" money: and
I was obliged to agree to these conditions. Mrs. Christison went with
me to the bazaar, outside the fort. It consisted of a long range of
"chopper" sheds, near the Delhi gate, divided into compartments.
The natives were now very glad to hire these little stalls from the
bazaar master, to sell their wares.

We had some difficulty in procuring a few things, for the natives
will bargain and charge you three times as much as the article is
worth; but, in spite of their jabbering and chattering, I got some
flannel and other warm materials to make some things for baby, and
some clothes for my *exigeant dhye*.

We did not leave Agra till Saturday, the 12th of December, as the
Raikeses had just gone, and we were obliged to wait for the return of
their *shigrams*. We had each 150*l*. given us by Government, as we could
not yet get our own money from Calcutta. The last day was a whirl
of excitement; for not only had we to pack up and prepare for our
journey, but all sorts of business to attend to, and papers to sign, at which
I was not an adept. My friends were very kind; Mrs. Nichols made me
some pillows, as we were to take our bedding with us; Mrs. Christison
made me a plum cake, baked in a tin biscuit-case; and Mrs. Campbell
fitted up and gave me a despatch-box and many other little necessaries.

We also had to send off our boxes that day, with the two *dhyes* (one was Mrs. Proctor's *dhye*) and their husbands and children by bullock train.

I must not omit to mention Muza, who had remained faithful to Mrs. Blake, waited on her in the fort, and had done all he could for her comfort: I often tasted some of his little cookeries. Government gave him only 25*l.*, though he had lost more than that at Gwalior. Mrs. Blake (who intended going to England), before she left the fort, gave him a valuable ring, which he said he preferred to money; Mr. Raikes, the judge, also gave him a handsome sum of money. Ever since the mutinies broke out he had always been telling Mrs. Blake to quit the country, as now it was no fit place for women.

We all dined that day with the Campbells, and at night we all assembled, and those we were leaving behind drank to our safe journey home in some champagne that Captain Campbell had just brought us, which had come in with some things recovered from Gwalior. I don't think we slept very well that night for thinking of our journey, and that, at last, we were really to leave our prison.

The next morning Mr. French came to say goodbye, and brought me a sermon which he had sat up the night before to copy, as I liked it very much. I had seen Mrs. French the previous evening, bat he was not in then.

Early in the morning we were accompanied to the Delhi gate by about twenty of our friends, who helped us to pack our *shigrams*. We had been allowed the great favour of a guard of two *sepoys*; but thinking they were not the most faithful guardians in the world, we dispensed with their attendance, Mr. Fitzgerald being well armed Mrs. Proctor, myself, our two babies, and *dhyes*, shared one *shigram*, and Mrs. Blake and Mr. Fitzgerald the other.

I could not agree with Shakspeare that "parting is such sweet sorrow," for it was with keen regret and swelling hearts that we bade goodbye to kind friends whom we might never see again.

CHAPTER 8

The Exodus

We crossed the bridge of boats, and gazed at the gloomy but faithful walls of the fort, till a turn in the road hid it from our sight. I now reflected on the past, and thought, what a good thing it was, that we, who had been so heavily afflicted, were thrown together amongst others all more or less afflicted by the same cause, instead of being left selfishly to brood over and cherish our sorrows; in which case we might have succumbed, and perhaps lost our. reason. But living in a constant state of anxiety, we were compelled to mix with others and sympathise with them; which opened our hearts, and made us feel less desolate. I had often read the essay on Despair, in *Friends in Council*, and felt the truth of this passage: "Some souls we ever find, who could have responded to all our agony, be it what it may. This at least robs misery of its loneliness."

All the way along we saw signs of the times, in the burnt and destroyed villages. We had telegraphed to Allyghur to know if the road was safe between Agra and Allyghur, and received a satisfactory answer "that we might venture." Still we felt we were running a risk when we passed large bodies of natives, armed to the teeth, who looked at us as if they would kill us any minute; but we also passed parties of our own soldiers.

We did not reach Allyghur till late. It was occupied by our troops, and Captain Murray, who had the command, rode out to meet us, and said he had got a tent pitched for our reception. The fort is a most miserable looking place, not at all like the one at Agra; though it is considered very strong. It is only a large space enclosed by thick high

177

mud walls, and a deep moat.

The encampment reminded me of the descriptions I had heard from officers of the Crimean camp, so bleak and wild looking was it, with tents pitched all about, and little mud huts. We drove into the fort, where we were greatly cheered, after our cold dismal journey, by the sight of soldiers cooking their suppers over the bright fires; and by hearing the neigh of horses and clang of arms. We found dinner ready in the tent; Captain Murray, Dr. Mackellar, young Hennessy, and Captain Fitzgerald of the Commissariat, another nephew of Mrs. Blake's, all dined together.

After dinner, the officers retired to their quarters and sent us some charpoys: the babies and *dhyes* lay on beds spread on the ground. The night was bitterly cold; and the *dhyes* were very bad-tempered, though we had given them a good supper; the babies were also fretful, so that we did not pass a very comfortable night. The next morning (Sunday), I walked round the fort with Dr. Mackellar. We heard that Colonel Greathed had come up with and defeated the flying remnant of the Gwalior Contingent, and taken fifteen of their guns; but that the road was still unsafe, and would be for long. We therefore determined to go on to Meerut: Captain Murray tried to persuade us to stay till we heard more news, for fear the remains of the Gwalior Contingent might be lurking about; but finding we were determined to go on, he gave us a guard of *sowars*.

We reached Meerut late that night, and slept at the *dâk* bungalow. The next morning we moved to the hotel; the master of which, Mr. Courtenaye, was very kind to us. He told us all about the mutiny at Meerut: he was not there at the time, but his wife and two of his children were cut to pieces in the outbreak. He also said he had lost eighteen relations in different parts of India, in the mutinies. We heard that the people at Meerut had been greatly alarmed about the ladies who had not escaped with the first party from Gwalior, and had even thought of going in a party to our rescue.

Our rooms were very comfortable, and we slept in real beds for the first time since our escape from Gwalior; we had sheets,—

an almost forgotten luxury,—and sat down to a properly spread dinner table.

They had had a false alarm a few days before our arrival at Meerut, and all the people had rushed out in their night dresses into the street; which was soon filled with carriages ready for escape. After staying a few days at Meerut we left, on Friday, for Delhi.

All round Delhi the country had a desolated look, and I could not help thinking how short a time it was since the road we were travelling was thronged with bloodthirsty wretches panting for more blood and plunder. It seemed strange that they should have been allowed to march on to Delhi, almost unimpeded, and surprise the poor people living there in peaceful security, when there were two European regiments at Meerut, one a cavalry regiment; perhaps it was better to be thus taken by surprise, instead of being kept in suspense. At Gwalior we lived a whole month in suspense, and the last fortnight in hourly dread of being murdered. "There is a pause near death when men grow bold towards all things else."

The modern city of Delhi, founded by Shah Ji-han, and called by him Shah Jehan-abad, is situated in the midst of a sandy plain, on the right bank of the Jumna. It is 956 miles from Calcutta, 880 from Bombay, and 400 from Lahore, surrounded by granite walls, seven miles in circumference, and having eleven entrances. We passed many skeletons of camels and bullocks, and parties of armed natives. We had left our guard, and Mr. Fitzgerald, at Meerut.

Early in the afternoon we reached the bridge of boats, where we paid toll to a native; which rather astonished us, for we thought all natives were now excluded from public offices. After crossing the bridge, which swarmed with natives, bullocks, and flies — the latter attracted by the scent of sweet-meats, of which large amounts are made in Delhi—we thundered through the Calcutta gate into the "City of Horrors:" every spot of which is consecrated as the death-place of some hapless victim, or brave soldier.

Passing through one or two deserted looking streets, we entered the "*Chandney Chowk* " (the principal street of Delhi), which quite astonished us by its gay appearance; for Delhi was in our minds associated with nothing but gloom and desolation. The natives either mingled in crowds or sat before their shops on pieces of carpet, with raised trays before them, on which were displayed embroidered shawls, skull caps, toys, shells, and sugar cane; here and there brilliant pieces of calico, just dyed, were hung to dry across the street.

The natives were all gaily dressed with bright turbans; and they had an impudent, self-satisfied expression on their faces, very irritating to us, when we remembered the merciless and cruel deeds so lately enacted here by their brethren. This street was the bazaar, and far more eastern in its aspect than any I had yet seen. The houses are picturesquely built, and very lofty; some whitewashed, and others adorned by gaily painted representations of elephants prancing with their legs in the air, camels with huge humps, flowers, stars, and crescents.

One picture I was most amused with; it represented an English officer, a short little man with a very red face and beard, and dressed in startling colours, riding on a horse standing almost upright, and fighting a lion rampant There were ladies running along, all out of perspective, and bowing politely to gentlemen, or picking flowers off prim-looking bushes. Certainly the oddest and most eccentric native mind had found development in printing these pictures. The houses were oddly decorated with curiously carved shutters, doors, and balconies, and there were queer little by-lanes leading into the principal street.

The street was crowded with English soldiers in their bright uniforms, Seiks on their wild looking steeds, funny little Ghoorkahs, European ladies riding on immense elephants, and gentlemen on camels, horses, and ponies. Altogether the gay crowds, the green trees, the bright pieces of calico, and the azure blue sky, formed an enlivening scene; and one might have forgotten the fearful things that had so lately taken place, but for two large gallows in the middle of the street

Down the centre of the "*Chandney Chowk*" runs a raised aqueduct; and an officer afterwards told me that when we were taking Delhi, the enemy placed a gun at the top of the "*Chandney Chowk*," which raked the street with grape, while a cross fire was kept up from the windows. A party forcing its way across to the Bankhouse was repulsed, and while rapidly retreating, a soldier fell wounded; one of his comrades actually leapt back again over the aqueduct and dragged the wounded man across it.

We alighted from our gharries at a native's house, temporarily used as a *dâk* bungalow, the proper one having been destroyed; and after traversing a narrow alley, mounted some steep steps into an extraordinary-looking place. On one side we looked into a garden, and on the other side, from a sort of gallery, we saw some officers comfortably eating their dinner; which was rather tantalising to us, as we were very hungry. We were then shown into some rooms, which looked dirty and forlorn, as if haunted by the ghosts of *pandies*; and a dead rat lay on the floor: we could not make up our minds to sleep a night there, and so agreed to go to Dr. Batson, a connection of Mrs. Blake's. We accordingly retraced our steps, and, before getting into our *gharries*, refreshed ourselves with a bottle of soda-water, much to the astonishment of the natives.

After many inquiries, and turning down many deserted by-lanes, we arrived at Dr. Batson's abode, which had formerly belonged to some grand native. We ascended a flight of narrow steps on to a terrace, and then entered a large room: like all native houses it consisted of one good room, with an intricacy of winding passages and narrow staircases. The doors at each end, and the *punkah*, were pierced by large holes caused by a cannon ball bursting in at one door and going out of the other. Dr. Batson, his wife, and daughters, received us very kindly, and after a refreshing tea, took us to a neighbouring native house which they had prepared for our reception.

The part fitted up for us must formerly have been the *Zenana*; and we reached it by a flight of steps, so narrow that no stout person could have ascended. The inner room, where we slept, was separated from the outer room or gallery by *"purdahs,*[1]" hung across archways.

Early next morning I was aroused by a message from Captain Garstone, the gentleman I had met at Agra in January; who, directly he heard of my arrival, had come to invite me to his quarters, where his wife and children were, in a mosque within the palace walls; but I was then too tired to move again that night

We breakfasted at the Batsons' house, and Dr. Batson gave us a most interesting account of his escape from Delhi,—one of the most wonderful on record. It is unnecessary for me to detail it, as his portrait and a narrative of his escape appeared in one number of the *Illustrated London News,* for 1857. He came into our camp on a camel, disguised as a *faquir,* sometime after the arrival of our forces before Delhi. He had passed himself off as a Cashmerian, on account of his blue eyes; but so well did he disguise himself, that, speaking the language and understanding the customs of the natives, he wandered amongst them a long time undetected. His wife and daughters, who were in cantonments when the mutiny broke out, escaped with the other fugitives to Umballah.

Captain Garstone again came, and drove me to the Palace, which is surrounded by lofty walls of red sandstone between fifty and sixty feet high, at the opposite end of the *Chandney Chowk.* Before the *barbacan* were patrolling a man of the 60th Rifles, that gallant regiment which had done such good service in the siege, and a diminutive Ghoorka, with a grotesquely solemn face, looking too small "to shoulder his musket." We drove into a small courtyard, and then through a magnificent gateway into a long and lofty arched corridor.

Here, in small recesses on each side, lived little Ghoorkas, who were cleaning their arms or smoking: their downcast looks harmonised with the gloomy solitude of this once luxurious palace. We turned out of this ante-like corridor down a narrow road, leading to the small mosque, which was surrounded by tumbledown, squalid-looking buildings.

I received a kind welcome from Mrs. Garstone, who was

1. *Purdahs,* quilted curtains.

much pleased with my baby; and they gave me one of the three compartments, into which the mosque was divided by *purdahs*. These *purdahs* looked like *arras*, and made me feel as if we had gone back to the old tapestry days; the effect was carried out by a large fire blazing on a brick hearth, which Captain Garstone had contrived out of one of the sacred recesses, some antique chairs, and a table and shelves.

On these was arranged some valuable "loot" which Captain Garstone had found in the king's palace; including a beautifully bound and illuminated Koran on vellum; a curiously carved sandal-wood cane, in which was concealed a dagger; a strange picture of some old Mogul, very like the present king; a splendid casket of ebony and mother of pearl, full of secret drawers (which Captain Garstone was very much disappointed to find contained no jewels); a solid silver enamelled flask for scent, and a variety of charms, bangles, signet-rings, &&

The next day (Sunday) we went to service in the *Dewan-i-Khas*, and drove through the vaulted corridor into a large courtyard, which reminded me of the Armoury Square at Agra, with its rows of guns. Mrs. Garstone told me that over the gateway leading into the corridor, were the rooms formerly occupied by Mr. Jennings; in one of which, where poor Miss Jennings and Miss Clifford were surprised quietly sitting at breakfast, and murdered, the stains of blood on the walls and floor are yet to be seen. It is now used for a mess-room. Several marks are seen all over the staircase, where the miscreants killed poor Captain Douglass, who was coming down to speak to them, they having sent for him.

We got out of the carriage, and walked through a large paved marble court into the *Dewan-i-Khas*.

This building was formerly used as a Hall of Audience; it now looked dirty and forlorn: the gilding was tarnished, the white marble dingy, and the walls, which, like those of the halls at Agra, had formerly been ornamented with a mosaic of precious stones, were much defaced. Along the top is a mosaic inscription in Arabic:—

If there be an Elysium on earth,
It is this—it is this!

The 60th Rifles, and another regiment, were there, and though tanned and sunburnt, they did not look much the worse for their long campaign.

In the centre, a little table was placed, from which Mr. Rotton, the chaplain, read the prayers and preached. This splendid hall, which once echoed to the mandates of a despotic emperor, with sole power of life and death over millions of submissive slaves, now echoed the peaceful prayers of a Christian people. Service over, the soldiers, at the word of command, marched out, the hall resounding to their martial tread.

Captain and Mrs. Garstone, after speaking to General Penney and Mr. Saunders, showed me over the rest of the Hall. I saw the block of crystal on which the matchless Peacock Throne had formerly stood, and the garden, now desolate and ruined, the trees all torn by shot, and the walks overgrown with rank grass and weeds. Beyond, a stretch of barren country extended to the horizon. We then went to the king's private mosque, near the palace, which he used for his daily prayers. It is built of pure white marble, and was now occupied by some officers, who were busy writing. We could not see the rooms formerly used by the king, as they were now inhabited by Mr. and Mrs. Saunders. All the buildings of the palace had a forlorn and dirty look.

In the afternoon Captain Garstone kindly offered to drive me round Delhi. We drove through some deserted streets, the houses of which were riddled, and the trees torn and broken by grape and round shot, and all redolent of a damp, nauseous smell. We ascended on to the ramparts, and had a good view of Hindoo Rao's house, the ridge of high ground behind which our force had encamped, the road leading to cantonments, and the open country, which lay spread like a map before us.

A little further on, I saw the cannon which the enemy had so cleverly turned on the column when forcing its way up the street, also the very spot where poor General Nicholson had fallen mortally wounded

184

We then drove down a street leading to the Jumna Musjid, a splendid building, standing on an eminence, and ascended by a flight of steps on each side. It is built of red sandstone, which, though too brilliant in the midday sun, glows richly in the mellow evening light The Musjid is surmounted by domes of white marble, and at each angle is a lofty minaret: it was erected by Shah Jehan, and took six yean to build. I could not see the inside, as it was occupied by the Belooch battalion.

This building and street were very difficult to take: our troops were once repelled; and, indeed, had the place been well defended, it never could have been taken. The enemy fired from the flat roofs of the houses, and from the narrow passages, angles, and corners, with which the street was filled, and did much execution amongst our troops. Captain Garstone told me that some dead bodies and skeletons of the *sepoys* were found in the houses and back-streets; but not so many as were expected, as nearly all had been flung into the Jumna. In the *Chandney Chowk* only one or two skeletons were found.

On our return home we called on Mrs. Blake and Mrs. Procter, who were still at the Batsons'. Mr. Fitzgerald had also come in from Meerut. Mrs. Procter was in great distress, for her *dhye*, having lost her husband, had gone to look for him. Captain Garstone met the *dhye* some days after, still in search of her husband, and she called out to him, "O *Sahib*, where is my *admi?*" [2]

On Monday Captain Garstone having to go to his house at Meerut on business, Mrs. Garstone drove me to the fort of Selimghur, which was connected with the Palace by a bridge over a small branch of the Jumna. It was occupied by some of our troops, and near it were pitched some tents inhabited by invalid soldiers. We stood on the bridge, the silence only disturbed by the whirr of a bird's wing, and looked on the dark water, on which were cast deep shadows from the frowning fortress and high banks.

I had time and quiet here to indulge in a reverie on the former grandeur of the Eastern Moguls, and the pomp and pag-

2. *Admi*, husband.

eantry of their magnificent court and its ceremonies,—so different to our practical and prosaic ideas of royal state.

On Tuesday Mrs. Garstone, two of her children, and I rode on an elephant lent us by Mr. Saunders, and the other children and my baby were taken for a walk by a numerous suite of servants and a *chuprassi*. The elephant was a docile creature, and would *salaam*, when told, by raising its trunk high in the air, and then slowly lowering it; and it was amusing to see the little Grarstones commanding this obedient mountain of an animal to *salaam*, which it did instantly. The *mahout* was a queer withered-looking little man: these *mahouts* are not long-lived, for as they almost live on the elephants' backs, the motion injures the spine. I believe the camel *sowars* suffer from the same cause.

We rode into the *Chandney Chowk*, which looked very gay: indeed, an Eastern crowd is always striking, from their long flowing white or coloured garments. Women were returning from the wells with large jars gracefully poised on their beads, the tinkling of their ornaments sounding very musical. *Bheesties* were staggering under their heavy burdens, and "*mollees*" [3] carrying trays of flowers and vegetables; some were washing themselves in the aqueduct and combing their hair, and a few (great dandies) had little looking-glasses, in which they kept admiring themselves, and then *pomatuming* and curling their black locks, and arranging their skull caps and turbans. They all looked impudently at us, as though they thought we had no right there. Oh how I detested them, and longed to turn them all out of Delhi!

We passed parties of Europeans riding on elephants like ourselves, or walking and driving: two pretty little children of Lady Campbell's, dressed in the Highland costume, were walking, attended by a number of natives. From our elevated position on the *howdah*, we could see into the upper stories of the houses; they were all full of dirt, rubbish, broken *ghurras* [4], and old clothes. Many of the houses in the *Chandney Chowk* were occupied by English officers and their families.

---

3. *Mollees*, gardeners.
4. *Ghurras*, earthen vessels.

We met a mad elephant, with its feet fastened together by an iron chain, and were obliged to cross the road. These animals are subject to mad fits, when they are very dangerous. Mrs. Garstone told me that when she was marching in the spring, an elephant was taken with one of these attacks, and became so dangerous, that a *coolie* was obliged to run before it to warn people to get out of the way; the poor fellow unfortunately coming too near, the furious animal seized him, and crushed him to death under his feet, and then threw the body away; but the *mahout*, a brother of the poor *coolie*, ordered the elephant to take up the body, and made him carry it the whole day for a punishment; though the elephant might at any minute have made the *mahout* share the same fate as his brother. This shows what power these *mahouts* have over the animals, which are very fond of them.

Mrs. Garstone pointed out to me all the places where our poor countrymen were so brutally murdered: the Kotwall [5], where several were killed, and where the bodies of the princes[6] were afterwards exposed; an open space outside the palace gate, near a tank, where twenty or thirty women were massacred; and the Bankhouse, where the poor Beresfords were murdered, which looked much devastated by fire, shot, and shell. It is said that when the bank was surrounded, the inmates took refuge on the flat root and Mrs. Beresford actually killed two or three of the wretches herself, who were attacking her daughters.

Most of these Europeans who were massacred were writers and clerks of the custom-house, or shopkeepers, living in the city: the officers had a better chance of escape, as they lived at cantonments two or three miles off. We also passed the magazine, and saw the marks of the explosion caused by poor young Willoughby attempting to blow it up.

In the evening, we again went out on the elephant towards the Cashmere Gate; and on entering the Mainguard, a small courtyard, it presented a strange spectacle of ruin. When the

---

5. *Kotwall*, police house.
6. Mirza Mogul, the king's nephew, Mirza Kishere Sultamet, Aba Bukt; this last said he died happy, for he had seen British women dragged through the streets of Delhi.

mutiny broke out, several officers were sabred here, and the trees were torn and broken by the shot and shell. A party of *sepoys* and an officer formerly took turns in guarding this place. We passed over a deep, wide moat through the gateway, which is so wide that a carriage can be driven along the top: its massive strength surprised me.

The road to the gate, which is commanded by the walls and bastions, winds round a raised mound immediately in front of the gate. When I perceived how difficult it was to approach the gate, and how well it was commanded by the guns of the city, I appreciated more than ever the noble deed that had been performed by that little band of heroes. I may be allowed briefly to relate this memorable exploit

Early on the morning of the 14th of September, when the head of the first column of stormers arrived close to the Cashmere Gate unperceived by the enemy, owing to the winding of the road, a small party, consisting of Lieutenants Salkeld and Home, and Sergeants Carmichael, Burgess, and Smith, with four sappers and a bugler, advanced, and went up to the gate. The instant that Lieutenant Home hid the powder at the foot of the gate, the enemy perceived them, and opened, from all sides, a heavy fire on the little band.

Sergeant Carmichael was just going to fire the fusee, when he was shot dead. Sergeant Burgess then took the fusee, and was also shot dead. Lieutenant Salkeld then seized it, but was shot through the arm, and fell over into the moat, breaking his leg in the fall; but when falling, he threw the fusee to Sergeant Smith, who fired the charge, which exploded, killing about seventeen of the enemy, and shattering the gate. The bugler instantly sounded the advance, and the column rushed on, and entered the city.

We went on by the road round Delhi, and saw the road leading to cantonments. The walls and bastions opposite Hindoo Rao's house were very much destroyed, and the Moree bastion was almost a mass of ruins. We also passed the Seiks' camp: these men are so dirty that they were obliged to be kept outside the walls; they certainly looked very wild, sitting in groups round their fires, the light flashing on their brigandish swarthy faces, ka-kee uniforms, and strange, fantastic weapons: they were cheering themselves by singing wild, but not unmusical, melodies.

We skirted the old city of Delhi, said to be the lurking place of many escaped *sepoys* and citizens, who quitted the city on the entrance of our troops to hatch further mischief under the shelter of deserted mosques, forming extensive ruins near an old Mussulman burial ground. Most of the natives hiding here are said to be *Gazees* — men who are brought up to think that by killing, mutilating, and exterminating all the *Feringhis*, they are fulfilling the wishes of their prophet, and gaining for themselves a happy place in paradise.

We re-entered the city by the Lahore Gate. Out of the eleven gates only three were allowed to be opened, the Lahore, Calcutta, and Cashmere Gates. Passing down the *Chandney Chowk*, we soon reached our quarters; they looked quite snug and home-like after the dismal scenes of desolation we had so lately passed through, and which were wound up by a funeral procession, chanting weird-like strains of lamentation, looking like a train of condemned spirits on their way to Hades.

Captain Garstone, having returned from Meerut, joined us at dinner; he brought me a nice little knitted hood for my baby—a very acceptable present

It was very strange to go round some of the back streets and alleys of Delhi at night, many of them so narrow that we had to go some distance before finding a place wide enough for the elephant to turn in. These lanes were pervaded by a noisome smell, and I often fancied that dead *sepoys* must be lying in the houses.

We saw bits of regimentals, shakos, and cartouche-boxes lying scattered about, and the only living things visible were some wretched cats, mourning over the ruins of their habitations. The houses were utterly deserted, and as "loot" had been found in them, I kept a good look out from my elevated position, into the rooms; but I saw nothing except a music-book, for which I instantly sent the *coolie* who waited on the elephant. It was full of chants and hymns copied in a lady's hand; and as I heard Miss Jennings played the harmonium in the church, I fancied it might have been hers, and thrown there by some plunderer as useless.

Poor Miss Jennings was engaged to be married; and all who knew her said she was a most amiable person. Major Reid called on Captain Garstone, he commanded the Ghoorkas, and had been at the mosque during the whole of the siege, and he talked pathetically of his little Ghoorkas, saying that they were pining for their blue mountains.

On Wednesday the 23rd the Nawab of Jhujjhur was hanged. He was purposely put to death before Christmas Day, to show our contempt for the natives, who had threatened a rising on that day. Captain Garstone went to see the execution, and said the Nawab was a long time dying. The provost-marshal, who performed this revolting duty, had put to death between 400 and 500 wretches since the siege, and was now thinking of resigning his office. The soldiers, inured to sights of horror, and inveterate against the *sepoys*, were said to have bribed the executioner to keep them a long time hanging, as they liked to see the criminals dance a "*Pandie's* hornpipe," as they termed the dying struggles of the wretches.

Delhi now seemed a place fitted to breed malaria and fever, its back streets were so dirty, and full of stagnant water and half-charred bricks. On Thursday (Christmas Eve), Captain Garstone drove me to see cantonments, about three miles from the city; and passing the church I observed it was riddled with shot, and the pillars broken: some soldiers, looking ill and worn, were walking about near it; the church being used as a hospital.

The windswept sharply across the plain, making us feel bitterly cold. As we drove on, Captain Garstone pointed out the places where our piquets were posted, showing how they had gradually drawn nearer to the city: also the spot where the general and his staff used to come out to reconnoitre with telescopes and field-glasses.

Sir Theophilus Metcalfe's house, where we had formerly stationed a piquet, was very much destroyed; it was a large *pucka* house, situated in the middle of a park-like compound.

All the houses in cantonments were burnt and ruined; amongst them the house of my uncle, Colonel Stuart Menteath, who had been brigade-major of Delhi for some years. Captain Garstone pointed out to me one of the bells of arms (small circular stone buildings for the *sepoys* to put their arms in at night), in which an officer's wife and children had lived during the whole siege.

Before the cantonment, which was situated in a hollow, was a high ridge of ground, covered with brushwood and prickly pear, and large blocks of stone; beyond this was the site of our camp, and indications of it are still to be seen on the bare plain,—the holes where the tent poles had been erected, and the places of camp fires; also broken bottles and all sorts of fragments. Captain Garstone pointed out the exact spot on which the general's tent had stood, and, further on, his own; and he told me that the cantonment cemetery was so full of our poor soldiers, that, before Delhi was taken, another piece of ground had to be marked out for a burial-ground.

We walked up to the flag staff; which, as the "crow flies," is only a mile from Delhi. It was here that people from cantonments had waited for some hours, hearing the firing, dying shrieks, and triumphant yells of the assailants in the city, not knowing what to do; till at last, finding all was over, they had made off to Kurnaul and Meerut I also saw the very place where the cart full of dead bodies had remained more than a month, they having been left a prey all that time to vultures and jackals.

Captain Garstone said he had frequently had to ride from our camp to the little mosque with orders; and he showed me the indentation in the earth caused by a shell which had exploded close to him, the space between the two places being much exposed to the enemy's guns. This mosque was marked all over with round shot and shell, and it was so near the walls, that our troops could hear the *sepoys* singing on the ramparts. It was very strongly built, with massive walls, and was held during the whole siege by a guard of the Simoor Battalion, commanded by Major Reid, and the 60th Rifles.

191

Hindoo Rao's house is a large *pucka* house, standing on an eminence, and bears many signs of the storm of shot and shell, in its broken windows, and shattered doors and balconies. I entered a room in the house, which looked gloomy and damp: here the poor wounded soldiers had been taken in to have their wounds dressed. Once a shell burst in it, and killed an officer and several men; and I shuddered when Captain Garstone told me he had seen the floor a pool of blood.

Near this house we had two batteries; and from this elevated ridge you look down on one side upon the city, and on the other upon cantonments. The ground and trees were torn by shot and shell. The broken and irregular ground formed a good cover for the enemy, who used, in the early part of the siege, to steal out, concealed by the ditch round the city walls, and surprise our piquets; but being without a leader, and having no fixed plan of action, they never knew how to follow up in advantage.

The stillness was quite painful, and when I looked on the city lying before me, with its white houses, lofty domes, and slender minarets, shining calmly in the sun, I thought of the strange contrast it formed to the terrible confusion that had reigned so short a time before within its now apparently peaceful walls. It was a thrilling sight to turn and look on the dreary waste, where our brave soldiers for months had endured the harassing attacks of a swarming enemy under a burning sun and scorching winds, and amidst death in various forms; knowing all the time that the fate of India, their own lives, and those of thousands besides, depended on their success: only the feeling that they must conquer or die, could have sustained them; like Hannibal's soldiers after the burning of their ships. We descended the hill and drove home, thinking of the aching hearts at home that must have waited, in fearful suspense, the news of victory or defeat; and of the many desolated lives and broken hearts the retaking of that city had cost

Sir Theophilus Metcalfe "*tiffed*" with the Garstones. He is a wonderful man in the eyes of the natives, who have a wholesome dread of him. When I was at Delhi he was busy hunting out, trying, and hanging mutineers and murderers: he has a lynx eye for detecting culprits. One day, when passing General Penney's house, amongst a guard of *sowars*, he detected a murderer, and instantly singled him out, tried, and condemned him: he also found out poor Mr. Frazer's murderer, and had him hanged.

One day, a native jeweller came to offer his wares for sale to Mrs. Garstone, who, thinking he charged too much, said, "I will send you to Metcalfe, *sahib;*" on hearing which, the man bolted in such a hurry that he left his treasures behind, and never again showed his face.

Hearing that Mrs. Procter had gone to Umballah, and that Mrs. Blake intended to stay over Christmas Day, I, at Mrs. Garstone's request, agreed to stay also. I wished to see the rooms where the "loot" was sold by the prize agents; but as it was a general holiday; being Christmas, they were not open. We often saw the commissioner, Mr. Saunders, and his wife driving about, and they seemed very popular.

Christmas Day was ushered in by troops of sleek, self-satisfied looking natives, covered with "caste marks," coming to the Garstones, followed by *coolies* bearing large trays of offerings— oranges, boxes of dried grapes and peaches from Cashmere, almonds, sugar-candy, and *kismuts* [7], which much delighted the little Garstones. These they offered in a whining, hypocritical way, till at last there was quite a pile of trays in the court-yard. It is customary with the natives to propitiate the "*Sahibs*" in this way on

Christmas Day, which is quite a gala day with them: they go round for *Bâksheesh*, and substitute garlands of yellow jessamine and tinsel for holly. We went to service in the Dewan-i-Khas, though we were rather nervous about the threatened rising. In the middle of service we heard a buzzing, chattering noise going on outside, and began to look uneasily at one another; till an officer went out and found the servants quarrelling and making a great noise, which soon ceased, much to our relief. They had a similar panic at Simla on Christmassy, only of a more serious nature.

7. *Kismuts*, dried fruit, like almonds.

In the afternoon, Captain and Mrs. Garstone and myself, with another officer and his wife, went to see the King of Delhi We drove down the Corridor into a dirty street, formerly occupied by the king's poor relations, of which he had a great number. It is customary amongst rich natives to live in large families, clustered together in one compound, as the rich natives support their poorer relations. At last we came to a small white house guarded by a Ghoorka, and then turned down a narrow passage into a large courtyard, in which were more houses occupied by prisoners of importance waiting for their trial, and guarded by Ghoorkas and men of the 60th Rifles: all places of importance inside the palace walls are guarded by these men.

We then came to a large, ruined, and broken-up garden, where we were joined by Mr. Omanney, a young civilian, who had charge of the king. We climbed some steep steps on to the terrace, where some more guards were walking before the door, and entered a dirty-looking house, then the abode of the "king of kings," the descendant of a long line of Moguls, including Shah Jehan, Aurungzebe, and Timour. Pushing aside the *purdah*, we entered a small, dirty, low room with whitewashed walls, and there, on a low *charpoy*, covered a thin small old man, dressed in a dirty white suit of cotton, and rolled in shabby wraps and *rezais*, on account of the cold.

At our entrance he laid aside the *hookah* he had been smoking, and he, who had formerly thought it an insult for anyone to sit in his presence, began salaaming to us in the most abject manner, and saying he was "*burra kooshee*" (very glad) to see us.

As we looked at him we thought how strange it was that this frail old man, tottering on the brink of the grave, could harbour such a plot and such deep revengeful feelings against us. His face was pale and wan, and his eyes weak and uncertain, seeming to shun our scrutiny; but an aristocratic expression of face reminded us of his noble descent.

He had a venerable-looking white beard, and he swayed about in a frail decrepit way, exciting feelings that were a mixture of contempt, abhorrence, and pity: contempt, for the degraded position to which he had brought himself by his wild scheme of reinstating himself on a throne which he could only hope to enjoy for a passing year or two; abhorrence, that he could give up our poor countrymen to be brutally murdered, and even, it is said, feast his eyes and ears on their dying anguish; and pity, that he should have so short a time for repentance, and that the descendant of a line of kings, whose splendour and power were boundless, should be thus degraded

We ladies, after gazing at the king and his son, Jumma Bukh, son of Zeenat Mahal, the king's favourite wife, who had a shrewd clever face for a boy of about fourteen, were allowed to see the queen, Zeenat Mahal,—a favour not granted to the gentlemen. It seemed absurd to humour thus their silly prejudices, when they had spared no European in their power any indignity or insult. However, we raised the *chick* which separated the queen's room from the king's, and entered a very small bare, shabby room.

Seated on a *charpoy* we beheld a large bold-looking woman, with not the least sign of royalty or dignity about her. She seemed about forty; her complexion was tawny, and her face large and coarsely featured, with daring black eyes and wide mouth, and dark hair partially concealed under her white cotton *chudda*. She wore a cotton dress of black print and but few ornaments; her small and well-shaped hands and feet were bare. Judging from her looks, she seemed capable of inciting the king on to deeds of blood, which she was accused of having done. She began asking Mrs. Garstone and the other lady about their husbands, and why Mrs. Garstone had not brought her children, as she wished to see them; then, looking at my black dress, she sneeringly asked me what had become of my "*sahib.*" I was so angry at her look and tone of heartless contempt, that I said, "*Chupero*" (silence), and walked out of her presence.

On the terrace outside the queen's room were some dirty native women cooking her dinner. I had noticed, sitting near the queen, a young nice-looking girl, dressed in white, who I believe was the wife of the king's son, the boy we had just seen. I afterwards heard that the king and queen did not live on very good terms. She said that he would still consider himself a king, and when she sent for things from the bazaar, he pronounced them not good enough for him; and that he would not smoke the tobacco when it came, because he did not consider it nice enough. He complained that she had plenty of concealed money and jewels, which she would not sacrifice to his comfort; so that Mr. Omanney was obliged to allow him four *annas* a day,—about sixpence.

On returning to our quarters, I laid my *dâk* to Umballah, and sent on my box with the *dhye's* husband and child, as we were to follow next day; and in the evening I had my last ride on the elephant I heard in one of the streets a party of soldiers, sitting round a fire, singing "Annie Laurie:" the cheerful chorus of voices sounded strange, rising from this "City of the Dead," for the greater part of Delhi deserved no better name.

We were also regaled by savoury smells; for I believe all our soldiers were allowed a certain sum to provide a Christmas dinner. Our celebration of Christmas Day was a strange contrast to the celebration of it at home, where happy people were going to church, cheered by the chiming of bells and surrounded by joyful faces. We, however, contrived to have a Christmas dinner, and Captain Garstone rejoiced his children by some Christmas gifts.

Early next morning my *gharry* came: even it bore marks of a siege, for the lining was torn, and the doors and windows shattered by bullets.

Mrs. Garstone kindly provided me with a plentiful supply of food, some oranges and boxes of grapes, and one or two little reminiscences of Delhi. After saying goodbye to my kind friends, I drove through the corridor, which echoed to the rumbling of the gharry, and took my last look of the moody little Ghoorkas sitting in the murky darkness of their "dens," smoking and eating their breakfasts: pawing through the *barbacan*, I drove to Dr. Batson's, where I found Mrs. Blake and Mr. Fitzgerald ready to start

We soon took a last view of the "City of Horrors." I could not but think it was a disgrace to England that this city, instead of

196

being rased to the ground, should be allowed to stand, with its blood-stained walls and streets,—an everlasting memorial of the galling insult offered to England's honour.

Many would forget this insult; but it cannot, and ought not to be forgotten. Yet the natives are actually allowed to ransom back their city, street by street; whereas, if it were destroyed, being their most sacred city, and one that reminds them of their fallen grandeur, it would do more to manifest our abhorrence of their crimes, and our indignation against them, than the hanging of hundreds.

Delhi ought to be rased to the ground, and on its ruins a church or monument should be erected, inscribed with a list of all the victims of the mutinies,—if it be possible to gather the names of all those who were massacred,—and the funds for its erection should be raised by a fine levied on every native implicated in the mutinies, but not openly accused of murder.

Not only our victories of 1857 must be remembered, but the cruel massacres of English men and women which preceded them. Such atrocities ought never to be buried in oblivion.

We travelled along the road by which our army had marched to Delhi a few months before; the plain near it, Mr. Fitzgerald said, was strewed with bones, as there was fought the first battle, when the rebels came out to attack our force. I saw the "*Serai*," which had cost us so much to gain; its high mud walls offering such resistance to our guns, and its court affording protection to the enemy.

On the 26th of December, we reached the *dâk* bungalow at Kurnaul, where General Anson had died of cholera: we stayed the night there. The next day we came to the end of our journey by *gharry*, and found our *dhoolies* waiting, as Mr. Fitzgerald had directed, by the roadside; and we arrived at the hotel at Umballah in time for dinner on Sunday, but too late to go to service.

On Monday Mrs. Procter came to see us before leaving for the Punjâb. Mrs. Blake then went to stay with Mrs. Hope Grant, and I, to Mrs. Fitzgerald, whose husband we had met at Allyghur. I then "laid" my *dâk* to Simla, and as my *dhye* was an incessant trouble to me, I changed her for an European soldier's widow, whose husband had been killed at Delhi. Here I bought for my baby some *putto*, a soft cloth made of camel's hair, which the Cashmerians brought to the door, as Simla was very cold.

I received a letter from my aunt, giving me directions about my journey, and saying, that a pony and servant would wait for me at the first *dâk* bungalow from Simla. Mrs. Blake agreed to stay with Mrs. Hope Grant till she heard of the arrival of the invalids at Ferozepore, or any other way of getting home; when I hoped to join her.

CHAPTER 9

The Journey Homeward

If thou art worn and hard beset
With sorrows that thou would'st forget,
If thou would'st read a lesson, that will keep
Thy heart from fainting and thy soul from sleep,
Go to the woods and hills: no tears
Dim the sweet looks that Nature wears.

I left Umballah early on the morning of the 31st of December. It was so cold I was glad to wrap myself in *rezais*; but the fresh wind reminded me pleasantly of home. Before me rose into the clear blue sky the sharply-defined Himalayah mountains. It was a glorious sight to see them, rising peak above peaky till your eye grew tired of trying to measure their wonderful height

I arrived in the evening at one of the hotels at Kalka, where I had ordered rooms; and, after the children (one was the nurse's) were put to bed, and arrangements made for proceeding early the next morning, I walked in the veranda and watched the sun setting behind the mass of mountains. It was truly a splendid sight to behold the hills illumined with rich crimson and golden tints, and the long shadows gradually creeping over the flat barren plain spread below. It was soon dark.

One certainly misses the twilight in India; the transition from light to darkness is so sudden. The next morning I travelled, with my retinue of about thirty natives, along the new road, planned, under Lord Dalhousie, to connect India with Thibet; it is rather longer than the old road, but better. We crossed a bridge which spanned a stream where the natives were bathing, and then began to ascend amongst the mountains. The hanging jungle near Kalka was very lovely: festoons of flowering creepers, ilexes, and rhododendrons in profusion, and lofty pines, far surpassing the dwarf-like imitations we have in Europe, presented a brilliant display of tropical vegetation.

As we wound gradually higher up the zigzag path, the scenery became wilder and more rugged, and, suddenly turning sharp angles, we came to pretty little villages clustered on the terraces formed on the hills, every available nook and crevice of which was diligently cultivated. Looking down on these cottages, with their curling blue smoke, and the ravines and dingles, reminded me of parts of the Tyrol, though on a more colossal scale.

We met parties of peasants, curiously muffled up, coming down the mountains; some bearing heavy loads of wood, and others riding shaggy little mountain ponies. I liked the independent look of these children of the hills, so different from the cringing, servile aspect of their brethren in the plains. They strode along with a vigorous tread, and looked hardy and athletic.

The air was so invigorating and delightful that I walked almost the whole day; and at noon we halted for refreshment by the side of a stream. These streams wind tortuously, " streaking the hills with a bright emerald thread." What impressed me most, was the intense silence and solitude that reigned: the echoing of our voices, and the tramp of the bearers, were the only sounds I heard. As I walked along, gathering wild flowers, the only thing I missed in this scene of surpassing beauty was a companion to enjoy it with me; for now the brightest scene, to me, had a shadow over it.

We reached the *dâk* bungalow at Kukkri Hutty lake, and I gave the bearers, who were very tired, plenty of *bâksheesh*. It was so cold here that I had a fire all night. At daybreak we continued our journey; still ascending into wilder scenery, amongst craggy hills, thickly wooded with firs; the snowy range now appeared in sight, tinged with roseate hues by the glowing light of the rising sun.

On passing a toll-house, I asked how far it was to Simla. The native answered me in very good English; and on my asking him how he came to know English so well, he said he had learnt it in the Agra college, and told me a good deal about that institution, and the masters, whom he seemed to like.

We again halted for the night at a bungalow, where my aunt's servant was waiting. On resuming our journey, I was tantalised all day by seeing Simla before me, and yet not being able to reach it till night. As we approached Simla it looked very pretty, with its white houses dotted about on the hills, which sloped down to a sort of valley. We now met people riding on horseback, or in *jâm-pâns*; the ladies rolled up in furs and the gentlemen in costumes of "*putto*." It was pleasant to meet Europeans with bright cheerful faces again.

My aunt's house was on the opposite hill, in "*Chota Simla*," three or four miles from the entrance of the station. After ascending a steep path, up "Jacko," the bright lights gleamed, and I was soon joyfully welcomed by my aunt and cousins. Only those who have long been separated from relations and have been leading a harassing anxious life, can know how cheering it is to meet your own kinsfolk. I was delighted to find myself in an English-looking, brightly-lighted drawing-room, and actually to go upstairs into a homelike bedroom, papered, carpeted, and curtained, warmed with a glowing fire, and having a little cot for my baby, and then to descend into a comfortable dining-room, where a Christmas dinner was spread.

We soon sat down to table, and were joined by two Delhi heroes; one was Lieutenant Eton of the 60th Rifles, who, having received a very severe bullet wound in the head, had his head enveloped in a cap something like an Esquimaux. I had hoped to see my youngest cousin's husband, who had been through the siege of Delhi; but he had rejoined his regiment, and was now engaged in active service under Sir Colin Campbell.

The next morning the first thing I did was to look out of my windows. One of them looked down upon Simla: the houses are perched about on such seemingly inaccessible places, one fancied that one must fly to get to them, no road being visible. I then stepped on to the veranda, which was two stories high, and looked up at "Jacko," its lofty peak towering sheer up into the sky.

After "*chota hazerai*," I went out to explore, and was charmed with all I saw. The air was fresh, and deliciously scented by the tall pine trees, many of which are 150 feet high. I then descended the steep path from my aunt's house on to the "Course" or "Mall." The houses here are very pretty, and built in the Elizabethan style, or like Swiss cottages; some, too, have pretty English gardens, with rustic fences and chairs. Peaches, apricots, and cherries grow luxuriantly in these gardens, which are gay with English flowers. All the houses have names, which is very unusual in India: my aunt's was "Closeburn," and another "The Rookery." Simla is the Cheltenham of India.

In the afternoon, I rode on a pretty Caubûl pony through the bazaar, and was much amused to see the numbers of ladies carried in *jâm-pâns*. These resemble large armchairs, having a movable hood and curtains, generally lined with scarlet cloth; and the ladies, who recline inside, wrapped in furs, look very luxurious. The *jâm-pânese*, four of whom and a mate are required for each *jâm-pân*, are dressed in livery: my aunt's wore black cloth tunics turned up with scarlet, and turbans, with her crest.

As carriages cannot be used at Simla, nearly all the ladies, as well as gentlemen, ride. It really required a little manoeuvring to manage a spirited pony amidst the crowd of equestrians and *jâm-pâns* on the narrow roads, which were only protected from the "*khuds*," or precipices, by low wooden fences; and even this protection is only in the immediate vicinity of Simla. Accidents often happen in the season: that year two ladies had been thrown over the "*khuds*," but escaped death by being caught in the bushes; their horses, however, were killed. One day my pony shied, and if a tree had not stood just on the edge of the "*khud*," I should have been over.

One morning I walked nearly to the top of "Jacko" and had a splendid view of the "snowy range." I was sorry I was not there when the rhododendrons were in bloom, for then the hill sides are a blaze of scarlet with their rich bloom.

I was much amused in my morning walks to see the *jâm-pânese* going out in parties to cut wood, which they are not allowed to do within five or six miles of Simla, and the natives coming in from the interior: some of them hill chiefs, dressed in sheepskins, and armed with primitive-looking weapons; and women, looking very different from those of the plain, dressed in coloured trowsers and jackets, their ears and noses loaded with silver ornaments.

On Sunday we went to church, and I heard service read again in a church for the first time since the 14th of June. There were two chaplains, and the choral part of the service was beautifully performed, "Mozart's Twelfth Mass" forming part of it. It is a very nice church, with stained glass windows and open benches. In fact, our little church at Gwalior, the beautiful new ones at Lahore and Umballah, and this at Simla, quite put to shame many of our neglected parish churches at home.

Life at Simla must be very pleasant to some. The climate, scenery, and society are all delightful; and balls, archery meetings, and picnics follow in constant succession during the season, when the commander-in-chief, his staff, and all who can afford it, leave the burning plains for the cool mountain breezes.

After scarcely a month's stay amongst my kind relations at this delightful place, where I received great kindness from many friends, I was again obliged to set forth on my journey. As all the boats were taken, and the invalids were not expected to reach Bombay till spring, I was advised to go by bullock train, *via* Lahore and Mooltan, and down the Indus by steamer to Kurrachee, and on to Bombay. I left on the 19th of January, 1858, a few days earlier than I had intended; as a fall of snow was expected, which would have snowed me up. I returned to Umballah by the old road, which is only a narrow path winding round the rocks.

It is utterly vain for me to attempt to give the most faint idea of the surpassing beauty of this mountain scenery. It would require the pencil of a Turner, and the pen of a Scott, to convey any idea of it

As I approached the flat dreary plain, stretching out into dim indistinctness, I parted with intense regret from the glorious hills, knowing that it was not likely I should ever again see them; but their beauty will have a lasting place in my memory. I reached Kalka on the second evening after leaving Simla, and after dining, continued travelling all night, and arrived at Umballah at 4 o'clock next morning. At gun-fire I left the hotel and went to Major Ewart's, he and his wife being great friends of my aunt's.

I was again troubled by my English nurse, who now gave up the idea of going to England with me as she had promised, so I was obliged to have recourse to another *dhye*. After great difficulty I procured one, who promised to go with me as far as Bombay, and perhaps to England. One afternoon, Major Ewart drove me to see the new church, which was not quite finished; the mutiny having prevented its completion. The architecture seemed very good, and inside all down the aisles were scrolls with illuminated texts of Scripture. This is principally done to gratify the native Christians; for in all the Mussulman temples, sentences from the Koran are inscribed. It was getting too dark to see much, but what I did see pleased me greatly.

This church had been fortified, in case of an attack from the rebels, with mud walls and small bastions, on which cannon were placed: the defences did not look very strong, but I remembered how Mr. Boyle's house at Arrah was defended for seven days by fourteen gentlemen, none of whom were military men, and fifty Seiks, against 3000 rebels well armed, and provided with cannon.

I could not go on for a day or two, as Mrs. Hope Grant, Mrs. Blake, Mrs. Ricketts (Mrs. Blake's sister-in-law, whose husband was killed in the mutiny at Shahjehanpore), and Mr. Fitzgerald, had taken all the *dhoolies* and bearers; but on the evening of the 27th of January, I set off for Lahore, and after travelling all night, reached Loodiana at noon. I rested and dined there, then went on to Jullunder, which seemed a nice station, with some large houses in it

The houses in the Punjâb are rather different to those in the

N. W. provinces, and are called "*kutcha* bungalows," being made of mud-bricks not coated with "*chunam*;" and there generally is a small room built on the roof, in which the residents sleep during the hot weather.

The variations of the thermometer in winter are very trying; at two o' clock p.m. it will be 75°, and at sunset and sunrise 30°. In the summer the heat is very oppressive; the weather at this time was very pleasant. The country round seemed very pretty and fresh, the fields all well cultivated, the crops green, and large trees shading the road; and the blue hills of Cashmere looking soft in the distance. Parties of Cashmerians were coming down to sell their wares in the plains, with shaggy camels laden with their goods.

I thought the Punjâbees a finer race of men than the natives of the plain: they are more robust, with a different expression of face, and fierce-looking eyes; they were also better dressed, in quilted *chogars* [8] and trowsers, generally of the gayest colours, and well armed with matchlocks, spears, and shields of buffalo hide studded with brass nails. We passed several villages surrounded with thick, high mud walls, which looked as though they could be easily defended. Altogether their persons, manners and villages, seemed more formidable than those in the plain.

It was very lonely to travel surrounded by natives, the only white person besides myself being my baby. At times I met officers going down the country; but ladies and etiquette are too closely allied to allow of my speaking to them: between gentlemen there is a kind of freemasonry, which is very pleasant, and indeed needful in a wild country with no Europeans near you.

At night it was particularly lonely; the darkness being so great, and the torches making it seem darker, and the stillness being only broken by the howling of jackals and pariah dogs. Then it was startling to be awoke out of a sound sleep, by the *dhoolie* being suddenly set down, and finding yourself surrounded by a dozen men shouting for *bâksheesh*, and the torches glancing on a dozen fresh ones preparing to go on with the *dhoolie*. I always

---

8. *Chogar*, a long loose cloak.

gave them double *bâksheesh*, and thus they gave me the character of being a liberal "*Mem-sahib*" at the next *chowki*, so I got on without trouble or delay.

On the 30th, late at night, I reached Umritsur. It is the holy city of the Seiks, and is thickly populated. In 1500, it was a great place for pilgrimages, Ramdas the fourth "*Guru*," or spiritual pastor of the Seiks, having had a fountain made here, called "*Amritsir Saras,*" (The Fount of Immortality). There is a large fort here, the fortress of Govindghur, built in 1809 by Runjit Singh, the batteries of which are very strong. During the alarms in the Punjâb, and the mutiny of the native troops at Lahore, all the ladies and children were sent into this fort

It is really marvellous, when one considers the populous state of the Punjab and the immense number of native troops there, that the mutiny did not more fully develop itself in this region. We cannot sufficiently admire the prompt, judicious, and decisive way in which Sir John Lawrence, Mr. Montgomery, and others acted. Though Sir John Lawrence had sent nearly all the European troops down to Delhi, yet he contrived with the few remaining, to keep the native troops and swarming population in check, by playing off the hatred of the Seiks for the Hindoos. As Euripides says:

One wise head is worth a great many hands.

After leaving Umritsur, I was surprised to see a *sowar* accompanying me, who changed every time the bearers changed: though this guard, I believe, was quite necessary.

On the evening of the 31st of January, I reached Lahore, or rather Mean Meer, which is the name of the military cantonments, about three miles from the city of Lahore. I thought it a dull, dreary place, with long rows of barracks, surrounded by flat arid country. I went to the house of the chaplain, Mr. Boyle, to whom my aunt had given me a letter of introduction, and who received me most kindly, as if I were an old friend, though he had never seen me before. On Sunday I went to the church, which is a beautiful building; the walls are coated with highly polished *chunam*, which has the effect of white marble, and the fittings up are all green, which is soothing and agreeable to the eyes, after the glare outside. Mr. Boyle had been chaplain at Sealkote; and in the mutiny there he had a narrow escape of his life.

All the "trucks" (*dhoolies* on wheels, drawn by one horse, the roads being too bad for the common *dâk* gharry) being engaged, we went to the officer who had the superintendence of the bullock-carts for bringing up troops from Mooltan, to see if I could have the use of one or two bullock-carts. These bullock-trains traverse the whole of India, and at times are very useful for conveying troops. I was rather startled when shown the carts which the officer very kindly allowed me to have, as they were common country vehicles, with a "*chopper*," or thatched top.

Mr. Boyle one day drove me to see the "*Pandy* Camp." But before giving a sketch of this encampment, it is necessary to explain how these rebels were kept chained, as it were, by a handful of Europeans. Lahore, being a city of great antiquity, and formerly the residence of the Mahommedan conquerors of Hindoostan, it is held in great veneration by Mussulmans on account of its mosques, tombs, and a splendid mausoleum. It is seven miles in extent, and surrounded by high walls; but it was far larger before the Seiks devastated it: even now, however, it contains 100,000 inhabitants.

In a military point of view, also, Lahore is a very important place; the fort being within the walls of the city. When news was received by telegraph of the mutiny at Meerut, Sir John Lawrence was away; but Mr. Montgomery and the other authorities at Lahore, having discovered that the native regiments, consisting of the 16th, 26th and 49th N.I, with the 8th Cavalry, were plotting to gain possession of the fort and kill all the Europeans, they formed a plan to outwit them, and this, probably, was the means of saving the Punjâb.

On the 12th of May a ball was given by the officers at Mean Meer; and the 15th was said to be the day fixed for a general rising of the *sepoys* throughout India: the plans of the mutineers having been altered by the premature outbreak at Meerut.[9] The *sepoys* intended,

9. Some say, however, that both these days were premature, as the natives intended to rise in rebellion on June 23rd, being the centenary of the battle of Plassey, gained by Clive, June 23rd, 1757.

when the guard was changed at the fort (for then a greater number would be together) to take possession of the fort, treasury, and magazine; and at the kindling of a bonfire, all the native troops at cantonments were to seize the guns, let out the 2000 prisoners from the jail, and enact a tragedy if possible worse than that at Meerut. The ball went on as usual; but, unknown to the *sepoys*, very different proceedings were being prepared for. Instead of the usual guard of *sepoys* being sent down to relieve the sentries at the fort, Europeans were sent, who turned out the sepoy guards, and disarmed them: thus showing them that their plot was discovered.

Early next morning all the troops were ordered on parade, and after the Governor-General's proclamation had been read, the whole of the native regiments were, by a skilful manoeuvre, brought in front of the guns, and confronted by five companies of the Queen's 81st. At a given signal, the *sepoys* were ordered to pile arms, and the *sowars* to unbuckle sabres.

At first they hesitated; but grape-shot and cannon are powerful to enforce obedience, and 2500 native troops were speedily disarmed by 600 European soldiers. The disarmed regiments were encamped on the parade ground, opposite the barracks, where their women and children lived till Delhi was taken; but between the barracks and the native regiments were encamped the European soldiers; parties of whom were always under arms, having a battery of guns kept loaded, and a body of Seik cavalry with their horses saddled. This state of guarded suspense lasted for months, until at last Sir John Lawrence telegraphed to General Wilson, to say that if Delhi were not taken directly, the Punjâb would be lost.

We drove round the "*Pandy* camp," Mr. Boyle giving me all the particulars as we went on. It was a most strange sight to see thousands of those powerful-looking men, most of them upwards of six feet high, thus kept under. Some were in uniform, and others in their native dress, and all were living with their wives and families in small thatched huts and tents. Many of them were going to fetch water, and I noticed the ferocious and sullen expression of their faces.

On Wednesday, the 4th February, I again started on my journey. Mr. Perkins, secretary to the Punjâb Relief Fund, previously called and gave me letters to obtain a free passage down the Indus to Kurrachee, and also one to the committee at Bombay for a free passage to England: those who had lost their property in the mutinies having free passages given them from the money sent out from England by Alderman Finnis, then Lord Mayor of London. Mr. Boyle supplied me with plenty of provisions for the journey. It took an hour to pack the carts, as one of them was destined to be our dwelling-place for four days. I covered the straw with *rezais* and a mattress; but still it was uncomfortably small for myself, baby, and *dhye*.

Mr. Boyle told me that on the road I should find European soldiers at the *serais*. These *serais* are native hostelries, consisting of large buildings surrounded by courts, where the natives, when on a journey, keep their animals and sleep at night. They were now used by Government for the troops coming up the country; and sergeants were stationed there to supply with fresh bullocks and provision the soldiers who rested and dined there, as these *serais* are a day's journey apart.

We travelled slowly along a dusty road for a whole day, the fine dust penetrating everything till we were covered with it. The bullocks, though they went very slowly, were fine large creatures, and clothed in coarse cloth on account of the cold. I often asked the natives we passed what time it was, but they spoke a different dialect; and, as far as I understood, always said it was twelve o' clock. The country was so desert-like I felt as if I had come to "a land where all things always seemed the same," and "in which it seemed always afternoon."

At last, about twelve o'clock at night, arriving at a *serai*, where we stopped to have the wheels of the cart greased, I was aroused by the light of several torches, and found myself in the middle of a courtyard full of carts and bullocks, having a large building at one end. The drivers said that the "*sahib*," meaning the sergeant, was coming, and presently the "*sahib*" appeared and offered me refreshments. At my request, he brought me a cup of tea, and gave the *dhye* a large supply. He was very kind; and as he said he had no butter, I gave him some potted meat and preserves, of which Mr. Boyle had given me a large supply.

I was much troubled with a whitlow which chose this inopportune time to torment me; and as I could get no water to bathe it in, it gave me much pain and prevented me from sleeping. I travelled on without resting more than a few minutes when the bullocks were changed, and passed parties of the 7th Fusiliers on their way to Lahore; they travelled in their fatigue uniforms, which were long white blouses like a carter's frock. They always took a look inside my cart, and seemed astonished to see an English lady-travelling in a cart no better than a gipsy's; some wished me "good morning," others asked if India was all like this? the road between Mooltan and Lahore being certainly an unfavourable specimen of the beauties of India.

At the last *serai* I passed, on the evening of the fourth day since leaving Lahore, the sergeant was very kind; he brought me a chair to sit on and have tea, and got me some cold water from the well to bathe my finger in.

As he complained of the intense dullness of the place, and said he had no books to read, I gave him *The Heart of Midlothian* and another novel which I had done with; and an officer, who afterwards passed, told me the sergeant had been so interested in Jeanie Deans that he had sat up all night to finish the end of her journey to London.

Early on Sunday morning I reached Mooltan, and passed the fort where ten years before poor Anderson and Agnew were so barbarously murdered. The *dâk* bungalow being full, I went to the chaplain's, Mr. James, and was much disappointed to hear that the steamer which was to sail next day was quite full, and that another was not expected for ten more days.

The country around Mooltan is both sterile and ugly, and being subject to inundations of the Chenab, it is covered with low sand-hills; but water fit for drinking is only to be found at a great depth: where the inundations cover the land it is very fertile, and rice is much cultivated. Mooltan, from its proximity to the Indus, must be the gateway of the northern part of India, and in time may become a flourishing station from the constant traffic.

On Monday evening we walked round the parade-ground, where the European soldiers were making preparations for games of cricket, pony-races, &c. Mr. James asked one man what they were going to do, and he replied that they were making ready for the soldiers' games; for it was right they should have a holiday and enjoy themselves once a year: he said this in a solemn way, as if it were more a sort of duty to enjoy themselves than a pleasure.

The next day Mrs. James and I drove to the parade-ground. On a flat dreary plain was collected an immense concourse of people, in the centre of which the English soldiers were commencing their sports, enlivened by a band; around them were grouped the European spectators, the ladies in carriages; and in the background a thick throng of natives, all gaily dressed in holiday attire, with bright turbans and *chogars*, looking like a bed of tulips: one man was robed in a *chogar* of yellow chintz, dotted about with peacocks with spread tails.

Cards with programmes of the games were handed round. Here I met a friend, who had come down from Simla by the mail-cart: gentlemen often travel by this conveyance, as there is a seat for one person beside the driver, and it is a much quicker mode of travelling. I had also the pleasure to meet Mrs. Blake again, who with her party was staying with different friends till the next steamer.

I thought the military cantonments very ugly; the houses being of *kutcha*, and the gardens not flourishing, as it was a new station. The civil cantonments, two or three miles off, were much prettier. Here, for the first time since leaving Bengal, I saw a great many date-trees.

On the 16th of February the steamer arrived, and an order was issued that anyone who wished to go must be on board the next day at 12 o clock. As all the carts had been engaged, I hired two camels to carry my boxes down to the steamer; but they did not like the rattling of the boxes and became unmanageable, so the bearer called them "*khrab-wallahs*,"[10] and told the man to take them away and bring donkeys in their stead. Next day I sent my baby and *dhye* in a *dhoolie*, and Mr. James drove me to the river, which was two miles off. Here I saw a small steamer towing a "flat." These "flats" were introduced by Lord William Bentinck, for communication between Calcutta and Allahabad: they are more comfortable and clean than the steamers. My berth was taken for me on board the steamer, by the manager of the relief fund at Mooltan. Everything was in confusion on board; not the least order or method were observed.

Mr. James having asked the captain to show me my cabin, he took me into what he called "the saloon," a dark, dirty place, and apologised for its untidy appearance, by saying that troops had broken all the chairs and lamps, when coming up the river, and he had not had time even to clean it out: it certainly looked as though a company of soldiers had had the "run" of it, from its battered, defaced appearance. The captain said that all the cabins were engaged, and pointed out a bench, about two feet wide, running round part of the saloon: "This is your share," he said, pointing to a chalk line marking out about six feet of the bench, with my name chalked on it.

I must say I was taken aback, even after my experience of fort life; for this space was all the accommodation for myself, baby, and *dhye*. A dirty, sail-cloth kind of curtain, separated my berth, from that of another lady's, and from the saloon; and behind this curtain we had to sleep and perform our toilettes. Mr. James, having ordered his bearer to unpack my bedding and carry down some of my smallest boxes and stow them under the bench, bade me goodbye.

I then went on deck and found Mrs. Blake, and several other friends; also Mr. Maclaine of the 3rd Europeans, who was wounded at Agra on the 10th of October. They were all, however, much to my vexation, located on the flat. I went to see their cabins, which, though small, were better than those on the steamer. The passengers on the steamer were all strangers to me; amongst them were two chaplains, and some officers of the 7th

10. *Khrab-wallah*, cross or ugly fellow.

Fusiliers, who were on their way back again to England, having only been a few weeks in India. All the gentlemen had to sleep on deck, as there was no room for them below.

As the steamer had to stop every evening to take in a fresh supply of wood, we thus got a walk before dinner; and the gentlemen sometimes went out shooting ducks, geese, teal, and other water-fowl which abounded in the neighbouring marshes. The country was so flat, that one evening a party of us, out walking, lost our way in the dusk; till at last, coining in sight of the funnel of the steamer (a conspicuous land mark in that flat region), we guided ourselves back.

We frequently met steamers coming up the Indus, and often with troops on board; and one evening, returning from our usual walk, we found a cheerful scene near the river. The soldiers from a steamer coming up, had gone on shore to amuse themselves: many of them, having just killed a bullock, were cooking their suppers over fires; this, with the wild groups of *coolies* running to and fro with wood, which was piled up in large quantities on the bank, formed a study fit for Rembrandt.

We halted for an hour or two at Mittun Cote, a dreadfully hot, unhealthy station, situated on the junction of the Chenâb and Jhelum with the Indus. The river is much wider here, and there are little islands on which are built heathen temples.

On the 28th we reached the sea, and as our steamer was not strong enough to breast the waves, we had to cross on to another over a narrow plank. We lay at anchor all night at the mouth of the river, as the entrance to the harbour at Kurrachee is rather difficult; and at daybreak we were off again and reached Kurrachee about noon. Now began the bustle of landing; which gave me much trouble, for my *dhye* was a novice at travelling, and I had her to take care of as well as the baby and luggage.

The brigade-major, however, who came down for Mrs. Blake, kindly took me in his boat, and promised to drive me to my friend's house. We had to wait some time at the landing-place; as a vessel which was anchored some way out was waiting for its cargo of *Pandies*, ready to take them to the Andaman Islands.

The *sepoys*, chained together in couples, and manacled, were coming down the steps into the boats. They looked a wretched, miserable, dirty set, and the clanking of their chains had a dismal sound. The captain of their vessel, a Yankee, said he would "break them in." They were to clean out their "dens" or "hutches" on board, and eat bacon or anything, regardless of caste. Some people said that few would reach their destination, as they suffer so much from sea-sickness and have such a devout horror of the "black water," and have been known to mutiny rather than go by sea from Calcutta to Bombay, or elsewhere.

The Andaman Islands, a group of four islands inhabited by savages, in the Bay of Bengal, are so unhealthy, that though the English tried to form a settlement there in 1791, they were obliged to abandon them in five years. It was said that each *sepoy* was to be allowed a knife, to defend himself against the savages, and some food; and if he behaved well, his wife was to be sent to him in two years.

When I saw Kurrachee, I thought of the prophetic words of Napier.

I see plainly, Kurrachee will be nothing, till a mole be made from the Bunder to Kamaree point: this mole will be ruinous, yet it will change Kurrachee from a mud-built hamlet to a large and flourishing city.

This has been done, and Kurrachee is now a "flourishing" town; and when the railway is finished and a direct communication with England by steamer started, it will become a place of great importance. The church here is a fine new one; the town is large, and contains several European shops. The cantonments are just like the Punjâb cantonments. The "course" runs along by the side of the sea, and its termination is called "Scandal point;" as all the carriages stop there for their occupants to enjoy the sea breezes and talk. The surrounding country is bleak and unproductive. We were again too late: for the steamer going to Bombay was quite full, but I heard that another would start in a few days.

On the evening of the 6th of March, Mr. Rawlinson drove me down to the harbour, which was some distance from cantonments; and on our way he pointed out the place where the railway to Indore was

214

being marked out. The steamer was anchored some way out, and it was not very pleasant to trust oneself to the mercy of a rough sea in a queer little boat, managed by a crew of natives, who kept furling and unfurling die sail in such an unskilful way that I thought we should be capsized every minute.

The *dhye*, who had never been beyond Umballah in her life, was dreadfully frightened. Mr. Rawlinson kindly accompanied me on board, where I again met Mrs. Blake and her party, and Lady Hope Grant; her husband having lately been made a K.C. B.

We reached Bombay on the 9th of March, the day the overland steamer left; and I thought of going to the Refugees' House; but, not knowing where it was, went to the Hope Hall Hotel. This was a most fatiguing day, from the difficulty of getting the boxes out of the hold, amongst the gesticulating and jabbering natives, and then procuring a carriage.

The harbour at Bombay is thought one of the most beautiful in the world. The entrance is between the Colabba and Caranja Islands, and there is a lofty lighthouse on the extremity of Colabba. Bombay appears to be one of the most densely and variously populated cities in the world: it is thronged with English, French, Persians, Arabs, Jews, Portuguese, and natives from the different islands, besides the large native population of Hindoos, Parsees, and Mahommedans.

This day it was particularly crowded, there being a fresh influx of people preparing to leave by the different steamers and sailing vessels. At the hotel I met Mrs. Blake, who had gone on shore earlier than I had; she was very anxious to leave that day, by the overland steamer, but found it impossible. The hotel was so crowded that the proprietress said she had not a room to spare; but she gave up her own room to Mrs. Blake, and to me a little place screened off from the hall, which was only just vacated; she said that people were even obliged to pitch tents in the "compound."

The next morning I received a large packet of home letters, which had been sent to my agents; and most welcome they were, as I had not received any since leaving the fort I was again worried with business, having agents to see, letters to write to the "committee," money matters to arrange, and clothes for my voyage to see after; and last, though not least, to persuade my *dhye* to go with me to England. Formerly people had large sums to pay before taking natives to England, as a security for their safe return; but now they are not considered so precious.

In the evening, Mrs. Blake, Mr. Maclaine, myself and another gentleman, drove to the Botanical Gardens, which are very beautiful, and the scent of the tropical plants is most delicious. The drive was a very pleasant one; everywhere the blue sea appeared, and date and cocoa-nut trees flourished; the sea breezes contributing much to their growth.

Bombay is a most amusing town, having much more of native character in its buildings and inhabitants than Calcutta. The streets are narrow, and thronged with motley groups of natives, amongst which the *Parsees* are most conspicuous, with their curious head-dresses, about which they are very fastidious; these head-dresses are horizontal tubes of stiff card, covered with silk of a peculiar pattern. Besides this headgear they wear a white linen or cloth *caftan*, and loose, flowing silk trowsers of the brightest hues: scarlet striped with orange, and other gay varieties; with a *cummer-bund* to match, and English boots or shoes of patent leather.

The *Parsees* appear predominant in Bombay; and many of them hold public offices. One day I went to my agents and asked to speak to the head of the firm, when an important looking *Parsee* appeared, and told me that since the death of the manager, he (the *Parsee*) carried on business in his name. The *Parsees* are immensely wealthy; they drive beautiful English carriages and horses, and have splendid establishments; their houses being furnished with English and French furniture of the most costly kind: chandeliers, mirrors, velvet-covered couches, rich carpets, marble tables, Buhl cabinets, pictures, books, pianos, and articles of *vertu*.

Their gardens, too, are very beautiful, and kept up at a great expense. They give splendid entertainments, and are particularly fond of iced champagne. Even the humblest *Parsees* know English, and the rich have their children regularly instructed in it. The *Parsee* ladies are generally richly attired in a *chudda* of the finest silk or gauze, wound round them: this *chudda* is called a "*sari*" in Bombay, and is so many

216

yards in length that it serves for a skirt as well as a veil. They wear a small bodice of velvet or silk, fastened with precious stones, and drawers of silk, or fine muslin; their arms and ankles are covered with costly bangles, and their noses and ears pierced with jewelled rings.

I was told that many of them are even richer than our merchant princes at home, and are very munificent in their charities. They say the reason Sir Jamsetjee Jejeebhoy gives such immense sums is, that he won't be outdone even by the governor. Some of their names are very odd, and can never be mistaken; many of them terminate in jee: as, Cursetjee, Bomanjee, Ruttonjee, Luxmonjee, &c

The *Parsee* religion is very curious. Zoroaster was the reformer of the ancient religion, or rather the founder of a new system, which became the dominant faith of the East, until the rise of the Mahommedan power and the conquest of Persia by the Arabs in the 7th century, compelled the Persians to abandon their ancient religion. Those who would not, fled to the deserts of Kerman, and to Hindoostan, where they still exist under the name of *Parsees*, a name derived from Pars or Fars, the ancient name of Persia: the Arabs call them "*Guebers*," signifying unbelievers.

The system of religion founded by Zoroaster teaches them the existence of an Almighty being, who created two archangels; one of these, Ormuzd, remained faithful to his Creator, and is the source of all good and light; the other, Ahriman, rebelled against his Creator, and became the author of all the evil upon the earth. Ormuzd created man, and supplied him with all materials for happiness; but Ahriman introduced evil into the world. The *Parsees* adore fire, light, and the sun, as emblems of Ormuzd, and keep a fire continually burning in their temples. They have a class of priests, called *Magi*. They carry their dead on biers, and expose them on lofty towers, called *Parsí Dakhma*, or Towers of Silence, until the vultures and other birds of prey have devoured the flesh, when they throw the bones into a deep well.

It was really quite a treat to visit the shops in Bombay; the china depository was very attractive, with its carved ivory chessmen and jars, deliciously scented sandal wood boxes, inlaid and carved like the finest lace; silver work from Dacca, and large china vases and monsters. Most of the shops are in the fort, which is like a small fortified town: the cathedral also is within the walls of the fort. The fortifications are extensive, and would require a large garrison to defend them. Near the sea the walls are very strong; but the houses are lofty, and many of them built of wood, so that there is great danger of fire. In 1803, a fire did break out in the fort, and burnt many houses.

The fort had a money-making look; most of the people seemed mentally adding up accounts, and all looked rich and flourishing. The *barbacan* was guarded by some highland soldiers, who looked strange with their fair faces and picturesque costume.

We visited the famous caves of Elephants. Starting early in the morning, we drove to the *"Bunder,"* and then had a pleasant sail of an hour and a half. The bay is surrounded by a beautiful range of well wooded hills, and contains the islands of Salsette [12] and Elephanta. The blue water, dotted about with different sized vessels, and picturesque native boats with lateen sails, formed a beautiful scene. On landing, we ascended to the caves by a rude flight of steep steps embowered in trees. The caves are certainly most wonderful The cave temple is supposed to have been excavated in the tenth century. It is 130 feet long by 110 wide, and the roof is the solid rock, supported by four rows of columns nine feet high.

On the walls are carved, in high relief, colossal figures of Shiva and his wife Parvati. The cave was agreeably cool and shady after the heat outside. Along the side are little cells, formerly inhabited by the priests.

We had some luncheon tables placed for the purpose. On our return we met a large school of girls, English and half-castes, with their teachers; they were all dressed neatly in white, but I noticed that they had no stockings on.

A few days after our arrival in Bombay, Mrs. Blake and Mrs. Shakespear went to stay with a friend of theirs, the Hon. Mr. Mallet,

---

12. The island of Salsette, in 1739, was in the possession of the Mahrattas, and separated from Bombay; it is now united by causeways.

a Member of Council, and Mrs. Mallet most kindly invited me also, thinking I should be uncomfortable at the crowded hotel.

Their house was at Mazagon, about a mile out of town, and the drive to it lay through a bazaar and along the shore. The house is a most spacious and comfortable one, situated in a large compound sloping down to the sea, and having a pretty garden. The sound of the waves and the fresh spray added beauty to the scene. The rooms were very large, lofty, and numerous, the drawing room was fifty feet long.

The houses at Bombay do not look so imposing outside as those at Calcutta, but they are quite as lofty and spacious: they are more like bungalows with thatched roofs, and only one story high. Instead of residing in the town, as at Calcutta, all the Europeans, and rich Parsees and natives, live either at Mazagon, Bycullah, or Malabar Hill; and some have houses in the hills, about fifty miles from Bombay, where they spend the hot months; but the climate of Bombay is not nearly so oppressive as that of Bengal, and there is almost always a fresh breeze from the sea. The houses are most richly furnished with white marble, and a wood that grows in the neighbourhood, something like ebony; and much of the furniture is English.

On Sunday we went to a beautiful new church, at Bycullah, built of a fine white stone. The bishop preached.

The drive from the Mallets' house to the fort was very amusing; we often stopped in the bazaar, when returning from a drive in the evening, to have the carriage lamps lighted. The gaily dressed crowds of natives and brilliant lights were very pretty.

The spirit shops are very attractive to the natives; the liquors being put in the window in beautifully coloured jars, over which gay lamps are suspended. The natives make toddy from the date trees, which abound in Bombay, and for each tree they pay a tax. They climb these trees by cutting notches in the trunk, and then hang up earthen vessels to collect the dropping juice, which they afterwards ferment; they also make an intoxicating drink from rice. The wells at Bombay are very pretty, and being mostly surrounded by motley groups of natives bearing large jars and earthen vessels on their heads, and *bhees-*

---

13. *Mussak*, a goatskin for carrying water..

ties filling their capacious *mussaks* [13], they look picturesque.

The Esplanade before the fort runs along the shore; it is a wide and extensive green, like the Maidân at Calcutta, and affords pleasant drives. A band plays twice a week, and every evening it is thronged with people riding and driving. Here too the inhabitants turn out at a certain hour, forming a curious medley of dress, language, and nations.

The *Parsees*, conspicuous with their unbecoming head dresses, are dotted about in groups, sitting on small pieces of carpet, eating and chatting with one another; the richer ones, lolling back in their luxurious carriages, looking the personification of ease and self-satisfaction, drive about bowing condescendingly to the Europeans, whom they always pass with a dash.

On the Esplanade, rows of tents are pitched called the "Strangers' Lines," which can be hired by people who prefer this mode of life; or, as is constantly the case, when the hotels are full. These tents are very large and comfortable, and contain several compartments used as sitting, sleeping, and bath rooms. Here, too, in the season, people often erect bungalows, which they remove when the rains begin; as the sea often overflows the coast.

The public buildings at Bombay are not so fine as at Calcutta; and the governor's house is at Pareil, some miles out. The town hall and church at Bycullah are handsome buildings, and there is also a comfortable club house at Bycullah, and a race course.

The steamer we were to leave by was an extra one; put on in addition, on account of the great number of passengers waiting to proceed to England, many of whom had been in readiness some time. The Relief Fund gave us free passages, and a sum of money for an outfit; these passages were given by the Peninsular and Oriental Company, to the managers of the relief fund, at a reduced rate. The passage *via* Bombay is not so expensive; mine, including the nurse's, only cost 150*l*.whereas, in coming out to Calcutta, a reserved cabin for two had cost us 300*l*.

A few days before we left, Colonel Greathed came to dine at the Mallets. He spoke of the battle on the 10th of October, and asked us if we were not very glad when he so opportunely arrived at Agra, only just in time.

On the 18th of March the *Oriental* was to leave, so we bade goodbye to our hospitable friends, and drove down to the Apollo Bunder; when finding the steamer had not yet come round, we put off in a boat, and were soon on board. Only those who have been on board a large vessel can know the bustle and confusion that goes on at first, and how soon people settle quietly down. We were a very pleasant party; and many who had come down the Indus with me were on board.

We sailed in the evening, and the moon which had just risen, cast a soft flood of light over the clear blue sea, and the white houses and green trees of Bombay sloping down to the water. I had soon taken my last look of India, and its myriads of people,—most of whom are black at heart,—its burning sun, and all the scenes of horror I had witnessed.

We had a prosperous voyage, but had to wait a week in Egypt; which, however, gave us the pleasure of seeing the pyramids, the bazaars, for which Cairo is celebrated, the petrified forest, Heliopolis, and other relics of this interesting land, which never can be surpassed or equalled in beauty, wonders, and grandeur.

At Alexandria, I parted with great regret from Mrs. Blake, who had been my kind friend and fellow-sufferer since the 14th of June, 1857. She was going *via* Marseilles to Paris.

On the 26th of April, 1858, the *Ripon* arrived at Southampton, where I was met by my father, and I again stood on the shore of dear old England; which, if I did not kiss, I embraced in my heart.

Ah! thought I, you who dwell in this had can never value enough the privilege of living in a country where freedom reigns in deed as well as in word, where Christianity is universal, and which is ruled by a sovereign, who sets to all her subjects a good and noble example.

LEONAUR

ALSO FROM LEONAUR
AVAILABLE IN SOFTCOVER OR HARDCOVER WITH DUST JACKET

A JOURNAL OF THE SECOND SIKH WAR by *Daniel A. Sandford*—The Experiences of an Ensign of the 2nd Bengal European Regiment During the Campaign in the Punjab, India, 1848-49.

LAKE'S CAMPAIGNS IN INDIA by *Hugh Pearse*—The Second Anglo Maratha War, 1803-1807. Often neglected by historians and students alike, Lake's Indian campaign was fought against a resourceful and ruthless enemy-almost always superior in numbers to his own forces.

BRITAIN IN AFGHANISTAN 1: THE FIRST AFGHAN WAR 1839-42 by *Archibald Forbes*—Following over a century of the gradual assumption of sovereignty of the Indian Sub-Continent, the British Empire, in the form of the Honourable East India Company, supported by troops of the new Queen Victoria's army, found itself inevitably at the natural boundaries that surround Afghanistan. There it set in motion a series of disastrous events-the first of which was to march into the country at all.

BRITAIN IN AFGHANISTAN 2: THE SECOND AFGHAN WAR 1878-80 by *Archibald Forbes*—This the history of the Second Afghan War-another episode of British military history typified by savagery, massacre, siege and battles.

UP AMONG THE PANDIES by *Vivian Dering Majendie*—An outstanding account of the campaign for the fall of Lucknow. This is a vital book of war as fought by the British Army of the mid-nineteenth century, but in truth it is also an essential book of war that will enthral.

BLOW THE BUGLE, DRAW THE SWORD by *W. H. G. Kingston*—The Wars, Campaigns, Regiments and Soldiers of the British & Indian Armies During the Victorian Era, 1839-1898.

INDIAN MUTINY 150th ANNIVERSARY: A LEONAUR ORIGINAL

MUTINY: 1857 by *James Humphries*—It is now 150 years since the 'Indian Mutiny' burst like an engulfing flame on the British soldiers, their families and the civilians of the Empire in North East India. The Bengal Native army arose in violent rebellion, and the once peaceful countryside became a battleground as Native sepoys and elements of the Indian population massacred their British masters and defeated them in open battle. As the tide turned, a vengeful army of British and loyal Indian troops repressed the insurgency with a savagery that knew no mercy. It was a time of fear and slaughter. James Humphries has drawn together the voices of those dreadful days for this commemorative book.

Lightning Source UK Ltd.
Milton Keynes UK
UKOW02f2256061014

239731UK00001B/99/P